SOCIAL WORKERS AND COMPASSION

Social Workers and Compassion is designed to assist social work students, social workers, social work managers, social care workers, and lecturers in developing knowledge, understanding, skills, and values related to various aspects of compassion.

Focussing on social work in the UK, the various elements of compassion – compassion, compassion fatigue, compassion satisfaction, self-care, self-compassion, and mindfulness – are clearly located in a systemic, organisational, and structural context. The chapters draw upon evidence-based and evidence-informed sources and present critical perspectives that are linked to existing practices in social work education, social work, and the author's own experiences.

Drawing upon literature from social work and health care, social, organisational, work, and positive psychology, and from sociology and social policy from various parts of the world, the book will be of interest to international social work readers as well as professionals and professionals in training in the criminal justice, health care, counselling, and clinical psychology fields. It will be essential reading for social work students, lecturers, social care workers, social workers, and their managers.

Stewart Collins was employed for ten years in probation in Leeds. He has been employed as a social work educator in Leeds, Bangor, and, until recently, in Glasgow. Stewart has worked as an External Examiner for many years with various social work courses and continues to do so. He has been, and is, on the editorial boards of various social work journals. Stewart has worked as a volunteer in a wide range of settings. In particular, he has worked for many years, and is currently working, as a volunteer with an agency that assists people experiencing alcohol problems.

SOCIAL WORKERS AND COMPASSION

Stewart Collins

LONDON AND NEW YORK

Designed cover image: © Getty Images

First published 2023
by Routledge
4 Park Square, Milton Park, Abingdon, Oxon OX14 4RN

and by Routledge
605 Third Avenue, New York, NY 10158

Routledge is an imprint of the Taylor & Francis Group, an informa business

© 2023 Stewart Collins

The right of Stewart Collins to be identified as author of this work has been asserted in accordance with sections 77 and 78 of the Copyright, Designs and Patents Act 1988.

All rights reserved. No part of this book may be reprinted or reproduced or utilised in any form or by any electronic, mechanical, or other means, now known or hereafter invented, including photocopying and recording, or in any information storage or retrieval system, without permission in writing from the publishers.

Trademark notice: Product or corporate names may be trademarks or registered trademarks, and are used only for identification and explanation without intent to infringe.

British Library Cataloguing-in-Publication Data
A catalogue record for this book is available from the British Library

ISBN: 978-0-367-63169-7 (hbk)
ISBN: 978-0-367-63231-1 (pbk)
ISBN: 978-1-003-11253-2 (ebk)

DOI: 10.4324/9781003112532

Typeset in Bembo
by codeMantra

CONTENTS

	Introduction	1
1	The Present Context of Social Work in the UK	6
2	Compassion	33
3	Compassion Fatigue	63
4	Compassion Satisfaction	88
5	Self-Care to Promote Self-Compassion	111
6	Self-Compassion	135
7	Mindfulness	159
	Name Index	*187*
	Subject Index	*195*

INTRODUCTION

In Voltaire's classic text, Candide (1759), the central character optimistically sought the best in the best of all possible worlds but suffered greatly as a result. Voltaire concluded the book with terse advice to work on cultivating the garden. This tantalisingly brief and ambiguously short conclusion is not explored or expanded upon in any depth. However, it led me to think about the place of gardens in my own early life. I considered my grandparents' garden in what was the then industrialised town of Halifax, West Yorkshire. Their "garden" comprised the paved yard of a back-to-back terraced house; it had no front entrance and no front garden. The yard contained an outside toilet; it was located opposite an iron foundry whose open doors revealed belching flames, considerable heat, smoke, and sulphurous odours; it seemed like a vision of hell to me as a small boy at the time. In my grandparents' back "garden" a few window boxes were located. They contained plants, flowers of a type which I cannot recall, but they did offer brief flashes of natural brightness amidst the bleak, oppressive backdrop. Inside the house, I also recall my grandfather grew bulbs at certain times of the year, in long glass jars filled with water and, if my memory serves me correctly, with long roots descending into the lower reaches of the containers.

Later, following the death of my grandmother and the passing of the years, my grandfather moved into a flat in "sheltered housing" for older people. Here he had no "outside" garden at all. But he continued to develop his plant growing activities with a wide, impressive array of plants located on a broad, and quite extensive, windowsill in his living room. The plants were a source of satisfaction, enjoyment, and pride to him. Looking after his plants seemed to play a large part in making his life worthwhile and purposeful. He gave a lot of attention to the plants and, to me, there rarely seemed to be a time when displays of greenery and colour were not present. The role of plants and gardens in my grandfather's

DOI: 10.4324/9781003112532-1

2 Introduction

life reminds me rightly or wrongly of the working lives of many social workers, which can be demanding, unpromising, and uncompromising, but also contain several moments of satisfaction, pleasure, and pride which light up the working week and make "doing the job" worthwhile. Interestingly enough, and perhaps surprisingly, while recently undertaking research on this book I discovered an article about compassion, which talked about the "bleak landscape [where] generosity and compassion still break through like wild and beautiful plants, giving us hope and meaning. It is up to us...to nurture and cultivate them [so] that we can create a garden where there is the possibility of harmony and human flourishing" (De Zulueta 2013, p.125).

For many years I reflected on, researched, and wrote about the various aspects of the mainly barren garden that comprises pressure, stress, and burnout in social work – but in recent times I have moved on to give attention to a more generally colourful, thriving garden – the positives of social work, to what "keeps us going" in social work and helps us to persist, "to keep on, keeping on". These ideas were developed in a series of articles and in a previous book – *The Positive Social Worker* (Collins, 2020) – which focused upon topics such as hope, optimism, commitment, resilience, support, coping, confidence, and control. While working on that book I became more aware of other associated ideas, other concepts that could be explored further, such as compassion, compassion fatigue, compassion satisfaction, self-care, self-compassion, and mindfulness. The chapters that follow focus on those topics. One of the chapters – self-care – is an updated version of, expanded and developed from, an article previously published in *Practice: Social Work in Action* (Collins, 2021). The other chapters are original material. I would like to express my thanks to Moira Godfrey whose work contributed much to providing foundations for my understanding of the ideas developed in the mindfulness chapter.

The contents of this book are based on a combination of evidence-based and evidence-informed research findings, a wide range of books and articles linked to the various aspects of compassion, my own experiences of social work in statutory and voluntary settings, in social work education, and the experiences of other social workers. Like much of social work, the book is a combination of "science" and "art". The ideas and concepts presented are drawn from social work, psychology, social, organisational, work, and positive psychology, health care, sociology, and some social policy literature. As the theoretical and literature bases underpinning this work come from a wide range of countries, the book should appeal to a wide range of international social work readers, for example, from the UK, Europe, the USA, Canada, Asia, Australia, and New Zealand, while the book has a "practical" focus upon a UK context.

The book is intended primarily for undergraduate and postgraduate social work students in the later stages of their programmes, social work lecturers, practice educators, recently qualified and experienced social workers, social care workers and their line managers. It may also be beneficial for workers training for, and working in, criminal justice contexts, for students and

Introduction **3**

practitioners in the health care and nursing fields, for counsellors and clinical psychologists.

The book is clearly located in an ecological systems, and network context. The aims of the book are:

- To assist readers to develop knowledge, understanding, skills, and values related to compassion, compassion fatigue, compassion satisfaction, self-care, self-compassion, and mindfulness.
- To consider individual, group, organization, socio-political, cultural, and structural perspectives on the various aspects of compassion.
- To consider the implications of these compassion-based concepts for social work education and social work practice.
- To explore relevant critical perspectives.
- To consider and explore links between compassion-based approaches and existing knowledge, values, and skills in social work.

Each chapter contains definitions, general and detailed exploration of the compassion-related concepts along with critical evaluation, accompanied by a committed consideration of their implications for social work practice. The linkage of theory, concepts, and ideas to the work of social work students, social workers, and social care workers is an important part of the approach taken in each chapter. We will also consider the impact of social divisions related to the compassion concepts such as culture, ethnicity, gender, sexuality, age, religion, (dis) ability, and language.

The contents of the chapters should provide valuable signposts and guidance for students, practitioners, line managers, and social work educators to establish, maintain, and develop critical, compassionate approaches in relation to themselves, service users, team members, colleagues, and the organisational, structural, and political contexts in which they work.

Like many other aspects of social work, the various perspectives on compassion discussed within this text are not without controversy, contradiction, arguments, disputes, and tensions. These will be considered in the contents of each chapter. Furthermore, compassion-related concepts are constantly evolving, growing, changing, and developing. Therefore, the comments in this book are by no means the "final word", but they do provide a foundation, a springboard for debate, encompassing a willingness to engage with the struggle to be open minded, to be curious to learn about compassion-related matters.

It would also be foolish indeed to pretend that by exploring compassion-related concepts we will have "answers" to the complexities of social work. This is most certainly not the case. We can only move towards the partial resolution of some of the "answers" to these subtle and intricate issues by considering compassion perspectives as part of a much broader, wider range of knowledge, skills, and values. Hence the importance of linking, blending the ideas underpinning, and associated with, compassion-related approaches to already existing, transferrable

4 Introduction

material. Therefore, the contents of this book should be seen as clearly located in a context of structural, political, legislative, and organisational policies, procedures, practice settings, a whole range of social theories, social work theories, social work processes, and anti-discriminatory and anti-oppressive approaches. At the same time, at an individual level, compassion-related concepts can be seen as linked to "character traits", as "state like", or as "practices", but these aspects would seem to be ultimately subject to change, dependent on time, place, and context; they can also be learned about and developed. All of the concepts can be "measured" either as part of one's own "personalised" professional development or as part of institutionalised professional development, as is the case with compassion in nursing. Nevertheless, as we shall see, there can be doubts, uncertainties, and questions about the appropriateness of the latter approach and about the reliability, the validity of some of the measurement scales, which tend to focus on individual practitioners at the expense of the organisational and structural context.

Each chapter of the book could probably be read independently of the other chapters; each could be valuable in its own right. However, a major, overall feature of the book is that the concepts presented in each chapter fuse and coalesce into a potent blend in assisting practitioners to develop a cluster of critical knowledge, understanding, and skills associated with compassion-related concepts, beliefs, attitudes, and behaviours.

As far as I am aware no comprehensive, collected literature source is available for social work practitioners, social work students, and social work lecturers centred upon the various aspects of compassion presented in this book. While much research, many books, and numerous articles have been compiled about compassion-related ideas generally, and more recently, particularly related to the health care and nursing fields, surprisingly little has been written in any depth about the various aspects of compassion and social work. Most of the topics covered in the chapters that follow have been mainly presented in a limited number of social work journal articles. However, some social work books have been published on a few of the chapter topics, for instance, on self-care and social work, while there are texts about mindfulness and social work. References to these books can be found within the relevant chapters.

All of the chapter topics that follow link aspects of compassion to social work. Some of the chapters have a very wide-ranging focus; others consider matters more narrowly. The first chapter sets the wider scene in introducing the current context of social work in the UK, including consideration of pressures, stress, and the impact of the recent pandemic. The second chapter, also wide-ranging, considers compassion, nursing, and social work; it is primarily focused upon workers being exposed to, exploring, and engaging with the strengths and the vulnerability, the suffering of service users. This is accompanied by a wish, a desire on the part of workers to alleviate that suffering, arising from a sense of common, shared humanity, in that we all experience vulnerability and suffering to varying degrees at different points in our lives. The third chapter, on compassion

Introduction **5**

fatigue, has a more negative focus than the other chapters; it concentrates on social workers' experiences of compassion fatigue, vicarious trauma, secondary traumatic stress, and burnout. These aspects are seen by some as the consequences of exposure to suffering – a core element of compassion. By contrast, Chapter 4 examines the rewards that are associated with compassion satisfaction in social work which, research shows, actually outweigh the demands of compassion fatigue. In Chapter 5, we move on to consider how social work practitioners and social work organisations can establish and maintain "officially sanctioned" self-care, which is one of the key requirements for social workers in England. In turn, self-compassion forms an important element in self-care for practitioners, which will be the focus of Chapter 6. Mindfulness, which will be the focus of Chapter 7, is perhaps the most highly popularised way in which social workers can maintain self-compassion.

The intention of this book is that it should help professionals associated with social work to feel more compassionate towards themselves both individually and collectively and to provide more compassionate services for service users. The social work garden may sometimes have poor soil, be challenged by disease, weeds, harsh weather, and a predominantly cold climate in the UK and elsewhere. But it is still capable of producing "wild and beautiful plants" that can be nurtured, nourished, and sustained in appropriate conditions with good soil, sun, warmth, and water. It is hoped that this book will contribute ideas that are nurturing, nourishing, and sustaining to enable people in the social work garden to flourish and thrive!

References

Collins, S. (2020) *The Positive Social Worker*, London, Routledge.

Collins, S. (2021) "Social workers and self-care; a promoted yet unexamined concept?", *Practice: Social Work in Action*, 33.2, 87–102.

De Zulueta (2013) "Compassion in twenty first century medicine; is it sustainable?", *Clinical Ethics*, 8.4, 119–128.

Voltaire, (2005[1759]) *Candide or Optimism*, trans. and ed. T. Cuffe, London, Penguin.

1

THE PRESENT CONTEXT OF SOCIAL WORK IN THE UK

Introduction

The purpose of this chapter is to firmly locate the topics focused upon in this book within a wider context of social work in the UK. We will reflect on the impact of discrimination, oppression, and intersecting social divisions upon service users and social workers. We shall also consider the impact of neoliberalism, new managerialism, and austerity involving cuts to the public sector, local authority budgets, and resources available to meet the needs of service users. We will look at the impact of the recent coronavirus pandemic upon society, service users, and practitioners, which has exaggerated and exacerbated existing problems and difficulties. In this chapter, we will also note the strengths and resilience demonstrated by service users, while simultaneously exploring the enormous pressures and stress imposed on them from so many directions and sources.

We will also examine the demands made upon social workers from service users, and from employing organisations, considering the possible negative impact on their professional and personal lives while, at the same time, not neglecting the rewards, the satisfactions associated with, and linked to, the profession – particularly work with service users. At the conclusion of this chapter, we will begin to consider the need to develop a more compassionate, more action-oriented social work approach to the vulnerability, the suffering of service users on both small scale, individual, family levels and at wider scale, structural, collective, and policy-orientated levels. We will also begin to recognise that in order to provide more compassionate services in partnership with, and on behalf of, service users and to be wary of, and to work to prevent compassion fatigue, practitioners need to be empowered to care for themselves and for each other – hard though that may be.

DOI: 10.4324/9781003112532-2

The Present Context of Social Work in the UK

At the time this chapter was written, the UK and most of the rest of the world had experienced and were affected by restrictions linked to the global pandemic – COVID-19. Most people had become much more isolated, experiencing loss of face-to-face, physical contact with extended families and friends, limits on short and long distance travel, direct access to restaurants, public houses, sports venues, and various group gatherings. Most children and young people had been prevented from attending school; people in residential care had only limited physical contact with their loved ones; many older people in residential care died. Loss had become a characteristic of the experiences of people during the pandemic; theories of loss are particularly important in understanding our increased, intensified moments of suffering (Turner, 2020). Many people have gone through varying degrees of suffering as part of shared, common human experiences during COVID-19 that will have impacted both social workers and service users. Furthermore, while many have worked to maintain and develop positive emotions, this has been difficult for everyone, as negative emotions have been in danger of predominating such as "helplessness, anger, grief, guilt, anxiety, fear, shame, sadness and disappointment" (IFSW, 2020, p.14).

Social work service users demonstrate resilience, perseverance, pride, and strengths in dealing with the difficulties and problems of day-to-day living (Saleebey, 2009). However, there is also considerable evidence of service users experiencing particular stress associated with discrimination, poverty, negative labelling and stigma, stereotyping, poor health, housing, and education provision, often living in areas with high incidences of material deprivation. Other structural matters, social divisions such as class, ethnicity, "race", gender, age, sexuality, physical and learning (dis)ability, language, and religion will impact service users and social workers. These divisions have also been reinforced and amplified during the recent pandemic (IFSW, 2020). For example, among ethnic minorities, a disproportionate percentage – around one third – of critically ill coronavirus patients in 2020 were Black Asian and Minority Ethnic people (BAME), although BAME people comprise only 14 per cent of the total population in England and Wales (Turner, 2020). Also, BAME people were more likely to be in "high risk" occupations such as health-care roles in the NHS (Turner, 2020). Deaths of BAME people in these roles have also been disproportionately high. At one point, over a half of over 200 deaths of NHS employees were from an ethnic minority background, while ethnic minority staff comprised 20 per cent of NHS staff (Ravalier and Allen, 2020). Overall, in 2020 in the UK, Black men and women were four times more likely to die after contracting the virus (Office of National Statistics, 2020). There were also issues about restricted attendance at funerals, backlogs, and delays with funerals which increased pressure and stress, especially on relatives and friends of Muslim people whose beliefs necessitated rapid burials in order to facilitate the

8 The Present Context of Social Work in the UK

grieving process. At the same time, Muslim men and women have experienced the highest fatality rates for COVID-19 of any religious community in the UK (The Guardian, 2021a).

Over the past ten years, there has been increased inequality in the UK, including rises in the rates of child and adult poverty (Marmot et al., 2020). Over one fifth of the UK population, around 14 million people, are classified as poor (Joseph Rowntree Foundation, 2017). Fitzpatrick et al. (2018) found around one and a quarter to one and a half million people in the UK were living in destitution, unable to buy essentials linked to housing, heating, and food. Harrop and Reid (2015) estimated two million more children in England will be living in poverty by 2030. In Scotland, almost one in four children are recognised as living in poverty, linked to low wages, under-employment, worklessness, and inadequate social security benefits (CPAG in Scotland, 2018).

By 2021 £37 billion less had been spent on working-age social security compared with 2010 (Butler, 2018; Lavalette, 2019). Therefore, poverty was obviously present amongst significant numbers of service users before COVID-19, but this increased during the pandemic, for example, with reduced working hours, increased rates of unemployment, and higher fuel bills as children and families were having to spend more time at home. Service users have suffered and/or will be suffering in a market-oriented society which tends to be highly competitive and highly individualistic with uncertainty and precariousness characterising daily living. This suffering has developed further with the impact of the coronavirus. The Legatum Institute (2020) found the pandemic had resulted in an increase of nearly 700,000 people living in poverty in the UK.

Service users may have experienced, or be experiencing, emotional problems, neglect, abuse, aggression, mental health, drug and alcohol problems, accidents, injuries, and unexpected, unanticipated losses. As might be expected, almost all social work respondents to two Community Care surveys (2020b and c) felt the recent pandemic had a negative effect on service users in mental health, adult social care, and children's services settings, with increased levels of need. A BASW (2020a) survey found first time presentations of service users experiencing mental distress to approved mental health professionals had increased by three quarters between Spring and Summer of 2020. A Community Care survey (2020b) suggested many service users with mental health problems linked to community teams were not seen face to face, with difficulties experienced when trying to conduct assessments mainly via telephone contacts. Anxieties have been increasing among families with children and young people experiencing mental health problems, with even more difficulties in accessing the long waiting lists of already stretched Child and Adolescent Mental Health Services. In 2021, an investigation reported by The Guardian (2021b) noted considerable increases in self-harm reports and suicidal ideation among secondary school children, while prescriptions for under-18s had risen in a period of four months by nearly a third.

The Present Context of Social Work in the UK **9**

Older people and people experiencing learning and physical disabilities have had restricted opportunities to physically socialise face to face with peers in day centre settings, while having limited access to relatives, the resources of others such as general practitioners, community groups, and "specialist" support agencies (Community Care, 2020b). A survey by MENCAP (2020) of over 1,000 families found care packages for people with learning disabilities had at least halved since the start of the pandemic, reducing their independence. Also, opportunities for respite care had become more limited, meaning that carers were subject to more strain and pressures. In all, group-based helping endeavours have been difficult to maintain because of social distancing requirements. Furthermore, as family activities outside the home have been restricted, families have had to spend more time together with only limited access to roles and support outside the home and rates of domestic violence and child mistreatment have escalated. An Association of Directors of Adult Social Services study (ADASS, 2020) revealed there had been a 69 per cent increase in domestic abuse referrals in just a few months following the commencement of the pandemic. Furthermore, after only the first three weeks of the first lockdown in the UK, the number of women killed by their partners had doubled, while the demands on the National Domestic Abuse helpline had risen by a half (BASW, 2020b). A study by the Office of National Statistics showed that women were also bearing the brunt of the demands of home-schooling activities during lockdowns in 2021, with a more negative impact upon their well-being than men (The Guardian, 2021c).

The poorest areas have been already hit by the deepest cuts to local authority budgets since austerity commenced around 2010. English councils have had average spending cuts of around a quarter; more than 30 council areas have seen cuts of around a third, with seven urban council areas experiencing over 40 per cent cuts (The Guardian, 2018). Overall funding for services was reduced by almost a half between 2010 and 2018 (NAO, 2018). Austerity policies have led to disinvestment in places and people, with the result that many local council services are at their most basic, which can affect the life chances of entire generations born or living in particularly deprived areas (Ravalier, 2019). Restricted social service budgets mean less resources are available to service users through social work organisations. Service users are more likely to have low self-esteem, limited status, security, and power, which can lead to minimal expectations, a sense of cynicism, hopelessness, abandonment, despair, depression, and anxiety (Charlesworth, 2000; Duschinsky et al., 2016). Emotional, physical, and financial precariousness characterises the lives of many service users. As Judith Butler (2009, p.25) puts it, this precariousness has been highlighted by a "politically induced condition in which certain populations [such as social work service users] suffer"; thus feelings of vulnerability are never far away (Duschinsky et al., 2016). Therefore, the impact of the suffering of service users forms part of the day-to-day reality of social work past, present, and future. Indeed, it can be easy to feel overwhelmed by individual, social, and structural problems, all of which have been exacerbated recently by the coronavirus.

10 The Present Context of Social Work in the UK

Impact on Social Workers

While some have argued that austerity measures may have led social workers to become closer to service users in a "shared traumatic reality" (Pentaraki, 2017), others have suggested that practitioners have become incorporated into the austerity process. Indeed, instead of being able to realise, to exemplify professional ethics in their practice, workers "frequently find themselves enacting a cutbacks policy…social workers… become, in effect, part of the austerity agenda, injecting neoliberalism into the lives of service users and communities" (Baines and Van Den Broek, 2017, p.126).

Social workers therefore also struggle with a variety of demands in their day-to-day work, which take place within a context of neoliberalism and new public managerialism (NPM) (Lavalette, 2019). Neoliberalism structures "policy, practice and relationships" (Garrett, 2018, p.64). It has been a long-term project dating from around the 1980s, "shrinking, privatising, and/or dismantling the public infrastructure supporting children, families and retirees" (Brown, 2015, p.105). NPM has played a significant role in embedding neoliberal practices (Garrett, 2018). It "systematically strips out the work of caring content" (Baines, 2004, p.26); it is the antithesis to social democracy and democratic participation in the workplace. Ideas transposed from the business and private sectors continue to be evident, including extensive use of surveillance, rigid rules, performance monitoring, standardisation, regulatory assessment tools, and gatekeeping mechanisms (Harris, 2003, 2019). As Cohen (2011, p.190) puts it

> Notwithstanding professional or compassionate concern… work and employment in social care settings is played out in the same territory as other work in capitalism. This territory is marked by persistent… conflict and constraint… increasingly the public sector is subject to pseudo market mechanisms incorporating targets, audits, and rewards for cost cutting.

Reduced professional autonomy, continuing negative media coverage often concentrating on social work's failings, its problems, and the recent coronavirus outbreak have all added to the demands made on social work practitioners.

With the recent impact of the coronavirus, an argument could also be made that this is another "shared traumatic reality", to which both welfare professionals and service users have been exposed together. There may well have been common feelings of loss, depression, anxieties, worries about personal safety, possible illness and hospitalisation, concerns about home schooling, restricted wider family, social contacts, and lack of social activities. But there are also differences; divisions in that social workers still occupy helping, professional roles, have knowledge, power, and acquired skills, carry out professional tasks and responsibilities such as assessment and evaluations. Social workers are in contact with service users for professional reasons; they may have statutory professional functions to perform; they have some degree of power as well as accountability to their organisations' policies and procedures. So, while practitioners may have become closer to service users in shared experiences of the coronavirus, they may remain "professionally distanced". We will examine this point further in the forthcoming chapter on compassion.

Social Workers: Pressure, Stress, and Challenge

It is not surprising that over the years extensive research evidence in the UK suggests in many instances social workers experience pressure and stress, linked to high, complex workloads, time constraints, excessive administrative require-ments, low control, sometimes limited managerial/supervisory support, poor physical environments, high rates of illness and absences, low retention and high turnover rates (see, for example, McFadden et al., 2015; Ravalier, 2019; Ravalier et al., 2021). Recent estimates suggest that overall vacancy and turnover rates in the children and family workforce stood at 16 per cent in England (DfE, 2019). Uncertainties also exist following changes in legislation, alterations to policy, lack of clarity about procedures, practices, and the ending of COVID-19 lock-down restrictions. Overall, social workers are often troubled by role conflict, ambiguity, and strain, while they struggle with traditional dilemmas of combin-ing care with control, when they are expected to work in a general context of conflict, contradictions, and risk (Collins, 2020).

In the midst of this difficult context, it is again not surprising that much of the literature about social work has focused on negative elements, i.e. on pressures and stress which we will consider in this chapter. For instance, as Duschinsky et al. (2016, p.32) pessimistically observe "The diversity of … different grounds of chronic, materialised suffering makes social work intervention tend to feel like a drop in the ocean". However, Collins (2020) notes pressure can be seen from both negative and positive perspectives. For instance, Robertson and Cooper (2011) discuss "hindrance pressures" which provide obstacles to achievement and to growth. These include poor work relationships, job insecurity, lack of control over one's functioning at work, unrealistic time demands and deadlines, all of which, as we have seen, are familiar to social workers. In their meta-analysis, Podsakoff et al. (2007) suggest that "hindrance pressures" were negatively asso-ciated with satisfaction, but positively to turnover and intention to leave work. However, in contrast, Robertson and Cooper (2011) also discuss "challenge pres-sures", such as worthwhile goals, undertaking meaningful and purposeful work which can "make a difference" and job flexibility. "Challenge pressures" link positively to commitment, to satisfaction and, as we shall see later, satisfaction is a key factor in the working lives of social workers. Van Heugten (2011) also observes in her research that pressure can be an important motivator; even high pressure can be found to be appropriately challenging for some social workers,

12 The Present Context of Social Work in the UK

who may be "exhausted, yet satisfied" (also see, for example, Graham and Shier, 2010; Stalker et al., 2007).

However, continued, extensive pressure can lead to stress. Work stress has been defined as "the harmful response people can have to undue pressure and demands placed on them at work" (Health and Safety Executive, 2017, p.3). Stress can increase feelings of depression, anxiety, and dissatisfaction with and attendance problems at work, with possible negative impact on workplace relationships and family and friends. Various physical difficulties are associated with stress such as disrupted sleep patterns, headaches, stomach pains, allergies, skin complaints, and heart disease (Shaufeli and Peeters, 2000).

Nevertheless, for many years, writers and researchers have criticised what they consider to be an excessive focus on stress (for instance, Wainwright and Calnan, 2002). These authors argue that the very nature of stress leads to pessimism, with a focus on negatives rather than positives, with insufficient attention to actions that might be taken to alleviate stress (Moriarty et al., 2015). Some authors and researchers regard stress as an inevitable part of life, but they also consider positive perspectives on stress. Going back to 1984 and beyond, Selye distinguished between "eustress", the more positive, creative aspect of stress, with its more harmful aspects. While Selye's approach has been criticised, others have argued that it has much to offer when considering its potential for improving health, with the emphasis on challenge appraisals which might enhance well-being (Beehr and Grabner, 2009; Dewe and Cooper, 2012; Simmons and Nelson, 2007). The latter helpfully suggest even "if the term eustress is not used, the idea of a multi-faceted notion of stress with *both* its healthy, positive and unhealthy negative features is both valuable and helpful" (Collins, 2020, p.4). Robertson and Cooper (2011) suggest "moderators" of stress include a range of protective factors which reduce it and increase well-being. These include, for instance, the rewards of social work, the compassion satisfaction social workers' regularly experience in their job, support from teams, colleagues, and supervisors which is sometimes undervalued, tending to receive less attention in social work literature and research (see Burns et al., 2020; Grant et al., 2019; Pithouse et al., 2019, 2021; Yuill, 2018).

As is the case with pressure, stress can also be seen as having both negative and challenging aspects. Lazarus and colleagues (Folkman and Moskowitz, 2004; Lazarus, 2006) have emphasised the importance of individual perceptions and cognitive appraisals of stress. Dewe and Cooper (2012) suggest that appraisal is a powerful construct that contributes to understanding the transactional nature of stress, advocating that it merits just as much attention as stress itself. Lazarus (2000) points out that people are constantly evaluating, frequently appraising situations in their environment; they do so even in the face of great difficulties. Such appraisals influence the emotions social workers encounter in stressful situations, impacting upon their personal and professional coping capacities and strategies.

Social Workers and Appraisals

Lazarus (2006) suggests appraisals involve two processes – primary and secondary. Primary appraisal occurs when individuals encounter stress, evaluate its meaning, analysing harm that has already occurred, while assessing threats in the future. Secondary appraisal takes place when people reflect on such encounters, assess "inner" resources such as their perceived controllability of a situation, their self-confidence, their expectations, along with "outer", practical and material resources beyond oneself. They consider again demands, threats, or challenges, deciding what to do, what action to take. Such appraisals are clearly influenced by environmental, structural contexts, organisational settings, and individual views. As Collins (2020, p.7) notes stress "entails complex, transactional interactions between environmental and organisational supports and constraints, individual perceptions and appraisal of perceived demands".

Nelson and Simmons (2003) note that a combination of negatives and positives, rewards, opportunities, threats, and harm can exist in the same appraisal, but usually either negatives or positives will tend to predominate. Lazarus (2006) described challenge appraisals as entailing "people committing themselves enthusiastically to work within and against obstacles while enjoying the benefits of such encounters" (Collins, 2020, p.138). Lefevre et al. (2003) found that responding with positive challenge appraisals tends to minimise distress, while negative appraisals are more likely to involve the development of distress. Lazarus (2006) perceived challenge appraisals to have numerous advantages. These included concentrating on opportunities for growth, for gain, for learning, for incentives to focus on positives in a situation, opportunities to locate, to contextualise, to place problems and problem situations into a much broader, wider-ranging, possibly global perspective over a longer period of time. These arguments ask workers to reframe and to refocus their thinking. While they may tend to be excessively individualistic, even seem somewhat trite, social work research has found that challenge appraisals are negatively related to such burnout elements as depersonalisation and exhaustion while being positively related to personal accomplishment (Ben Zur and Michael, 2007). Kearns and McArdle (2012) also highlight the benefits of appraisals for practitioners in reframing problems as challenges and in appraising organisational constraints more positively.

Several authors (for instance, Collins, 2020) also highlight that the appraisal process is essential for developing insights into the negative and positive emotional consequences of situations. Atkins and Parker (2012) advocate that attention should be given to the role of appraisals in developing understanding of the emotional implications of individual compassion in organisations, which will be discussed in the next chapter. Dewe and Cooper (2012, p.84) suggest that appraisals "offer a direct and theoretical understanding of the emotional process" involved, acting as a trigger, as a bridge to help us develop awareness of how we feel both in, and about, interactions with colleagues, managers, and service users

14 The Present Context of Social Work in the UK

in various situations. They also suggest, in common with social work writers, that organisational settings and cultures can have a limiting influence on the acceptability of, and need for expression of emotions by workers, with a tendency to focus on the rational, the procedural, and the technical (Ingram, 2015; Ruch et al., 2018). Interestingly, this tendency is also seen in some of the coping and social work literature (such as Acker, 2010), which perhaps surprisingly questions the importance, validity, and excessive use of emotional coping, while placing more emphasis on action-oriented, problem-solving coping.

Nevertheless, despite the importance of positive appraisals and coping in dealing with stress, we cannot ignore the fact that prolonged chronic stress can lead to burnout, which is discussed further in the third chapter on compassion fatigue. Burnout has been found to be strongly associated with human service, helping professionals such as social workers. Burnout can involve feelings of depersonalisation, limited empathy for other people, feelings of a lack of accomplishment at work and emotional exhaustion (Maslach, 2003). Compassion fatigue is seen as linked to stress and burnout and sometimes seen as an alternative to these terms. This will also be explored in Chapter 3. The chapters that then follow on – compassion satisfaction, self-care, self-compassion, and mindfulness – all explore means for reducing the incidence of compassion fatigue, associated stress, and burnout among social workers.

Recent Research and Surveys about Stress and Social Workers

The need to explore these ideas is emphasised by a Health and Safety Executive study (2017) in the UK which indicated professional social workers experienced higher levels of work-related stress than other workers. Studies of practitioners using the General Health Questionnaire (Goldberg and Williams, 1988) have suggested that the incidence of psychological distress, for example, anxiety and depression, varied between a third to a half (Moriarty et al., 2015). Furthermore, during this century, there has been a great deal of research related to stress and social work both in the UK and internationally (for instance, Lloyd et al., 2002; Ravalier, 2017, 2019; Ravalier et al., 2021; Ting et al., 2011). By comparison, studies of satisfaction experienced by practitioners, the benefits of working with service users, have been fewer; they have received comparatively little attention. In particular, studies of local authority social work in England since the turn of the century have tended to produce disturbing, difficult findings describing a persistent, continuing "crisis", on-going suffering, high emotional demands, often commenting about "defeated", "ill", "tearful" social workers (Jones, 2001). For instance, Coffey et al. (2004) surveyed two local authorities in England, finding high rates of job dissatisfaction, especially with management, little recognition for good work and perceptions of limited opportunities for promotion.

Multiple surveys since then, in the UK and elsewhere, have also found a wide variety of sources of stress for social workers such as concerns about the work environment, lack of support for decision making, poor quality supervision and unmanageable caseloads (Mickel, 2009). Another survey revealed extreme levels of stress, with large numbers of social workers thinking of leaving their jobs as well as leaving the profession (Shraer, 2015). An extensive study by McFadden (2016) discovered high levels of emotional exhaustion among practitioners, even those with smaller caseloads and supportive supervision, with two thirds of workers experiencing feelings of depersonalisation, a lack of feeling, a lack of empathy for other people, and uncaring responses to service users. A Guardian survey (2017) found that a third of the social workers perceived their caseloads to be unmanageable, a half were dissatisfied with work/life balance, with a quarter wanting to move away from a work culture which emphasised the appropriateness and the acceptability of a culture of long working hours.

Practitioners in Ravalier's (2017) wide-ranging study also found working conditions to be unacceptable, with high demands made upon them, experiences of low levels of control, strained workplace relationships, a culture of blame, with a lack of managerial support and of reflective opportunities in supervision. Half of the practitioners were wanting to change their jobs; they only wished to stay in the social work profession for a brief period of time. Particular concerns surrounded large, complex workloads, time demands required for administrative work, poor workplace conditions such as the undermining of opportunities to share experiences with fellow team members and to undertake "quiet" work such as telephone calls, recording and report writing as a result of "hot desking", with no fixed location for individual work and little contact with social work colleagues in the immediate vicinity. Practitioners in the UK were working on average around an additional ten hours beyond their contracted hours (Ravalier, 2017). Garrett (2018) has described this as unpaid voluntary work for organisations to fill the gaps created by cutbacks and lack of financial resources. Studies of social workers in Scotland and mainly in England and Northern Ireland also found excessive work hours to be a particular concern (Grant et al., 2019; McFadden et al., 2020). Johnson et al. (2021) discovered respondents were working five hours beyond their contracted hours, with three quarters doing this most of the time. However, pay and financial remuneration appear to be less of a concern for UK workers with only moderate increases sought – a point also emphasised in Donovan's (2017) survey. More recently, however, Johnson et al. (2021) discovered that one in four social workers were dissatisfied with their pay.

The Impact of COVID-19

Research into the impact of COVID-19 upon social workers in the UK so far has produced a plurality of varying, confusing, and, sometimes, contradictory results. During the initial stages of the pandemic, most practitioners started to work at home, "at a distance" from colleagues, managers, and service users, with some essential home visits involving, for example, adult/child protection. In a survey in May 2020, three quarters of social work respondents perceived

16 The Present Context of Social Work in the UK

that they were unable to do their jobs properly, with the pandemic significantly affecting the ability of social work agencies to carry out their roles (Community Care, 2020a). Over a half were concerned that conducting their duties caused anxiety because of the potential risk of infection from the coronavirus. It is perhaps surprising that this figure was not even higher, but presumably this was because a considerable proportion of respondents were working with service users via video or telephone contacts. In the same survey, over three quarters of respondents saw positives in increasing online activities. Nevertheless, at that time, a third thought their ability to meet statutory responsibilities had been compromised because of increasing demand either for services and/or from colleagues' illnesses or self-isolation.

A study focused on over 1,000 social work practitioners in late 2020, surprisingly, found that social workers' levels of well-being and quality of working life were significantly *higher* during the pandemic compared to 2018 (McFadden et al., 2021). Practitioners also scored high in relation to the overall quality of their working life, job, career satisfaction, and coping with demands from the work-life interface. Positive coping strategies were more prevalent than negative ones, with acceptance, positive reframing, emotional and instrumental (practical) support being amongst the most common coping strategies, but as the pandemic progressed decreases occurred in positive coping strategies and increases in negative strategies (McFadden et al., 2021). Findings from a qualitative study suggested that practitioners were accustomed to operating in, and dealing with, adversity, and were well motivated to maintain services, while it was again noted they were resilient in reframing interventions during COVID-19 as positive challenges, which also links in with our earlier comments about appraisals (Kingstone et al., 2021).

Research undertaken with 2,000 social workers in late 2020 noted that about three quarters of respondents were satisfied with their work and with their sense of achievement, although this proportion had dropped slightly from 80 per cent in 2018 (Johnson et al., 2021). High overall satisfaction levels had declined slightly in three areas – in a sense of achievement with the work, the work itself, and with less opportunities available for skills development. A further survey in November 2020 indicated that nearly two thirds of social workers were still satisfied with how their services had responded and had adapted to the pandemic (Community Care, 2020b).

However, a Community Care survey (2020c) also carried out near the end of the year indicated that three quarters of practitioners were by then feeling more negative about their work compared to earlier in the year. But again, perhaps this is not surprising, as this would have applied to most of the UK working population. Large numbers of social workers felt only slightly more negative, although around a third to a quarter felt worse or significantly more negative. The survey findings were similar across adult and children's services but did not consider other variables in any depth. There were also continuing, contrasting, varied differences in the late 2020 survey of workers' perceptions of the impact of

The Present Context of Social Work in the UK **17**

colleagues' absences through illness or self-isolation, with half of the practitioners feeling the service had only been slightly affected, while similar numbers felt the service had suffered (Community Care, 2020c; Silman, 2020).

In late 2020, around a half of practitioners believed they had maintained at least a similar level of contact with service users compared to one year ago, with one in ten feeling their communication with recipients of services had increased (Community Care, 2020b). Some studies confirmed increasing frequency of contact with service users using digital technology, which was seen as particularly effective in working with children and young people (for example, Baginski and Manthorpe, 2021; Cook and Zschomler, 2020; Ferguson et al., 2021). However, other studies also raised questions about the limitations of video and telephone contacts in relation to dealing with new referrals, assessments, especially of risk, and working with sensitive issues (Cook and Zschomler, 2020). Nevertheless, Pink et al. (2021) and Ferguson et al. (2021) argue for the future use of "hybrid" social work practices combining the best features of thoughtful, sensitive use of technology with traditional, active, direct, "physical", face-to-face contacts with service users.

There has also been evidence of increased levels of material help, support to families linked to food poverty and practical assistance, with examples of the use of creative, innovatory practices to maintain close relationships with children and families, encouraged by government guidance (for instance, Ferguson et al., 2021; Pink et al., 2021; Silman, 2020).

A BASW (2021) survey discovered that three quarters of social workers believed their employers had taken reasonable steps to ensure they could work safely during the pandemic, having responded well to the swiftly changing context of COVID-19. A half of the respondents believed they were able to carry out their work with confidence and support, while a third did not. Interestingly, two thirds of social workers in Johnson et al.'s (2021) study felt *increasingly* valued by their employing organisation during the pandemic.

In three surveys, perhaps not unsurprisingly, around three quarters of those responding believed workloads had started to increase not only numerically but also in terms of complexity, with changing rules and regulations, increasing anxiety, ethical and moral dilemmas, especially concerning assessment work (BASW, 2021; Community Care, 2020c; Johnson et al., 2021). In the first two surveys, a half of respondents commented about the difficulties experienced as a result of physical separation from team colleagues, as formal and informal contacts had declined, despite attempts to maintain these online. In the BASW (2021) survey, three quarters of respondents believed the COVID-19 crisis had a significantly negative effect on workplace morale, while over a half believed the pandemic had negatively impacted their mental health. Yet, in contrast, a half of practitioner respondents did not seem to perceive a negative impact upon their mental health – for reasons that were not clear but appeared to relate to different perceptions of the increased use of online and telephone contacts with service users, team managers, and colleagues and, perhaps, perceptions that the pandemic would

18   The Present Context of Social Work in the UK

abate and a return to previous ways of working would not be delayed beyond a few months.

Variations in responses to experiences during the pandemic may also have been linked to the levels of poverty and deprivation, urban and rural locations in the areas where the social workers were employed. They may well have been also attributable to differences between local authority organisations' policies, procedures, and practices, variations in emotional and practical support from team and colleague relationships, individual differences between workers, and other variables such as differences in workload, amount of worker autonomy, and independence (Antonopoulu et al., 2017; Silman, 2020). For example, Johnson et al. (2021) found workers' perceptions of support from managers were highly contradictory: they varied a great deal; over a third perceived it to have increased, nearly a third thought it had remained the same, while over a third perceived such support to have declined!

Apart from stress and more recent COVID-19-oriented studies, longer-term studies of social workers in Norway have indicated deteriorating conditions for practitioners. An interesting, unusual, follow-up piece of research by Tham (2018a), *11 years* after a first study, found increased stress on workers with higher workload demands, increased role conflict, less opportunities to influence decision making, stronger intentions to leave the job and the social work profession, with on-going work focused more on undertaking investigations, assessments, and reports, accompanied by less opportunities for on-going work with service users. There appears little reason to suspect that the findings might be any different around the UK. However, the research works of Burns et al. (2020) in Ireland and Pithouse et al. (2019, 2021) in Wales do provide more positive, optimistic grounds about the ability, the willingness of social workers to find satisfaction, and to remain for longer periods in their jobs. Tham (2018b) also indicated how the situation had got worse for those Norwegian workers located in "low income" districts with high incidences of poverty and deprivation, compared to those working in "higher income" districts with lower incidences of poverty and deprivation. Workers in the "higher income" districts seemed to be more satisfied with the support they received and with the organisational climate in their employment setting. These studies emphasise the importance of environmental, local geographical areas, as well as the organisational and individualistic aspect of stress and satisfaction.

Social Workers, Threats, Violence, and Complaints

Social workers can receive verbal abuse, threats of violence, and, more rarely, physical abuse.

For instance, Littlechild (2005) found more than one in ten child protection workers reported physical violence, while nearly a half were subject to threats from parents or other family members. In 2011, a Community Care survey indicated that well over a half of practitioners had experienced threats. Van Heugten

The Present Context of Social Work in the UK **19**

(2011) suggested research studies indicated at least half, if not most, of the workers had experienced significant violence during their careers, while verbal abuse and intimidation were common. The same author observed that around a quarter of the workers did not report incidents of violence, while support and supervision after such incidents was insufficient, with organisational responses varying a great deal. There is also evidence that social workers experience fear and anxiety about complaints. Littlechild et al. (2016) found that three quarters of practitioners in their research had been threatened with complaints. A BASW (2018) survey in Northern Ireland found 80 per cent of workers had experienced intimidation, three quarters had received threats, and a half had been subject to physical violence. In a large-scale UK survey, Ravalier et al. (2021) found almost two thirds of respondents had been exposed to verbal abuse, with well over a third encountering negative behaviours at least once in the past month.

As a consequence of receiving threats and aggression, some practitioners experienced an undermining of morale, of motivation, along with a lack of confidence in carrying out their work. Some felt this had impaired their ability to work with, and to challenge parents and children. Others experienced a significant impact on their health and well-being (Cooper, 2011; Littlechild et al., 2016; Skills for Care, 2013). Such events described above, accompanied by reactions to them, are clearly a cause for considerable concern, as they can significantly contribute to stress and compassion fatigue. They highlight the need for social workers' self-care to be supported by positive organisational responses and for practitioners to be assisted to develop and maintain self-compassion.

All these studies reinforce the idea of many social workers sometimes suffering in their day-to-day work with service users and experiencing difficulties in their organisational and environmental contexts. While service users will usually have experienced more direct, intensive, extensive, multi-faceted suffering related to structural problems, low incomes, poor housing, poor health, more limited educational opportunities, and personal problems, social workers also suffer because of structural problems, coping with their workloads, the resource strapped organisational and community environments in which they work, and having to react to recent UK wide crises such as COVID-19.

Social Workers, Stress and Trauma in Their Personal Lives and Past Histories

Social workers may also have experienced, or do experience, stress and suffering in their personal lives to varying degrees. This could involve life events related, for instance, to discrimination and oppression as members of minority groups, losses of significant loved ones, other personal losses, accidents and injuries, unanticipated house moves or job changes, limited incomes, and the recent impact of the coronavirus.

A great deal of debate exists about the impact of early life traumas upon social workers. There is clear evidence that some practitioners have suffered as a result of,

20 The Present Context of Social Work in the UK

for instance, past experiences of child abuse, neglect, parental violence, parental mental illness, drug taking, and alcohol problems. Some research emphasises the high incidence of adverse childhood experiences among, and their impact upon, social workers (see, for example, Thomas, 2013; Thomas and Otis, 2010; Tosone et al., 2012). Other researchers suggest the impact of such experiences may have been limited, or worked through, leading to better understanding of, and more empathy for, service users' circumstances (see Adams et al., 2008; Bourassa, 2012; Howard et al., 2015; Killian, 2008; Way et al., 2004). However, among others, Martin- Cuellar et al. (2018) have argued that the nature, the type, the impact of past personal trauma upon social workers are often varied, uncertain, and unclear – which makes it difficult to make generalisations about these matters.

Social Workers and "Service User Groups"

In statutory social work, there seem to be contradictory findings about demands placed upon social workers in working with different service user "groups". Many studies suggest that child-care workers experience specific demands and difficulties in coping, which lead to stress, less job satisfaction, and support (for instance, Coffey et al., 2004; Ravalier et al., 2021). Other research contradicts these findings. For instance, Evans et al. (2005) and Hudson and Webber (2012) discovered that nearly a half of mental health social workers (and approved mental health professionals) in their samples were said to be experiencing psychological distress, while among newly qualified children and family workers the figure was around a third (Carpenter et al., 2015). McFadden's (2016) research suggested that social workers working with adults experiencing physical disabilities experienced the highest levels of emotional exhaustion, followed by those working in mental health, while those working in child-care scored much lower. Other studies have found working in child-care or with a particular service user group was *not* the most significant variable in practitioners' perceptions of stress (for example, Ramon and Morris, 2005). Researchers over the past 20 or so years have tended to emphasise the impact of the organisational context, along with individual differences, in determining levels of job stress and satisfaction (for instance, Lloyd et al., 2002; Morris, 2015; Ravalier, 2017; Storey and Billingham, 2001). Interestingly, Antonopoulu et al.'s (2017) study of five local authority teams – *all* in child-care – revealed quite different patterns of stress levels, ranging from very low (one in ten workers) to very high (over a third of workers), which reveals the complexity of this matter.

The Organisational Context

These contrasting, different, sometimes contradictory findings would seem to indicate that stress and satisfaction levels among social workers in the UK are not primarily influenced by the service user group with whom a practitioner works,

The Present Context of Social Work in the UK **21**

but rather by the organisational context in which they are located. Therefore, in looking at ways to develop, to improve opportunities for workers to provide compassion to service users and positively experience compassion-related concepts themselves, such as compassion satisfaction, self-compassion, and self-care, which are discussed later in this book, we should look perhaps towards the organisational settings within which social workers are located, rather than focusing on work with particular service user groups. At the same time, in order to develop compassion-related concepts, we should also consider and work with interactions between environmental, organisational demands, and the abilities of individuals, including their interaction with wider structural, societal, political, legislative, and policy contexts (Collins, 2008; Wilberforce et al., 2014).

Structural Pressures and Social Workers

A structural focus would involve consideration of the important impact of intersecting social divisions such as "race", gender, age, sexuality, (dis)ability, language, and religion upon social workers in the UK. In response to a question about the influence of ethnicity upon social workers' functioning in the job, Ravalier (2017) found that institutional racism was prominent. Participants described their perceptions of having been the victims of institutional racism from management and their local authorities, with individuals being "undermined and overlooked" when being considered for promotion on account of their "race". Some instances of racism occurred in interactions with social work colleagues and service users. During the pandemic, Tedam (2021) found that Black African social workers experienced racism, less favourable application of rules and policies in their organisations, compared with white peers, while also experiencing discrimination from managers and some peers. However, more positively, Ravalier (2017) suggested BAME workers felt they were able to empathise more easily, to work together in closer relationships, in more genuine partnerships with service users from a wide range of ethnic backgrounds. Also, McFadden et al. (2020) in their large-scale study of health and social care workers that included over 1,200 social workers, mainly in England and Northern Ireland, found BAME practitioners reported the highest well-being scores. Similarly, Johnson et al.'s (2021) research with child and family social workers in England noted that BAME workers were more satisfied with their work, enjoying a higher sense of achievement than white workers. In both these instances, the reasons for these findings were unclear.

In response to a question about disability in Ravalier's (2017) research, participants noted a lack of understanding of disability by both fellow social workers and their managers, with problems in obtaining reasonable adjustments needed in the workplace, which led to difficulties in undertaking their work. In McFadden et al.'s (2020) study, significant well-being scores were related to disability; workers reporting no disability had higher well-being scores, while those practitioners experiencing disability recorded lower quality of working life

22 The Present Context of Social Work in the UK

scores. Similarly, social workers who had physical or mental health conditions were less satisfied with their work than those who did not – and this dissatisfaction increased over several years (Johnson et al., 2021). These findings illustrate that structural matters clearly influence and impact upon the suffering of BAME workers and disabled practitioners.

Similarly, women, who clearly comprise the vast majority of the social work workforce, are much more likely to experience sexual harassment in their personal lives and at work; they may experience conflicting demands from social work roles and major responsibilities when caring for children and for dependent relatives. The latter responsibilities have been exacerbated during the coronavirus crisis. In McFadden et al.'s (2020) study, male workers experienced significantly higher levels of well-being and quality of working life scores than females, who also seem more likely to experience compassion fatigue which will be discussed further in Chapter 3. However, on the other hand, in Johnson et al.'s (2021) study, females enjoyed higher levels of job satisfaction than men. Younger, single, inexperienced female social workers have been found to be more prone to stress and burnout, linked to high expectations of the job, excessive emotional involvement, and possible preoccupation with social work (Collins, 2008; Stanley et al., 2018). Gay workers, workers whose first language is not English, and workers from religious minorities are also more likely to experience discrimination, stress, and suffering (McLean and Andrew, 2000; Rajan-Rankin, 2014.)

The Work-Life Interface

It has also been pointed out that social workers' home lives may suffer, as demands from work can spill over into home life, eroding time spent at home, with a negative impact on home-based roles such as acting as a partner, parent, or carer (Beer et al., 2021; Kalliath and Kalliath, 2015). Research findings suggest social workers may experience higher levels of work-life conflicts than other professionals and workers (Kinman et al., 2014). Helping professionals, including social workers, apparently have tendencies to think more, to ruminate more about work in the home setting than many other occupational groups (Newsome et al., 2012). While this can be helpful in sometimes possibly bringing new perspectives on problems, it can also have negative effects, such as the practitioner anxiously, irritably brooding about, dwelling upon, difficulties at work when at home, at the expense of family relationships (Aaronson et al., 2014; Beer et al., 2021).

Kalliath et al. (2012) discovered high levels of time, role strain, and behavioural conflicts in a large sample of Australian social workers, with negative emotional reactions to work especially notable in the way they spilled over into home life. Excessive, negatively focused discussions about work while at home, extensive ventilation of bad feelings, such as complaints about poor conditions in the workplace, the difficult circumstances of some service users, and problems with work colleagues can lead to overloading partners with bad, negative feelings, accompanied by their increasing unhappiness (Duschinsky et al., 2016). Alternatively, workers may tend to withdraw from their personal relationships and, if living with a partner, increase their partner's levels of anxiety and distress about this (Kinman et al., 2014). Excessive work-life conflict can also involve increased risk of a range of emotional and physical problems, including anxiety, depression, exhaustion, sleep problems, weight, and drug and alcohol problems (Beer et al., 2021; Grant and Kinman, 2014). Many researchers argue that the maintenance of emotional regulation and containment, with clear boundaries between professional and work life, is particularly important as we shall see in later chapters (also see, for example, Thomas, 2013; Wagaman et al., 2015; Yi et al., 2019). Interestingly, social workers in Johnson et al.'s (2021) study found that over three quarters of the respondents perceived their line managers to be considerate of their home and family lives outside the work/organisational context.

During the demands of the COVID-19 pandemic, a UK Community Care survey at the end of 2020 indicated that eight out of ten social workers were working from home (Silman, 2020). In a BASW (2021) survey, over two thirds of respondents observed that it was more difficult working there than in the office, finding it harder to switch off when working remotely. Some saw benefits from this such as reduced demands from travelling time, lower travel costs, fewer "face-to-face" physical meetings, more control over use of time and, for some, less interruptions to professional social work tasks. But the majority of respondents expressed concerns about overlapping boundaries between work and home life, sometimes experiencing difficulties in finding an appropriate space and a location to work at home, problems when discussing sensitive issues with service users, greater isolation from colleagues, a temptation to work longer hours and trying to balance work obligations with commitments to caring for children or relatives and, at times, home schooling. A study of probation workers produced more negative perceptions of home-based working (Phillips et al., 2021). However, these pieces of research did not differentiate, for example, between those working in urban and rural areas and the extent of demands from family commitments linked to number and ages of children, elderly, and/or disabled relatives.

Rewards and Satisfaction in Social Work

At the same time that work problems can negatively overlap with practitioners' personal lives, it is also clear that social work can also involve enriching, enjoyable experiences, which are discussed in depth in the compassion satisfaction chapter that follows. These rewarding, satisfying work experiences can also "spill over" into, enhance and enrich family and life satisfaction, protecting mental health (Kalliath et al., 2019). In turn, emotional and practical support from family and friends is acknowledged as having a significant role to play in maintaining job satisfaction. This is also discussed at length in Collins (2020).

24 The Present Context of Social Work in the UK

As we have seen, and will see, research findings indicate that while practitioners may experience suffering and personal and professional stress, this occurs together, simultaneously in a dialectical relationship, with positive experiences and job satisfaction, in a manner which balances out, or usually outweighs, the negative demands of social work. For a recent example, see Yuill's (2018) qualitative research where social workers felt disenchanted about various aspects of their work but, at the same time, were committed to it and enjoyed it. Social workers often feel they can "make a difference" in their job and, as noted earlier, can find it positively challenging. They have passion for, and pride in, many aspects of their work, in professional competences and accomplishments (Beddoe et al., 2019; Savaya, 2022). There is extensive, detailed, prolonged evidence of this in much research and many surveys, in particular, in various parts of the UK and Ireland (for example, Burns et al., 2020; Cooper, 2015; Grant et al., 2019; Johnson et al., 2021; Kinman and Grant, 2020; McFadden, 2016; Pithouse et al., 2021; Ravalier, 2017; The Guardian, 2017). Social workers in the UK enjoy well-known, considerable satisfaction especially from their interactions, their work with service users, despite some of the pressures involved (for instance, Antonopoulu et al., 2017; McFadden et al., 2015). Similar findings of high levels of social workers' satisfaction have been seen in a range of international studies in Canada, the USA, and Europe (for example, Cuartero and Campos-Vidal, 2019; Hermon and Chahla, 2019; Karpetis, 2015; Senreich et al., 2020; Stalker et al., 2007).

Yet again, as we have already seen, the workplace, the organisational context, has been found to significantly impact upon practitioners' satisfaction (see recent studies by Bae et al., 2020; Baugerud et al., 2018; Ravalier, 2017, 2019; Senreich et al., 2020). This is explored in more depth in the compassion satisfaction chapter. Furthermore, positive factors such as supervision and support from teams and colleagues are well-acknowledged; it can usually be quite extensive; it is significant. For a detailed discussion of the role of support, see Collins (2020). Also, although its length, frequency, focus, and quality may vary, reflective, emotion-focused supervision provides another opportunity to buttress and develop compassion satisfaction. Furthermore, organisational and individual resilience both have a part to play, although there are clear dangers in over-emphasising the role of individual resilience, self-care, and self-compassion at the expense of the social, structural, and organisational context (Garrett, 2018).

Hence, despite the emphasis on stress in much research work, Ravalier and Allen (2020, p.14) also acknowledge the widespread evidence of enjoyment, fulfilment, and rewards in social work, commenting on "a distinct sense of vigour, dedication and absorption in spite of negative working conditions" – a quote which uses the language of positive work engagement and positive psychology. It is easy either to forget, or underemphasise, the joys of social work – a phrase very rarely used by social workers themselves – and that social work is one of the most rewarding and satisfying of occupations, despite its limitations, restrictions, and frustrations (Pooler et al., 2014a, b; Rose, 2003).

Conclusion

Taking this further, as Duschinsky et al. (2016, p.156) put it, "a sustaining social work is one in which we seek and find sufficient replenishment for ourselves and others both in the immediacy of face-to-face encounters and what we can alter of the wider infrastructure". Sustaining, thriving, and flourishing social work involves many elements to enable us to work competently in a wide range of ways. These elements include hope, realistic optimism, commitment, a sense of professional self-confidence, coping skills, and a sense of control (Collins, 2020), along with compassion, compassion satisfaction, self-compassion, self-care, and mindfulness – which are discussed in the forthcoming chapters.

Along with the strengths in service users' lives, in view of the negative labelling, stigma, stereotyping, stress, suffering, and vulnerability that are faced, experienced, and endured by so many service users, the need for kindness, understanding, and empathy, accompanied by actions by both the individual practitioner and at a wider scale collective level to alleviate such suffering, means that compassion is one of the major vehicles social workers can draw upon to further develop a sense of meaning and a sense of purpose to aid their helping efforts in supporting some of the most marginalised people in society. Practitioners need to continue to be "ethically vigilant, practically creative, and compassionate in their practice… practising new ways to continue to advocate for social justice, shared responsibility, care, and compassion" (Kong and Noone, 2021, p.5). Compassion is the topic that we will explore in the next chapter.

References

Aaronson, G., Astvik, W. and Gustafsson, K. (2014) "Work conditions, recovery and health: A study among social workers within pre-school, home care and social work", *British Journal of Social Work*, 44.6, 1654–1672.

Acker, G. (2010) "How social workers cope with managed care", *Administration in Social Work*, 34, 405–422.

Adams, R., Figley, C. and Boscarino, I. (2008) "Compassion fatigue and psychological distress among social workers: A validation study", *American Journal of Orthopsychiatry*, 26.1, 103–108.

ADASS (2020) *Autumn Survey Report*, London, ADASS.

Antonopoulu, P., Killian, M. and Forrester, D. (2017) "Levels of stress and anxiety in children and family social work: Workers' perceptions of organisational structure, professional support and workplace opportunities in Children's Services", *Children and Youth Services Review*, 6, 42–50.

Atkins, P. and Parker, S. (2012) "Understanding individual compassion in organizations: The role of appraisals and psychological flexibility", *Academy of Management Review*, 37.4, 524-546

Bae, J., Jennings, P., Hardeman, C., Kim, E., Lee, M., Littleton, T. and Sasa, S. (2020) "Compassion satisfaction among social work practitioners: The role of work life balance", *Journal of Social Service Research*, 46.3, 320–330.

26 The Present Context of Social Work in the UK

Baines D. (2004) "Caring for nothing", *Work, Employment and Society*, 12.2, 267–295.

Baines, D. and Van Den Broek, D. (2017) "Coercive care: Control and coercion in the restructured care workplace", *British Journal of Social Work*, 47.1, 125–142.

BASW (2018) *Violence against Social Workers*, Belfast, BASW.

BASW (2020a) *The Impact of the Covid-19 Pandemic on Approved Mental Health Professionals (AMHP) Services in England*, Birmingham, BASW.

BASW (2020b) *Domestic Abuse and COVID-19*, 13 May, Birmingham, BASW.

BASW (2021) Social Work during the COVID-19 pandemic: Initial Findings, Birmingham, BASW.

Baginski, M. and Manthorpe, J. (2021) "The impact of COVID-19 on children's social care in England", *Child Abuse and Neglect*, 116, 104739.

Baugerud, G., Vangbaeck, S. and Melinder, A. (2018) "Secondary traumatic stress, burnout and compassion satisfaction among Norwegian child protection workers: Protective and risk factors", *British Journal of Social Work*, 40.1, 215–235.

Beddoe, L., Staniforth, B. and Fouche, C. (2019) "'Proud of what I do but often… I would be happier to say I drive trucks': Ambiguity in social workers' self-perception", *Qualitative Social Work*, 18.3, 530–546.

Beehr, T. and Grabner, S. (2009) "When stress is (less) harmful" in Antoniou, A., Cooper, C., Chrousos, G., Spielberger, C. and Eysenck, M. (eds), *Handbook of Managerial Behaviour and Occupational Stress*, Cheltenham, Edward Elgar, pp.65–82.

Beer, O., Phillips, R., Letson, M. and Wolf, K. (2021) "Personal and professional impacts of work-related stress among child welfare workers in a child advocacy centre", *Children and Youth Services Review*, https.//doi.org settings 10.1016/jchildyouth 2020, 105904.

Ben Zur, H. and Michael, K. (2007) "Burnout, social support and coping at work among social workers, psychologists and nurses: The role of challenge/control appraisals", *Social Work in Health Care,* 45.4, 63–80.

Bourassa, D. (2012) "Examining self-protection measures guarding adult protection workers", *Journal of International Violence*, 27.9, 1699–1715.

Brown, W. (2015) *Undoing the Demos*, New York, Zone Books.

Burns, K., Christie, A. and O'Sullivan, S. (2020) "Findings from a longitudinal qualitative study of child protection workers retention: Job embeddedness, professional confidence and staying narratives", *British Journal of Social Work*, 50.5, 1363–1381.

Butler, J. (2009) *Frames of War: When is life grievable?*, New York, Verso.

Butler, P. (2018) "Welfare spending for UK's poorest shrinks by £37 bn", *The Guardian,* 23 September.

Carpenter, J., Shardlow, S., Patsios, D. and Wood, M. (2015) "Developing the confidence and competence of newly qualified social workers", *British Journal of Social Work,* 45.1, 153–176.

Charlesworth, S. (2000) *A Phenomenology of Working-Class Experience*, Cambridge, Cambridge University Press.

Child Poverty Action Group in Scotland (2018) *Child Poverty in Scotland*, www.cpag.org. uk /Scotland/child-poverty-facts-and figures

Coffey, M., Dudgill, L. and Tattersall, A. (2004) "Stress in social services; mental well-being, constraints and job satisfaction", *British Journal of Social Work*, 34.7, 735–746.

Cohen, R. (2011) "Time, space and touch at work: Body space and labour process (re) organisation", *Sociology of Health and Illness*, 33.2 189–205.

Collins, S. (2008) "Statutory social workers: stress, job satisfaction, social support and individual differences", *British Journal of Social Work*, 38.6, 1173–1193.

Collins, S. (2020) *The Positive Social Worker*, London, Routledge.

The Present Context of Social Work in the UK   **27**

Community Care (2011) "Social workers struggle with hostile and intimidating parents", 30 September.

Community Care (2020a) "Most social workers say COVID-19 has negatively hit their work and the lives of those they support", 28 May.

Community Care (2020b) "Worsening mental health, domestic abuse and poverty as support falls: Social workers count the cost of COVID-19", 18 December.

Community Care (2020c) "Coronavirus: 75% of social workers feeling more negative about their work than last year, survey finds", 11 December.

Cook, L. and Zschomler, D. (2020) "Virtual home visits during the COVID-19 pandemic: Social workers' perspectives", *Practice*, 32.5, 401–408.

Cooper, J. (2011) "Most social workers threatened in past six months", *Community Care*, 14 November.

Cooper, J. (2015) "Exhausted social workers on the edge of burnout, but still achieving positive change", *Community Care*, 14 July.

Cuartero, M. and Campos-Vidal, J. (2019) "Self-care behaviours and their relationship with Satisfaction and Compassion Fatigue levels among social workers", *Social Work in Health Care*, 58.3, 274–290.

Department for Education (DfE) (2019) *Experimental Statistics: Children and Family Social Work Workforce in England, Year Ending 30 September, 2018*. London, Department for Education.

Dewe, P. and Cooper, C. (2012) *Wellbeing at Work*, London, Palgrave.

Donovan, T. (2017) "Social workers too stressed to do their jobs according to one survey", *Community Care*, 15 February.

Duschinsky, R., Lampitt, S. and Bell, S. (2016) *Sustaining Social Work: Between Power and Powerlessness*, London, Palgrave.

Evans, S., Huxley, P., Webber, M., Katona, C., Gately, C., Mears, A., Medina, J., Pajak, S. and Kendall, T. (2005) "The impact of statutory duties on mental health social workers in the UK", *Health and Social Care in the Community*, 13.2, 145–164.

Ferguson, H., Pink, S. and Kelly, L. (2021) "Social work and child protection for a post-pandemic world: the making of practice during COVID-19 and its renewal beyond it", *Journal of Social Work Practice*, DOI:10.1080/02650533.2021.1922368.

Fitzpatrick, S. Bramley, G., Sosenko, E., Blenkinsopp. J., Wood, J., Johnson, S., Littlewood, M. and Watts, B. (2018) *Destitution in the UK 2018*, York, Joseph Rowntree Foundation.

Folkman, S. and Moskowitz, J. (2004) "Coping: Pitfalls and Promise", *Review of Psychology*, 55, 745–774.

Garrett, P.M. (2018) *Welfare Words*, London, Sage.

Goldberg, D. and Williams, P. (1988) *A user's guide to the General Health Questionnaire*, Windsor, NFER-Nelson.

Graham, J. and Shier, M. (2010) "The social work profession and subjective wellbeing: The impact of a profession on subjective wellbeing", *British Journal of Social Work*, 40, 1553–1572.

Grant, L. and Kinman, G. (2014) *Developing Resilience for Social Work Practice*, London, Palgrave.

Grant, S., McCulloch, T. Daly, M. and Kettle, M. (2019) *Newly qualified social workers in Scotland: A five -year longitudinal study, Interim Report 3*, Dundee, SSSC.

Harris, J. (2003) *The Social Work Business*, Abingdon, Routledge.

Harris, J. (2019) "From Seebohm factories to neoliberal production lines? The social work labour process" in Lavalette, M. (ed.), *What is the future of Social Work?* Bristol, Policy Press, pp.132–142.

28 The Present Context of Social Work in the UK

Harrop, A. and Reid, H. (2015) *Inequality 2030: Fabian Policy Report*, London, Fabian Society.

Health and Safety Executive (2017) *Work Related Stress, Depression and Anxiety Statistics in Great Britain*. Liverpool, Health and Safety Executive.

Hermon, S. and Chahla, R. (2019) "A longitudinal study of stress and satisfaction among child welfare workers", *Journal of Social Work*, 19.2, 192–215.

Howard, A., Parris, S., Hall, J., Call, C., Razuri, E., Purvis, K. and Cross, D. (2015) "An examination of the relationships between the professional quality of life, adverse childhood experiences, resilience and work environments in a sample of human service providers", *Children and Youth Services Review*, 57, 141–148.

Hudson, J. and Webber, M. (2012) *The National Approved Mental Health Practitioner 2012: Final Report*, London, King's College.

Ingram, R. (2015) *Understanding Emotions in Social Work*, Maidenhead, Open University Press/ McGraw Hill.

International Federation of Social Workers (2020) *Practising During Pandemic Conditions: Ethical Guidance for Social Workers*, Rheinfelden, IFSW.

Johnson, C., Sanders-Earley, A., Shannon, E., Winterbotham, M., McLaughlin, H., Pollock, S., Scholar, H. and McCaughan, S. (2021) *Longitudinal Study of Local Authority Child and Family Social Workers (Wave3)*, London, Department for Education.

Joseph Rowntree Foundation (JRF) (2017) *UK Poverty 2017: A Comprehensive Analysis of Poverty Trends and Figures*, New York, Joseph Rowntree Foundation.

Jones, C. (2001) "Views from the front line: State social workers and New Labour", *British Journal of Social Work*, 35.7, 1063–1079.

Kalliath, P., Hughes, M. and Newcombe, P. (2012) "When work and family are in conflict: Impact on psychological strain experienced by social workers in Australia", *Australian Social Work*, 65, 355–371.

Kalliath, P. and Kalliath, T. (2015) "Work-family conflict and its impact on the job satisfaction of social workers", *British Journal of Social Work*, 45.1, 241–259.

Kalliath P., Kalliath, T. and Chan, X.W. (2019) "Linking work-family enrichment to job satisfaction and job wellbeing and family support: A moderated median analysis of social workers across India", *British Journal of Social Work*, 49.1, 234–255.

Karpetis, G. (2015) "Psychological distress among mental health social workers", *European Journal of Social Work*, 18.5, 745–755.

Kearns, S. and McArdle, K. (2012) "Doing it right? Assessing the narratives of identity of recently qualified social workers through the lens of resilience – I am, I have, I can" *Child and Family Social Work,* 17, 385–394.

Killian, K. (2008) "Helping till it hurts? A multi-method study of compassion fatigue, burnout and self-care in clinicians working with trauma survivors", *Traumatology*, 14, 32–44.

Kingstone, T., Campbell, P., Andras, A., Nixon, K., Mallen, C. and Dikomitis, L. (2021) "Exploring the impact of the first wave of COVID-19 on social work practice in England, UK", *British Journal of Social Work,* DOI:10.1093/bjsw/bcab66.

Kinman, G. and Grant, L. (2020) "Emotional demands, compassion and mental health in social workers", *Occupational Medicine*, 70.2, 89–94.

Kinman, G, McDowall, A. and Uys, M. (2014) "The work/home interface: building effective boundaries" in Grant. L. and Kinman, G. (eds.) *Developing Resilience for Social Work Practice*, London, Palgrave, pp.33–53.

Kong, S-T. and Noone, C. (2021) *Social Work During COVID-19: Learning for the Future: Challenges, Best Practice and Professional Transformation,* Birmingham, BASW.

The Present Context of Social Work in the UK **29**

Lavalette, M. (2019) "Austerity and the context of social work today" in Lavalette, M. (ed.) *What is the Future of Social Work?* Bristol, Policy Press, pp.3–22.

Lazarus, R. (2000) "Toward better research on stress and coping", *American Psychologist*, 55, 665–673.

Lazarus, R. (2006) *Stress and Emotions: A New Synthesis*, New York, Free Association.

Lefevre, M., Matheny, J. and Kelt, G. (2003) "Eustress, distress and interpretation in occupational stress", *Journal of Managerial Psychology*, 7, 726–744.

Legatum Institute (2020) *Poverty Has Risen as a Result of the Pandemic*, London, Legatum Institute.

Littlechild, B. (2005) "The nature and effects of violence against child protection social workers: Providing effective support", *British Journal of Social Work*, 35.3, 387401.

Littlechild, B., Hunt, S. Goddard, G., Cooper, J., Raynes, B. and Wild, J. (2016) "The effects of violence and aggression from parents on child protection workers personal, family and professional lives", *Sage Open*, 6.1, 1–2, DOI: 10.1177/2158244015624951.

Lloyd, C., King, R. and Chenoweth, L. (2002) "Social work stress and burnout: A review", *Journal of Mental Health*, 11, 255–265.

Martin-Cuellar, A., Atentio, D., Kelly, R. and Lardier, D. (2018) "Mindfulness as a moderator of clinical history of trauma on compassion satisfaction", *The Family Journal*, 26.3, 358–368.

Maslach, C. (2003) *Burnout: The Cost of Caring*, Cambridge MA, Malor Books.

Marmot, M., Allen, J., Boyce, T. Goldblatt, P. and Morrison, J. (2020) *Health Equity in England. The Marmot Review 10 years on*, London, The Health Foundation.

McFadden, P. (2016) *Measuring Burnout among UK Social Workers*, Belfast, Queen's University, Belfast and Community Care.

McFadden, P., Campbell, J. and Taylor, B. (2015) "Resilience and burnout in child protection social workers: Individual and organisational themes from a systematic literature review", *British Journal of Social Work*, 45.3, 1546–1563.

McFadden, P., Gillen, P., Moriarty, J. Mallett, J., Schroder, H., Ravalier, J., Manthorpe, J., Harron, J. and Currie, D. (2020) *Health and Social Care Workers Quality of Working Life and Coping While Working during the COVID 19 Pandemic, 7 May-3 July 2020: Findings from a UK survey*, Belfast, Ulster University.

McFadden, P., Neill, R., Mallett, J. et al. (2021) "Mental well-being and quality of working life in UK social workers before and during the COVID-19 pandemic: A propensity score matching study", *British Journal of Social Work*, DOI:10.1093/bjsw/bcab108.

McLean, J. and Andrew, T. (2000) "Commitment, job satisfaction, stress and control among social services managers and social workers in the UK", *Administration in Social Work*, 23.4, 93–117.

MENCAP (2020) *My Health, My Life: Barriers to Health Care for People with a Learning Disability during the Pandemic*, Belfast, MENCAP.

Mickel, A. (2009) "Surveys reveal social workers' poor working conditions", *Community Care*, 29 July.

Moriarty, J., Baginsky, M. and Manthorpe, J. (2015) *Literature review of the roles and issues within the social work profession in England*, London, Social Care Workforce Research Unit, King's College.

Morris, L. (2015) "The process of decision making by stressed social workers: To stay or leave the workplace?", *International Review of Psychiatry*, 17.3, 357–364.

National Audit Office (2018) *Financial Sustainability of Local Authorities 2018*, London, NAO.

30 The Present Context of Social Work in the UK

Nelson, D. and Simmons, P. (2003) "Health psychology and work stress: A more positive approach" in Quick, J. and Tetrick, L. (eds.) *Handbook of Occupational Psychology*, Washington DC, American Psychological Society, pp.97–119.

Newsome, S. Waldo, M. and Gruszka, C. (2012) "Mindfulness groupwork: Preventing Stress and increasing self-compassion among helping professionals in training", *The Journal for Specialists in Group Work*, 37.4, 297–311.

Office of National Statistics (2020) *Coronavirus (COVID-19) Related Deaths by Ethnic Group, England and Wales, March 2020 – 15 May 2020*, London, ONS.

Pentaraki, M. (2017) "'I am in a constant state of insecurity trying to make ends meet, like our service users': Shared austerity reality between social workers and service users: Towards a preliminary conceptualisation", *British Journal of Social Work*, 47, 1245–1261.

Phillips, J., Westaby, C., Ainslie, S. and Fowler, A. (2021) "'I don't like this job in my front room': Practising probation in the COVID-19 pandemic", *Probation Journal*, 68.4, 426–443.

Pink, S., Ferguson, H. and Kelly, L. (2021) "Digital Social Work: Conceptualisng a hybrid anticipatory practice", *Qualitative Social Work*, DOI: 10.1177/14733250211003647.

Pithouse, A., Brookfield, C. and Rees, A. (2019) "Why are social workers in Wales the 'Happiest'? A conundrum explained", *British Journal of Social Work*, 49.7, 1987–2006.

Pithouse, A., Rees, A., Brookfield, C. and Djupvik, A. (2021) "Understanding social work workforce satisfaction", *Journal of Social Work*, 21.1, 107–127.

Podsakoff, N., Lepine, J. and Lepine, M. (2007) "Differential challenge hindrance-stressor relationships with job attitudes, turnover intentions, turnover and withdrawal behaviour; a meta-analysis", *Journal of Applied Psychology*, 92, 438–454.

Pooler, D., Wolfer, T. and Freeman, M. (2014a) "Finding joy in social work: Interpersonal resources", *Families in Society*, 95.1, 34–42.

Pooler, D., Wolfer, T. and Freeman. M. (2014b) "Finding joy in social work: Intrapersonal resources", *Social Work*.59.3, 213–221.

Rajan-Rankin, S. (2014) "Self-identity, embodiment and the development of resilience", *British Journal of Social Work*, 44.8, 2426–2442.

Ramon, S. and Morris, L. (2005) "Responding to perceived stress in a social services department: Applying a participative strategy", *Research, Policy and Planning*, 23, 43–54.

Ravalier, J. (2017) *UK Social Workers: Working Conditions and Wellbeing*, Birmingham, BASW.

Ravalier, J. (2019) "Psychosocial working conditions and stress in UK social workers" *British Journal of Social Work*, 49.2, 371–390.

Ravalier, J. and Allen, R. (2020) *Social Worker Wellbeing and Working Conditions: Good Practice Toolkit*, Birmingham and Bath, BASW, Bath Spa University and The Social Workers Union.

Ravalier, J. McFadden, P., Boichat, C. Claburn, O. and Moriarty, J. (2021) "Wellbeing: A large mixed methods study", *British Journal of Social Work*, 51.1, 297–317.

Robertson, I. and Cooper, C. (2011) *Wellbeing, Productivity and Happiness at Work*, London, Palgrave.

Rose, M. (2003) "Good deal, bad deal? Job satisfaction in occupations", *Work, Employment and Society*, 17.3, 503–530.

Ruch, G., Turney, D. and Ward, A. (2018) *Relationship Based Social Work*, London, Jessica Kingsley.

Saleebey, D. (2009) *The Strengths Perspective in Social Work Practice*, Boston, Allyn and Bacon.

The Present Context of Social Work in the UK **31**

Savaya, R. (2022) "Shame and Pride among Social Workers in Israel: A Concept Map", *British Journal of Social Work*, DOI:10.1093/bjsw/bcacf026.

Senreich, E., Straussner, S. and Steen, J. (2020) "The work experiences of social workers: Factors impacting compassion satisfaction and workplace stress", *Journal of Social Service Research*, 46.1, 93–109.

Selye, H. (1984) *The Stress of Life*, New York, McGraw-Hill.

Shaufeli, W. and Peeters, M. (2000) "Job stress and burnout among correctional officers: A literature review", *International Journal of Stress Management*, 7, 19–47.

Shraer, R. (2015) "Social workers too stressed to do their jobs according to survey", *Community Care,* 15 January.

Silman, J. (2020) "'Before there were peaks and troughs-with COVID-19 its relentless': Social work eight months into the pandemic", *Community Care*, 18 December.

Simmons, B. and Nelson, D. (2007) "Eustress at work: Extending the holistic model" in Nelson, D. and Cooper, D. (eds), *Positive Organisational Behaviour*, London, Sage, pp.40–65.

Skills for Care (2013) *Violence against Social Care and Support Staff Summary of Research*, Leeds, Skills for Care.

Stalker, C., Mendell, D., French, K., Harvey, C. and Wright, W. (2007) "Child welfare workers who are exhausted yet satisfied with their jobs: How do they do it?", *Child and Family Social Work*, 12, 82–191.

Stanley, S., Buvaneswari, G. and Arumugam, M. (2018) "Resilience as a moderator of stress and burnout: A study of women social workers in India", *International Social Work*, 64.1, 40–58.

Storey, J. and Billingham, J. (2001) "Occupational Stress in Social Work", *Social Work Education*, 20, 659–671.

Tedam, P. (2021) "To shield or not to shield? There should be no question-black African social workers experiences during COVID-19 in England", *British Journal of Social Work*, DOI:10.1093/bjswbcab107.

The Guardian (2017) "A ray of hope for social workers", 29 March.

The Guardian (2018) "Poorest councils have seen deepest budget cuts", 9 October.

The Guardian (2021a) "BAME deaths: Muslim body says exclusion policy led to tragic results", 23 February.

The Guardian (2021b) "Self -harm rate among young children in the UK doubles in six years", 16 February.

The Guardian (2021c) "Home schooling: Women's lockdown burden growing compared with men's share", 20 February.

Tham, P. (2018a) "A Professional Role in Transition: Swedish Child Welfare Social Workers descriptions of their work in 2003 and 2014", *British Journal of Social Work*, 48.2, 449–467.

Tham, P. (2018b) "Where the need is greatest: A comparison of working conditions of social workers in Swedish low-, middle-and high-income areas in 2003 and 2014", *Nordic Social Work Research*, 18.2, 185–200.

Thomas, J. (2013) "Association of personal distress with burnout, compassion fatigue and compassion satisfaction among clinical social workers", *Journal of Social Service Research*, 39.3, 365–379.

Thomas, J. and Otis, M. (2010) "Intrapsychic correlates of professional quality of life: Mindfulness, empathy and emotional separation", *Journal of the Society for Social Work and Research*, 1, 83–98.

Ting, I., Jacobson, J. and Sanders, S. (2011) "Current levels of perceived stress among mental health social workers who work with suicidal clients", *Social Work*, 56, 327–336.

32 The Present Context of Social Work in the UK

Tosone, C., Nuttman-Shwartz, O. and Stevens, T. (2012) "Shared trauma? When the Professional is Personal", *Clinical Social Work Journal*, 40, 231–239.

Turner, D. (ed.) (2020) *Social Work and COVID-19: Lessons for Education and Practice*, St. Albans, Critical Publishing.

Van Heugten, K. (2011) *Social work under Pressure*, London, Jessica Kingsley.

Wagaman, M., Geiger, J., Shockley, C. and Segal, A. (2015) "The role of empathy in burnout, compassion satisfaction and secondary traumatic stress among social workers", *Social Work*, 60.3, 201–209.

Wainwright, D. and Calnan, M. (2002) *Work Stress: The Making of a Modern Epidemic*, Buckingham, OU Press.

Way, I., Van Deusen, K., Martin, C., Applegate, B. and Yandle, D. (2004) "Vicarious trauma: A comparison of clinicians who treat survivors of sexual abuse and sexual offenders", *Journal of Interpersonal Violence*, 19.1, 49–71.

Wilberforce, N., Jacobs, S., Challis, D., Manthorpe, J., Stevens, M., Jasper, R., Fernandez, J.-L., Glendenning, C., Jones, K., Knapp, M., Moran, N. and Netten, A. (2014) "Revisiting the causes of stress in social work: Sources of job demands, control and support in personalised adult care", *British Journal of Social Work*, 44, 812–830.

Yi, J., Kim, M., Choi, K. and Droubay, B. (2019) "Compassion satisfaction and compassion fatigue among medical social workers in Korea: The role of empathy", *Social Work in Health Care*, 58.10, 970–987.

Yuill, C. (2018) "Social workers and alienation: The compassionate self and the disappointed juggler", *Critical and Radical Social Work*, 6.3, 275–289.

2
COMPASSION

Introduction

Of all the concepts explored in the different chapters of this book, compassion is perhaps the longest established, most well known and most well used. However, more detailed consideration reveals controversies about the meaning and purpose of compassion and attempts to distinguish it from other core concepts such as care and empathy. Furthermore, surprisingly, although it has been referred to briefly in many social work texts over the years, compassion has received little in-depth attention either in social work research or in social work literature. This has led to it being described as "a relatively new but still unknown concept" (Ortego-Galan et al., 2021, p.1350).

In this chapter, we will examine briefly the religious, spiritual, philosophical roots of suffering and compassion, and the more recent development of compassion as a "scientific", psychological concept, which has made considerable impact in the field of health care – in contrast to its limited impact upon social work. We will consider different definitions, education and training about compassion and critical perspectives, including the tendency to neglect the structural and organisational contexts in which it is located.

We will explore how social workers' intentions to be compassionate in response to suffering can be thwarted by inequalities, government policies, agency policies and procedures, the impact of outcome-based rational/technical approaches, and a lack of resources. We will also consider debates about the impact, the influences of professionalism upon social workers' abilities to express compassion in their day-to-day practices. While there is a need for compassion to receive more attention in social work, issues about the pros and cons of "institutionalising" it will be explored, accompanied by the possible dangers of it becoming an excessively quantifiable, measurable, standardised, codified,

DOI: 10.4324/9781003112532-3

34 Compassion

accountable concept – as in the case of nursing. We will move on to look at the limited attention given to compassion in qualifying and post-qualifying social work education and training, considering ways in which the situation might be progressed to resolve this issue. For instance, we will explore the links between compassion and other concepts learned in social work education – aspects which tend to have been neglected in existing literature and practices.

The Foundations of Compassion and Definitions of Compassion

As human beings, despite our often individualistic, competitive, cruel, callous, and self-absorbed behaviours both in the past and in the present, we can also be understanding, helpful, supportive, co-operative, and compassionate. Compassion is "one of the most important and distinctive qualities of the human mind" (Gilbert, 2013, p.xiii). Compassion has a long history in philosophy and of several thousand years in religious traditions such as Islam, Hinduism, Christianity, Judaism, and Buddhism (Davidson and Harrington, 2002). For instance, the Dalai Lama (1997) sees compassion as the "essence" of Buddhism, which itself has been called "a religion of compassion" and has also influenced psychological literature (Price, 2010; Ivtzan et al., 2016, p.138). While Gilbert (2013) acknowledges the impetus for the development of compassion coming from religious, spiritual, and philosophical roots, at the same time he comments on the development of "the science" of psychology and its approach to compassion in recent years.

Van de Cingel (2009) argues that compassion is derived from theories of virtue. It is one virtue amongst many, such as wisdom, courage, and humility, but is "central to improving the human condition...[it] is consistent with social work's commitment to vulnerable populations" (Collins et al., 2015, p.101). Nussbaum (1996, p.37) views compassion as "an essential bridge to justice". Ledoux, (2015) notes that Seneca, Rousseau, and Schopenhauer perceived compassion to be a fuel for social justice. Schopenhauer (1995) explored compassion as a solution to the "great mystery of ethics", a fundamental incentive for action, and as the foundation for any moral framework, "because people care in a deep ... way about the suffering of others" (Ivtzan et al., 2016, p.138). Armstrong (2010) and Doris (2010) also argue "there is a moral component to compassion... to be affected and moved to action by another's distress is a basis for living a moral life" (Ledoux, 2015, p.2044). Therefore, "in moral behaviour...we ourselves as persons and as ... workers ...highlight our responsibility and actions based upon, and emphasised by, compassion" (Collins, 2018, p.11). Gregory (2015) also provides an extensive discussion emphasising that compassion extends beyond the requirements of professional rules, regulations, and roles.

Compassion therefore is seen as a cornerstone of morality, cohesion, and solidarity – for a passionate, inspiring account of its development, see von Dietze and Orb (2000). Ozawa de Silva et al. (2012, p.148) go on to cite the Dalai Lama when they conclude that compassion is "a foundation for secular ethics...

Compassion **35**

an ethics based on fundamental human values irrespective of a person's religious beliefs", with a decreased, limited emphasis on the self, and enhanced feelings of interconnectedness with other people, the environment and surrounding world.

One of the other important foundational aspects of compassion is that we are all vulnerable; we all experience suffering during our lives, both ourselves and other people – we share mutual experiences of suffering as human beings such as illness and loss in similar and in diverse ways (Ling et al., 2020; Ovrelid, 2008). We recognise parts of our suffering in other people's suffering. As the Dalai Lama (2002, p.76) emphasises "people have... ability to connect deeply and spontaneously with the suffering of others". Nussbaum (1996) also points out that compassion rests on the argument that we have experienced, or will experience, vulnerabilities ourselves, as well as seeing that the suffering of other people is important, significant, is not justified, can be worked on, and perhaps resolved. Compassion is therefore a response to human frailty "that informs and motivates [us]...towards others" (O' Connell, 2009, p.3) So, we all have been, are, or will be, subject to different degrees of suffering that can be alleviated.

Compassion has been defined in different, ambiguous, multi-faceted ways (for example, see Ozawa de Silva et al., 2012). However, the Latin roots of the word compassion combine "com" meaning "with" or "together" and "pati" meaning "to suffer". Hence "the essence of compassion is suffering with others" (Tanner, 2020, p.1689). Nouwen et al. (2002, p.4) suggest that "compassion asks us to go where it hurts, to enter into places of pain, to share in brokenness, fear, confusion and anger". It entails experiencing anxiety, disappointment, frustration, and sorrow (Gilbert, 2013). However, scholars also point out, although compassion may be mainly, and usually, focused on vulnerability, pain, and alleviating suffering, it is not necessarily restricted to sharing negative emotions; it can also entail sharing pleasure and joy with people (Gilbert, 2013; Ivtzan et al., 2016; von Dietze and Orb, 2000). Gilbert (2019) goes on to argue therefore that the emotions associated with compassion are complex and clearly context dependent.

Gilbert (2019, p.109) points out that while there are different views about compassion, "it is linked to engagement with distress and suffering and a wish to alleviate it". Another recent definition of compassion states it is "a virtuous and intentional response to...ameliorate suffering through relational understanding and action" (Sinclair et al., 2020 p. 2). The Charter for Compassion (2009, para.1) also adds a further, wider dimension, which links to social work values, in suggesting compassion:

> Impels us to alleviate suffering...to honour the inviolable sanctity of every human being, treating everybody without exception with absolute justice, equity, and respect.

Compassion recognises people can, and do, have genuine concern for each other (Ivtzan et al., 2016); "it creates a desire to act on behalf of others" (O' Connell,

36 Compassion

2009, p.3). It is "an opposite of disgust, condemnation and rejection" (Nussbaum, 2001, p.50). People are perceived as fundamentally, inherently compassionate (Gibbs, 2017). Hence compassion also includes a nurturing element, linked to expressing concern for others which is one of its central features (Gilbert, 2005; Ledoux, 2015; Ling et al., 2020). Gilbert (2013) suggests desires to be genuinely supportive lie at the roots of compassion. The intention is to be helpful, not harmful, to develop one's own compassion which can be directed towards other people without necessarily wishing for, or expecting, reciprocation. However, Gilbert (2013) also notes that it is important to be concerned about, to care for oneself, to be compassionate, to be kind to oneself. This will be explored in considerable depth in the self-compassion and self-care chapters that follow.

However, it is important to consider debates about the place of "the self" in relation to compassion. Most approaches to compassion encourage altruism, a reduced emphasis on individual egoism and the self (for example, Ling et al., 2020; Sinclair et al., 2017). Indeed, some Buddhist perspectives on compassion take this further. They advocate the idea of "no self", with the self-being seen as either an unhelpful construct or a destructive "illusion", with the self constantly, moving, changing, and reconstructing itself (Epstein, 1988). For a stimulating, provocative perspective on this argument, the work of Ovrelid (2008) is worth exploring. Ivtzan et al. (2016, p.145) go as far as to say that "the individualistic model of self-hood-the idea that we exist as separate, fixed, and bounded entities can be regarded as an incorrect fiction but a fiction that underlies many... problems". We will also explore further aspects of the limitations of preoccupation with the self in the final chapter on mindfulness.

Some perspectives on compassion go on to argue that one way to overcome suffering is by transcending the self, by moving beyond the self, towards selflessness, creating a more expansive identity – involving other people and connection with people (Ovrelid, 2008). Thus, compassion entails positive thoughts, warmth, understanding, concern for people's well-being and a desire to improve it. This arises from a sense of altruism and shared, common humanity (Batson, 2011; von Dietze and Orb, 2000). However, while these ideas recognise interconnectivity, intersubjectivity, and collectivism, ultimately many compassion theorists do not undervalue people as individuals with agency, rather that individuals, intersubjectivity, and collectivism are not seen as dichotomies, but as dialogical, as interacting with each other (Harris, 2020; Ivtzan et al., 2016). Nussbaum (1996) argues that compassion is linked to the interconnectivity, for example, of individuals, institutions, and communities. Taking the theme of interconnectivity further, Fernando and Consedine (2014) discuss a helpful, transactional, system-based model of compassion linked to interactions between service users, their families, the environment, cultures, organisational perspectives, professional affiliations, and practitioners themselves.

Kirby (2017) suggests research about compassion has only really developed in the past 20 years or so, but this research highlights compassion's many positive aspects. Kirby et al. (2017) point out compassion has benefits for both physiological and mental health and emotional regulation. Benefits include increased feelings of well-being, affiliation, reward, reduced conflictual and aggressive behaviours, a growing sense of identification with other people, concern for other people, and pro-social behaviours (for instance, Jinpa, 2016). In a rare study of service user perspectives, Bramley and Matiti (2014) carried out a small-scale study of patients' experiences of compassion in a UK hospital. They found patients valued workers getting to know them, giving them time, demonstrating understanding of their experiences, and the importance of communicating compassion. While active commitment to relationships, to spending time with patients was valued, patients also valued fleeting contacts and small acts, brief demonstrations of compassion.

Debates about Compassion

Ozawa de Silva et al. (2012) and Ivtzan et al. (2016) confirm compassion involves various components. These can include motivational, affective, cognitive, and behavioural elements. Motivational elements involve the desire, the will to reduce another person's suffering. Affective and cognitive elements involve recognising suffering, offering sympathy and empathy related to responses to people's suffering. Behavioural elements include desires to then take actions to attempt to resolve suffering. Therefore "we learn to direct our attention compassionately, to think and reason compassionately, to feel compassionately, to behave compassionately" (Gilbert, 2013, p.218).

However, debates are evident, for instance, about "whether compassion is an *affective* state that motivates compassionate behaviour or is a primary *motive* that gives rise to emotion" (Gilbert, 2019, p.108). Goetz et al. (2010, p.341) defined compassion as "a distinctive affective experience whose primary function is to facilitate cooperation and protection of … those who suffer". Yet when Ekman (2016) surveyed emotion researchers only 20 per cent of respondents, agreed that compassion is an emotion. Also, within some Buddhist approaches to compassion, there is a focus on attending to suffering, a commitment to relieve it, with compassionate intentionality and motivation being perceived as central. Indeed, some Buddhist approaches to compassion specifically argue that it is not an emotion, although Buddhist traditions can also locate compassion within motivational constructs involving loving kindness and equanimity (Dalai Lama, 2001; Macbeth and Gumley, 2012).

Goetz et al. (2010) and Gilbert (2019) appear to conclude that, ultimately, compassion is neither "just" an emotion nor "just" motivation; it involves both a blend of motivation, reason, emotion, and behaviour.

From a behavioural perspective, Gilbert (2013, p.217) suggests "compassion can be defined as behaviour that aims to nurture, look after, teach, guide, mentor, soothe, protect, offer feelings of acceptance and belonging-in order to help another person". Kindness and warmth should be allied with courage, with an ability to tolerate distress, so that compassionate tolerance can become a focus

38 Compassion

(Gilbert, 2013; Kanov et al., 2017; Strauss et al., 2016). Courage and tolerance entail experiencing difficult emotions in oneself when working with suffering, without becoming too preoccupied with one's own responses or feeling overwhelmed. Acceptance entails non-judgment; it involves accepting other people even when another person's attitudes and behaviours might provoke feelings of frustration, fear, distaste, or disgust in the practitioner (Gilbert, 2013; Strauss et al., 2016). These ideas clearly link well to "traditional" social work values which we shall consider later. Compassionate attitudes and behaviours also require attributes, competences, and skills allied to knowledge of the causes of suffering and with efforts to acquire the means to help. Therefore, tolerance and acceptance of suffering are seen as very different to passive resignation, to feelings of powerlessness or hopelessness; they involve action elements (Gilbert, 2013). Gilbert et al.'s (2017) compassion scales reflect this commitment to action.

While not all compassion theorists would agree with the following summary, Strauss et al. (2016) go on to suggest compassion contains five elements, which have been incorporated into recent compassion scales (Gu et al., 2020; Pommier et al., 2020). These are:

- Recognition of suffering.
- Understanding the universality of experiences of suffering.
- Having feelings for the suffering of persons and connecting with them emotionally and cognitively.
- Tolerating and accepting uncomfortable feelings when responding to suffering, including frustration, anger, and distaste.
- Having the motivation to act to alleviate suffering.

Further Debates Surrounding Compassion

Debates are also evident about distinctions between sympathy, empathy, and compassion. Sympathy can be seen as the ability to be emotionally moved by, to feel for other people (Larkin, 2016). Gilbert (2013) suggests sensitivity and sympathy towards distress operate together and are important components of compassion. However, sympathy may involve feelings of pity, may have patronising or condescending elements, it does not necessarily entail communication of understanding to people or "closeness" in relationships; it can involve distancing and self-protection of a worker (Sinclair et al., 2017).

Empathy is perceived as a cognitive and affective endeavour through which we feel or sense the emotions of other people; we communicate our understanding to them. It is widely and clearly recognised as a vital, central skill in counselling. At the core of empathy are workers' efforts to convey to other people understanding of their feelings through non-verbal and, particularly, verbal responses, to tune in, to mirror, to reflect back their immediate and hidden feelings, experiences, and viewpoints (Egan, 2010; Rogers, 1967). In contrast, while compassion has an affective component, i.e. awareness, sensitivity, responsiveness to the feelings and suffering of other people, what distinguishes it from empathy is that it involves *a desire to act to alleviate suffering*. The desire to act or acting to alleviate suffering goes well beyond verbal communication in an interview situation. It goes beyond words; it involves an intention to act, to accompany and follow-up words with empowering deeds in partnership with service users (for example, Canda et al., 2020; Gilbert and Choden, 2013; Kinman and Grant, 2020; Steffen and Masters, 2005; Tsang, 2017). Thus, compassion involves a desire to act, to resist, to struggle, to persist, to persevere, to improve, and to change situations. In addition to a nurturing, concerned orientation, compassion also can focus on social justice approaches associated with its philosophical foundations (Nussbaum, 1996; Ovrelid, 2008; von Dietze and Orb, 2000). Many writers who advocate an action element to compassion therefore highlight wider perspectives, based around working within, and against, government policies, social policies, and organisational policies and procedures (such as, Collins et al. 2015; Gilbert, 2013). Nevertheless, other writers debate and dispute the necessity to actually act, arguing "wider" compassionate action may not always be possible, suggesting perhaps reasonably enough, that "being there", sharing feelings about experiences of suffering with people can clearly be beneficial in, and of, themselves (for example, Dutton et al., 2014; Hay, 2019; Jinpa, 2016; Stickle, 2016).

There are also interesting, quite extensive debates surrounding the relationship of compassion with, or to, care (for example, Collins, 2018; Tanner, 2020). This contentious area appears to be one that merits further investigation, but the approach taken here in this chapter is to focus on compassion. Compassion is distinguished from care by many researchers and writers on account of its more direct emphasis on suffering, on sharing, preventing, and alleviating suffering (Younas and Madigan, 2019).

Criticisms of Compassion

Some sociologically based writers have raised questions about the implications of compassion when set within hegemonic structures, where compassionate intentions to be helpful can also be associated with problematic aspects. Thus, it is argued compassion and policy can become intermingled – which sometimes can produce positive interactions, but at other times can also produce harm. Berlant (2004), Hoggett (2006), and others warn about the dangers of "compassionate conservatism", which can involve an excessive focus on the individual, ideas about the "deserving" and "undeserving", and disengagement from the state's positive responsibility for people. Singleton and Mee (2017) quote an extreme example of a nurse at the Nuremberg trials following the Second World War who had administered lethal doses of drugs to people experiencing learning disabilities in a hospital setting. She said: "When giving the… medicine I proceeded with a lot of compassion… I told people they would have to take a cure…I took them lovingly and stroked them" (Ebbinghaus, 1987, p.239). Singleton and Mee

40 Compassion

(2017, p.139) point out that this was obviously a grossly uncompassionate act, state murder, carried out with alleged compassion, supported by the "social, political and institutional context". Therefore, this striking, very extreme example illustrates compassion is not always associated with good; it can be associated with harm and negative actions, even being used to justify and to enable suffering.

Expressions of, and discussions about, suffering and hopes for compassion can also involve taking risks. They may involve revealing uncertainties, vulnerability, doubts, fears, lack of trust, and issues of whether, when, how to open up, and how far to go in discussion about suffering and compassion (Dutton et al., 2014; Gilbert, 2013; Kanov et al., 2017).

Berlant (2004), Vittelone (2011), and Singleton and Mee (2017) all raise important questions regarding the meaning of compassion, about the way compassion is actually enacted, who is being compassionate, what practices might be seen as compassionate in interactions between workers and service users. In contrast to many compassion theorists who argue, as we have seen, that we all experience suffering together, Berlant (2004) and Simpson et al. (2014) argue "the compassionate" is often enacted by those who have power, authority, influence, "social privilege", and do so "at a distance"; a comment that could well be applied to social work.

Many writers and researchers have raised questions about the organisational setting for compassion (for example, Crawford et al., 2014; de Zulueta, 2013; Harris, 2020; Henshall et al., 2017). They have expressed concern about practitioners trying to work compassionately in organisations experiencing the long-term impact of austerity, cuts, staff shortages, staff changes and illnesses, long working hours, often limited supervision, restricted professional development opportunities with an emphasis on targets and outcomes, rather than process. It would therefore be helpful to know more about the contribution organisations, their cultures, and climates make to attitudes and behaviours of workers, supervisors, managers, and leaders surrounding compassion and vice versa. We shall briefly consider these aspects later in the chapter when examining compassion and social work organisations.

Furthermore, compassion takes place under the influence of a structural context linked to a wide range of oppressions. While individual compassion may be associated with heightened imaginative awareness of, and sensitivity to, inequality and intentions to weaken hierarchies of oppression, compassion can also be considered to be "a highly political and cultural [concept] used in the service of seeming to promote equality while reproducing asymmetries ...[as] compassion, far from being politically neutral, reflects and distributes relations of inequality and difference" (Singleton and Mee, 2017, p.131 and p.140).

Hence, Whitebrook (2002, 2014), Berlant (2004), and Vittelone (2011) are all concerned to go beyond small-scale practices of individual compassion, sympathy and empathy "to a politics of compassion that promotes an understanding of the structural conditions of inequality and injustice and creates potential for social change" (Singleton and Mee, 2017, p.141). The aim is to link personal relationships to a politics which entails the practice of equality, "to create possibilities for intervention in the structural conditions that provoke suffering" (Singleton and Mee, 2017, p.141). Compassion is performed in a societal and cultural context. Therefore, a convincing case is made for moving compassion beyond the individual worker, service user, and a mainly individualistic and family-oriented approach, to one which also firmly locates compassionate interventions in a wider systemic, organisational, political, and structural setting (for instance, Harris, 2020).

The emphasis on individualised approaches to compassion is seen partly, for example, in the arguments that individualistic compassion should be "measured" more carefully, specifically, and comprehensively in order to clarify its nature, prevalence and contribution (Kirby et al., 2017; Ling et al., 2020; Sinclair et al., 2022). The reliability and the validity of a range of existing scales used to assess compassion were questioned extensively in a comprehensive survey by Strauss et al. (2016). The latter also point out the heavy emphasis on quantitative questionnaires at the expense of the limited use of qualitative research about compassion. Strauss et al. (2016) and Singleton and Mee (2017) also warn about other dangers of the measurement, quantification, codification, and standardisation of compassion. They, and Flores and Brown (2018), suggest such "measures" could lead to the "institutionalisation" of compassion. This involves surveillance and control of practitioners to "prove" they are compassionately competent as part of their professional development and continuing accreditation – as is the case in nursing. Singleton and Mee (2017) argue that nursing policies surrounding compassion in the UK links compassion with "calculation" and should move away from this focus on quantification.

It is perhaps surprising that research into an apparently well-established concept such as compassion is a very recent phenomenon; it is in its "infancy" compared to more recently developed concepts such as compassion fatigue (examined in the following chapter). There are a number of areas which might be developed in the future (Fernando and Consedine, 2014; Ling et al., 2020; Sinclair et al., 2020). These include not only exploration of workers' ability to offer compassion, but also, more attention could, and should, be given to working in partnership with people on the so-called "receiving end", i.e. the contributions, perceptions, and experiences of compassion by service users (Simpson et al., 2014; Sinclair et al. 2022). This should involve more detailed attempts to assess the intensity, the frequency, and the impact of compassion upon service users (see, for instance, Kirby et al., 2017). The latter, in their meta-analysis also suggest much more attention should be given to experiences of compassion in relation to organisational contexts, gender, sexuality, ethnic minority groups, younger, older, and disabled people. For example, a study by Singh et al. (2018) indicated very little research had been undertaken that focused upon compassion and ethnically diverse populations.

Education and Training for Compassion

It is not surprising that, if there are many different definitions of compassion, there will also be many different forms of compassion training. Some writers celebrate the positives of these differences (such as Gilbert, 2019; Stickle, 2016; Tanner, 2020) while others are more critical. Therefore, Ledoux (2015) raises questions about compassion training as do Kirby et al. (2017), Sinclair et al. (2020), and Ling et al. (2020). The latter point out that there is a wide variety, a broad range of competencies linked to compassion training, for instance, sympathy, empathy, distress tolerance, compassion meditation, loving kindness meditation, and breath awareness. The relevance of some of these concepts to compassion is, rightly or wrongly, questioned.

Compassion training can also vary greatly in length as well as content. Training experiences include a range of learning experiences linked to didactic teaching, experiential work, reflective and homework exercises. Some training programmes are one year long. Others such as Compassion Cultivation Training and Cognitively Based Compassion Training are about eight weeks long (Jinpa, 2016; Ozawa de Silva et al., 2012). Compassion cultivation programmes have promoted improvements in compassion for others (Jazaieri et al, 2014). One eight-week long programme resulted in participants being more likely to help a person suffering (Fernando and Consedine, 2014). There are also short, two weeks courses, for example, which have resulted in increased altruistic behaviour (Weng et al., 2013) and positive psychological changes in well-being (Matos et al., 2017). Compassion training is said to develop a worker's ability to: be more aware of the suffering of other people; develop concern for others; encourage desires to relieve suffering; and be ready to take action to relieve it (Jazaieri et al., 2014). Stickle (2016) and Tanner (2020) also highlight positive research findings. They note Klimecki et al. (2012, p.8) found that compassion training mapped the activation of "neural correlates of love, affiliation and positive affect" in participants. Researchers also discovered the use of various forms of meditation-related approaches in compassion training-enabled participants to learn how to better express compassion to other people, with compassion responses reflecting increased resilience, altruism, and stronger connections with the suffering of others, while maintaining positive feelings in themselves such as joy and warmth, rather than experiencing distress (Engen and Singer, 2015; Singer and Klimecki, 2014). The beneficial effects of viewing videos of the sufferings of others also helped to heighten aspects of compassion, such as nurture and positive affiliation with other people, as evidenced in MRI scans (Lutz et al., 2008). Also, recently, health-care workers viewing video scenarios linked to common humanity experiences demonstrated increases in levels of compassion, enhanced feelings of connection, and common bonds with other people (Ling et al., 2020).

Sinclair et al. (2020) explored the views of palliative care workers about possible future contents of compassion training. They identified self-awareness, experiential learning opportunities, effective and affective communication skills as significant areas, while the culture, the climate of the organisational context was seen to play a key part, with compassionate role modelling from members of staff at all levels seen as important. The workers argued that experienced, skilled mentors could support individuals in developing knowledge, understanding of, and reflections about, compassion. Workers also highlighted the contribution of self-care, which will be discussed in Chapter 5, but were clear that this should not be at the expense of organisational responsibilities for this matter.

Compassion, Health Care, and Nursing Professions

Compassion has been strongly supported in, and by, the health-care professions in the UK. The DoH (2008) review of the NHS demanded health care should be delivered compassionately. The King's Fund (Firth-Cozens and Cornwell, 2009) and the BMA (2011) also advocated for the cause of compassion in health care, as has the Nursing and Midwifery Council (2007). NHS England (DoH, 2012) emphasised, and defined, compassion in a vision and strategy for nurses and midwives, whereby compassion was one of the "six Cs" strategy, with guidelines for practice, training, and evaluation of practitioners. Compassion was a key part in the "Culture of Care" barometer to measure culture in organisations (DoH, 2013b). The Francis Report (DoH, 2013a, p.4) noted "a lack of ... compassion and humanity" more generally in the NHS, accompanied by a need for compassionate staff. Subsequently the government identified "compassion and care as the first of five key policy recommendations for the NHS", which followed the publication of a revised NHS constitution defining compassion as central to one of the six core values underpinning it (Singleton and Mee, 2017, p.134). Therefore, compassionate care for patients and staff is seen as a key, central purpose, and priority in the NHS (Schaub et al., 2022). However, putting such ideas into practice has proved to be difficult, with variations between NHS trusts and increases in "perceived organisational threats" around the manner of implementation of changes without adequate consultation, with familiar points about work overload, limited resources, poor work relationships with upper management, and communication difficulties reducing staff ability to provide compassion (Henshall et al., 2017). Alternatively, these researchers found that in NHS organisations where a culture of "perceived organisational compassion" was evident, this was a significant predictor of compassion for other people.

As regards nursing, in Canada, the provision of compassion is a cornerstone of professional nursing practice (Canadian Nurses Association, (2003), which gives "context and direction to nurses' decisions and actions" (von Dietze and Orb, 2000, p.166). Watson (2006) has described "the real nature of nursing as including the tasks of providing compassionate ... healing services and the transformation of suffering" (Ledoux, 2015, p.2045). In the UK, the idea of compassion as a nursing virtue has been incorporated into the curriculum; compassion has taken up a prominent place in nurses' education and training and, as we have already seen, so has the idea of "measuring" compassion (Bradshaw, 2011). NHS England

44 Compassion

emphasised compassion in the vision and strategy for nurses in Compassion in Practice (DoH, 2012). The attempts to codify, to quantify compassion were supported by one of the recommendations of the Francis Report that nurses should evidence "compassion …as part of their professional revalidation" (DoH, 2013a, p.1696).

Singleton and Mee (2017, p.135) argue compassion "was enacted primarily as a characteristic of the individual practitioner, with practitioners 'responsibilised' within a context of surveillance, threat of failure and loss of their professional status". Hence individuals were focused on, thus neglecting an overall lack of resources and wider inequalities (Strauss et al., 2016). Having discussed the role of responsibility in compassion, Tsang (2017) also concludes with cautions about the concern of exploitation of individual workers' responsibility at the expense of oppressive organisational, social, and structural contexts. Clearly, there is an anxiety that a focus on lack of compassion by an individual practitioner can lead to them being held responsible for the restrictions, the limitations of policy and practice matters which are, in fact, related to organisational and state provision and accountability – or lack of it (Crawford et al., 2014:Henshall et al., 2017; Horsell, 2017).

Interestingly, in view of the focus on individual practitioners at the expense of the wider context and earlier comments about the different perceptions, the various definitions of compassion, Papadopoulos et al. (2016) conducted a survey of over one thousand nurses. The nurses were asked to select one of three definitions of compassion. Nearly two thirds defined compassion as "a deep awareness of the suffering of others and a desire to alleviate it" – the most commonly accepted definition. Nearly a third selected "empathy and kindness" – a restricted definition, somewhat removed from that commonly accepted and devoid of any action element, while one in ten selected "a deep awareness of the suffering of others". These findings indicate that, despite the considerable attention given to compassion in the nursing field, there are uncertainties about its definition, its meaning from the practitioners' perspective, with a lack of attention to institutional implications and perspectives, especially as in this survey, only about one in 20 of nurses perceived that they received compassion from their managers.

Compassion and Social Workers

In contrast to nursing and health-care professionals, compassion has received little attention in the UK in either social work literature or social work research (Clark and Jen, 2020; Whiting, 2022). Furthermore, the position of compassion in relation to social work values and ethics appears to be an ambiguous one. Rhodes (1986) and Wulfekuhler and Rhodes (2021) are among the few writers about social work values and ethics who appear to have commented about the possible importance of compassion as a virtue-based approach. A place for compassion has, however, been identified in the BASW (2014, p.11) Code of

Ethics which recommends social workers "should act with integrity and treat people with compassion", while the Northern Ireland Social Care Council (NISCC, 2019, p.4 and p.7) also requires practitioners to include "compassion" in their approach. The recently revised Standards in Social Work Education in Scotland (SSSC, 2019, p.3) include a statement about the need for social work students to "demonstrate compassion as appropriate to the situation".

Radey and Figley (2007, p.207) in the USA are amongst the few social work researchers and writers to highlight the importance of compassion, concisely stating that "in a most basic sense...social workers are guided by compassion for humanity and an altruistic desire to improve individual and societal conditions". Yet their article and Figley's research is, in fact, focused much more upon compassion fatigue rather than compassion. In the UK, Bilson (2007) has touched on the significance of compassion. Nillson (2014), from Sweden, while considering some aspects of compassion, examines empathy and compassion fatigue in more depth rather than the role of compassion per se in social work. However, this author does make the valuable point that, when providing compassion, social workers do not necessarily experience suffering either as a plight or as a burden. Stickle (2016) writes about social work, compassion, and compassion training. She, like Nillson (2014), places emphasis on its distinction from empathy but takes an individualistic focus. Brill and Nahmani (2017) also discuss compassion and self-compassion with an individualised focus centred on two narrowly based social work case studies. From a much wider, broader, social policy and practice perspective, Spandler and Stickley (2011) and Horsell (2017) discuss compassion, policy, recovery-focused mental health services and work with homeless people, respectively, while Collins et al. (2012, 2015) consider compassion, social policies, and the social work role, partly linked to domestic violence. Yuill (2018), in a piece of qualitative research in the UK linked to a Marxian analysis, explores social workers' compassionate motivation in initially choosing social work as a profession. He also considers the contribution of compassion to a sense of on-going professional identity, with practitioners getting rewards from their work, but with their wish and desire to function as social change agents undermined by disillusionment with, and alienation from, organisational constraints.

A recent research study undertaken in Spain poses basic questions about social workers' knowledge and understanding of compassion, raising more concerns than the study of nurses' varying perceptions of compassion outlined earlier in this chapter (Ortega-Galan et al., 2021). A majority of social worker participants disliked the use of the term compassion, demonstrating a lack of knowledge and understanding of it, associating it with "weakness" and pity. A minority did see compassion in realistic, more positive terms, linking it more appropriately with the relief of suffering and distress.

Recent international book chapters have also explored the contribution of compassion to social work (for instance, Canda et al., 2020; Hugman et al., 2020). However, it is Tanner (2020) in the UK, who has written a recent, most comprehensive overview of compassion, its relationship with, and its contribution

46 Compassion

to, social work. She explores definitions, obstacles to compassion in social work practice, compassion in organisational and policy contexts along with ways of developing compassionate approaches to social work at both micro and macro levels.

Social Work Education and Training

In view of the limited research and literature focused upon compassion and social work, it is perhaps unsurprising that little attention has been given to its implications for social work education in the UK (Whiting, 2020). Michael Sheppard and colleagues (2015, 2018) are amongst the very few UK researchers to consider the contribution of compassion, seeing it as one of several "interpersonal dispositions" that are central to social work. Generally, perhaps assumptions may have been made, as with nursing, that social work students and practitioners will have compassionate attitudes, that they will present compassionate behaviours without needing to undertake much learning about the topic, with compassion seen as a trait, a disposition, which is an inherent part of one's personality (Bramley and Matiti, 2014; von Dietze and Orb, 2000). For instance, Sheppard et al.'s (2018) research indicated that qualifying social work students scored much higher on compassion than the UK "norm". However, compassion also can be seen as a state that changes, depending on time, activities, situations, context, culture, and circumstances; in turn, it can become a trait (Strauss et al., 2016; Wulfekuhler and Rhodes, 2021).

Therefore, as we have already seen, it is clear that compassion as a concept can be learned about, although details about how such learning should be accomplished are less clear. Nevertheless, writers such as Nusssbaum (1996) and Gibbs (2017) have argued for the importance of raising awareness about compassion in a wide range of educational contexts, such as in social work training. Younas and Madigan (2019) and Worline and Dutton (2022), while acknowledging a place for didactic and cognitive aspects of learning about compassion, also emphasise affective learning, student-centred, actively engaged, experiential learning, the use of small groups, dyads, reflection, reflective thinking linked to case studies, role plays, and practice experiences. These are all well-established learning approaches on social work programmes. Zembylas (2013) makes a strong, well-argued, inspiring, and thought-provoking contribution to the literature in emphasising the significance of critical perspectives surrounding compassion, which interrogate its meanings, understandings, and uses. This links well with the emphasis of social work education on critical thinking in order to ensure a curious, questioning, challenging approach to the complexities of the compassion concept. Interestingly enough, Sheppard and colleagues (2015, 2018) found students who were highly rated for compassion were rated lower in their capacity for evaluating arguments, seeing this as an area of tension, with great variations amongst students in their critical thinking capabilities.

Compassion also ties in with other existing, transferrable knowledge, skills and values presented on social work programmes which can be developed further. For example, programmes provide opportunities to learn about interviewing or counselling interactions. These include skills in attending, listening, non-verbal communication, and in maintaining sensitive responses to service users' feelings. Attention is usually given to the skill of empathy. This provides a good opportunity to introduce, to explore the role of compassion in relation to empathy and the debates surrounding this topic. Furthermore, compassion is also closely allied to the importance of other Rogerian-based qualities such as genuineness, warmth, and positive regard which may well be learned about in interview skills, psychology, or human growth and development modules (Egan, 2010; Rogers, 1967). However, in view of some of the apparently critical research findings about social work students and compassion, which emphasise aspects of "heart", "involved", "engaged", feeling-based approaches, rather than considering "head", "detached", analytical approaches, the contribution of social work process teaching and learning experiences about assessment, re-assessment, recording, report writing and also organisational, law, and social policy requirements, can provide a balance (and/or tensions and contradictions) to an approach that might be thought to be too heavily focused on compassion.

Another module in which compassion could be explored is in values classes, where "traditional" social work values are discussed such as respect, acceptance, non-judgmental attitudes, and the emphasis on the uniqueness and individuality of each person, which "fit" closely with the compassion concept. Furthermore, justice-oriented, and wider, more radical social work values also link with the broader aspects of the compassion concept, including anti-discriminatory and anti-oppressive approaches.

These wider-ranging aspects of compassion, which include not only intra-personal and inter-personal features, but also community, organisational, policy, and political perspectives are also closely associated with systems, network, and ecological approaches to social work (Collins et al., 2012, 2015; Gilbert, 2013; Harris, 2020; Whitebrook, 2002, 2014). Indeed, compassion could be said to add a more values-based, humane, human, relationship-oriented, more "feelings-focused" approach which is said to be lacking in traditional systems thinking – and is one of the major criticisms of it.

Finally, social work educators and practice teachers/educators also have an important role to play in modelling compassion, accompanied by the characteristics associated with it. They too may wish to raise their consciousness and awareness about compassion. Practice teachers have a particularly valuable contribution to make when students encounter the realities of service users' feelings about suffering first-hand in practice learning opportunities, through sensitive, reflective discussions in supervision about the emotional impact that makes upon students. Practice teachers' compassionate reactions, explorations about what emotions students themselves might experience, and actions they

48 Compassion

might take to alleviate service users' suffering form an important part of learning experiences about compassion.

The above examples are just some of the ways in which compassion could be integrated and be developed more extensively in social work programmes. Clearly, evaluation of learning opportunities might be presented through the use of assessment of knowledge and understanding of compassion in traditional, formal written assignments, in unassessed reflective exercises, and reflective writing about compassion.

Dilemmas Surrounding Compassion's Contribution to Social Work

Bourdieu (2012) considers social suffering. He draws attention to the experiences of public service workers as reflecting "the consequences and frustrations of a neoliberal state that has abandoned welfarist principles" since the 1970s, "accompanied by a retreat from an ethic of public service" (Smith et al., 2017, p.978). Bourdieu (2012, p.4) suggests those employed in a neoliberal state experience "all kinds of ordinary suffering (la petite misere)", but not the absolute poverty (la grande misere) of many people with whom practitioners work. However, the everyday feelings encountered by practitioners "whose mission is to deal with poverty and talk about it" has a significant impact in that social workers can "feel abandoned, if not disowned outright… in their efforts to deal with… material and moral suffering", as they are expected to act as society's "conscience"; they can be seen as mainly responsible for "dealing" with service users' suffering whilst working in cash strapped, resource stripped, organisations (Bourdieu, 2012, p.5 and p.183). Furthermore, as Bourdieu (2012, p.4) puts it, "using poverty as the sole measure of suffering keeps us from seeing and understanding a whole side of suffering characteristic of the social order". He goes on to draw attention to inequality and suffering, not only related to poverty but also to people's experiences of domination and of oppression, including feelings of humiliation, resentment, despair, and annoyance that can be associated with other forms of discrimination (Frost and Hoggett, 2008). The latter authors emphasise social suffering lies at the heart of subjective experience, the lived experience, of the hurt, damage, misery, and pain inflicted by late neoliberalism and late capitalism, accompanied by internal and relational wounds. In other words, both the inner worlds of suffering and the outer worlds of structural oppression impact upon the pain of the users of social work services and social workers are expected to cope with this.

Against this backcloth, social work students and practitioners can have positive compassionate intentions, but, in fact, may have to carry out actions which reflect negative consequences. Our intentions as students, our wishes as practitioners may be morally "good", but what we actually have to do might involve providing only a limited, perhaps inadequate service. The recognition of service users' suffering by practitioners does not necessarily lead to oppositional consciousness, agency, and action. McNay (2008, p.281) points out "there is a significant difference between recognising injustice, identifying systemic domination and common interests, devising strategies for action and finally feeling able to act". Tanner (2020) highlights the desire, the intentions to help to alleviate suffering, to "practice what one preaches", "to walk the talk" may be evident, but the desire to help can be frustrated, impeded, restricted, or internalised – which may be an element that contributes to compassion fatigue discussed in Chapter 3.

Compassion and Social Work Organisations

In statutory social work, the desire to be compassionate can be frustrated by legal duties and obligations, national policies, and organisational policies and procedures, whereby practitioners are often in contact with involuntary service users, with an emphasis on statutory tasks, rationing, and gatekeeping (Munro, 2011; Yuill and Mueller-Hirth, 2019). The practices of statutory social work agencies often encourage time limited, brief, fleeting contacts in short-term interventions. Within such contacts it may be hard to demonstrate compassion; compassion may not even be thought to be necessary. Statutory workers are often responsible for surveillance, control, protection of service users from various forms of risk and harm to themselves and other people (Collins, 2018). This is especially the case with some aspects of work with children and young people, older people, people experiencing learning disabilities, mental health problems, and in criminal justice contexts. Therefore, contradictions, dilemmas, tensions, and paradoxes surround compassion; compassion becomes a less prominent feature when it is subservient to, subsumed by, control demands (Barnes, 2012). The practitioner can be seen by the service user as another "technician", as another "official", who is carrying out highly focused, very specific, bureaucratic tasks that might not be seen to require compassion either by the worker or the service user.

A compassionate approach reinforces arguments that a major focus of the social work practitioner should be on the activities of compassion – including interacting and engaging with service users in relationships, giving high priority to these tasks and responsibilities when and where possible, rather than a focus on administrative demands (Ovrelid, 2008; Tsang, 2017). However, although earlier in the chapter we briefly considered general organisational contexts for compassion, we should examine further the contributions of social work organisations to compassion, although very little has been written on this matter. There is also a need to develop compassionate social work organisations where all levels of staff are committed to compassion as a part of agreed policies and practices, with a willingness to provide, to use training opportunities to develop awareness of compassionate approaches, and to put these approaches into action. Recently, early efforts have been made to advocate for compassionate leadership in social work organisations, proposing educational models based on health-care literature (Schaub et al., 2022).

50 Compassion

Kanov et al. (2004) provide an interesting analysis of the role of compassion and suffering in organisations, focused upon three aspects – firstly, collective noticing, secondly, collective feelings, and thirdly, collective responding, which are shared between workers. These three aspects can be inter-related and not sequential, but are legitimised, co-ordinated, propagated, and enabled by organisational values and practices. First, the collective noticing stage – the need for a collective sensitivity to, an acknowledgement of, compassion and suffering, the provision and use of a language to identify key elements, along with opportunities to discuss and communicate about them. Secondly, the collective feelings or connecting stage – staff share feelings about compassion and suffering with each other; they explore their mutual experiences rather than suppressing and internalising such feelings as anxiety, hurt, or anguish. Encouragement is given to staff openly talking about, openly sharing feelings about compassion and their work both informally and in team meetings, with leaders and managers modelling compassionate behaviours. The focus could be upon positive expectations and experiences of suffering and compassion, with encouragement given to expressions of kindness, warmth, and concern. Thirdly, collective responding – entails engaging in compassionate acts which are co-ordinated and endorsed by members of the organisation, working together in groups and/or as part of team meetings, to act in order to reduce or eliminate suffering. More recently others, for example, Dutton et al. (2014) and Kanov et al. (2017) have suggested modifications to Kanov et al.'s (2004) original model, such as including a purposeful, sense making or meaning aspect, while Dewar et al. (2011) and colleagues have done much work in promoting compassion in nurse education in organisations. They advocate focusing on positive compassionate acts, reflecting extensively about them, offering feedback on, and taking pride in reinforcing, good practice surrounding compassion that might otherwise be lost or neglected. The idea is to develop organisational commitment to compassion, not only in intentions in written policies, in written procedures, but in actual practices, in activities which are shared, discussed, acknowledged, and celebrated in a positive spiral.

Compassion, Power, and Professionalism

At the same time, it would be unwise to neglect the fact that social workers enact social policies, work within organisational procedures, have professional knowledge and skills that give us some degree of power, authority, and possible "privilege" discussed earlier. How these policies and procedures are *actually* carried out is, of course, subject to varying degrees of professional autonomy, practitioners' interpretations, job crafting, and sometimes, tactics in resisting "official" policies and procedures, accompanied by our desires to work in partnership with, and in empowering, service users. The point noted earlier remains, however, that we may well become separated, distanced from service users by perceptions of power, by knowledge and skills acquired during social work education and training, occupying the social work role, and the professional practices associated with social work.

Warner (2015) suggests that a key point about compassion is its concentration upon suffering, which helps to focus attention on power as "suffering results from what political, economic, and institutional power does to people... and how these forms of power... influence responses to social problems" (Kleinman et al., 1997, p. iv). Social suffering draws attention to what those without power have to endure, accompanied by tendencies towards unintended perceptions of the difficulty and dangers of service users being perceived as objects, lacking in agency, passive, "different", and as "the other" (Frost and Hoggett, 2008; Horsell, 2017). Hence, one contribution that compassion can make is to remind us, to encourage us, to think about, to reflect on, and carry out, our interactions with service users in more thoughtful, sensitive, responsive ways – ways which intend to raise our consciousness, to reduce power differences, to empower service users, to acknowledge mutual experiences, while placing more emphasis on partnership work (von Dietze and Orb, 2000). These matters will be discussed further later in this chapter.

Additionally, there are other dangers of an over-emphasis on excessively "detached" professionalism, an encouragement to maintain very strong, very clear professional boundaries, the restrictions imposed by a possible heavy emphasis on distancing and controlled emotional involvement, as discussed elsewhere in this book. For a striking example of the difficulties and the problems of over-emphasising professional boundaries in mental health work, see Morgan (2018). These elements can hinder, restrict, impede efforts to maintain ideas of sharing between workers and service users which characterises one of the key features of compassion. Compassion involves a closer "coming together", a developing "connectedness" in interactions between workers and service users, a diminution of professional distance, while an excessive emphasis on professionalism, professional power, knowledge, the resilience, and perhaps the "hardiness" of the worker may restrict compassionate endeavours and the idea of the approachable, humane professional.

Active Compassion

In my own experiences in social work in criminal justice it became clear that sometimes in certain situations "actions speak louder than words" in terms of not just believing in compassion, in being committed to it, but also carrying it out, enacting it, "doing" it (for example, Beddoe et al., 2019; Collins, 2018). As a social work student while I believed in compassion, while my intentions were to provide compassion when working with a young person on a supervision order who would not verbally communicate with me in office-based interviews, I began to realise that alternative, active expressions of demonstrating compassion, interest, and ways to build up trust were needed. These included playing games, the young person showing me around his home area where he played games,

52 Compassion

went cycling, where his school was located, where his relatives and friends lived. Hopefully, the young person experienced these activities as a demonstration of concern and compassion. Later, as a qualified worker, engaging in such activities with young people was rarely possible on account of time and workload pressures. Much of my work with young people became routinised and, in reality, rather mechanical, limited surveillance. Intentions to be compassionate were often frustrated by professional priorities which required fulfilment of statutory obligations to complete required written work and other bureaucratic time demands. For a recent, vivid research account of the stresses of "paperwork" or "computer" time made upon social workers compared to "compassionate" time and attention to service user suffering, see Yuill and Mueller-Hirth (2019).

I did manage to learn through experiences that criminal justice service users valued compassionate behaviours; *actions* which went beyond words in individual or family interviews. I began to realise many service users wanted/needed me to help with financial, furnishing, housing, and other practical problems which imposed suffering; these compassionate acts had considerable meaning for service users beyond verbal discussions, as did offers of lifts to family members to keep medical and other appointments such as visits to relatives in penal institutions. I also began to realise "ongoing" service users wanted/needed me to be present as a "familiar face" in what could be a crisis when they made further Court appearances (despite the presence of other criminal justice workers on Court duty) in order to support them, to sometimes provide verbal information to courts, and to be available if institutional sentences followed. This is not to say that these interventions were necessarily "effective" in terms of reducing offending behaviour, rather that they were practical displays of compassion, concern, and interest to try and alleviate suffering. The quality and impact of such relationship-based work cannot be easily measured (Munro, 2011) and does not fit well with organisational requirements to quantify or assess the impact of interventions. Interestingly, during the COVID-19 outbreaks, Ferguson et al. (2021) found practitioners were providing increased levels of material support to families such as helping to reduce food poverty problems, picking up shopping and medication, helping to provide furniture, and helping families to get online. Both families and social workers reported how these activities developed the "shared, common humanity" aspects of practice, which helped to build and reinforce positive relationships.

In my experiences, the perceptions of service users of previous practitioners with whom they had been working suggested that they valued workers who "put themselves out", who "went the extra mile", as did service users in studies of palliative care, looked after children and care leavers (Brown et al., 2019; Roberts et al., 2021; Sinclair et al., 2017). This involved doing often simple, ordinary, practical, everyday things like workers eating their sandwiches in service users' houses in order to give adequate time and appropriate space for service users to express their concerns This was also seen in practitioners making visits to homes when soaked through by rain in order to fulfil expectations and commitments. O'Leary et al. (2013, p.142) have also written about more flexible professional boundaries involving connecting with, rather than separating from, service users, again including very ordinary, apparently mundane, everyday social practices, which might be considered trivial, "such as sharing tea… with clients [which] may play an important part in developing the social worker-client relationship".

Behaviours mentioned above were "noticed", were remembered by service users, were appreciated even when, in some instances, they made little impact on their own life circumstances. Some of these actions might be seen as "unprofessional", unnecessary, unproductive, unfocused, producing little in the way of tangible, measurable outcomes. But it was clear such compassionate acts were valued, helped develop relationships of trust, movement towards more purposeful partnership work with service users who had experienced "let-downs" by authority figures and may have had little reason to trust a practitioner. They began to appreciate workers had a genuine desire, a real wish to help to improve conditions, to "alleviate suffering". Some years ago, a study by Farnfield and Kaszap (1998) showed how children in the mental health system valued practitioners who would go beyond "just" listening and talking, to acting on their behalf. More recently, Beddoe et al.'s (2019) research emphasised how practitioners in New Zealand were alive and alert to the need for such active engagement. Taking advantage of informal or unexpected opportunities to help to act to alleviate suffering is also seen in the "opportunity led approaches", advocated, for example, by Ward (2006). Brown et al. (2014) and Walsh (2018) also comment about practitioners' "practical compassion" in sharing activities, as seen in regular visits to a café, going for drives with mental health service users – a point emphasised by Morgan (2018). In the nursing field, Pearson (2006, p.22) has also pointed out that compassionate actions were often "simple not clever; basic not exquisite, central not peripheral".

In social work research, while there have been many studies of service users' views and experiences over the years, there have been few studies considering compassion (such as Beresford et al., 2008). An exception is Barnes (2012) who found that young people in her study wanted workers who actively demonstrated that they felt compassion towards them, were empathic, while concentrating on the process of working in partnership together. Social workers in this study were seen to have a lack of quality time for compassion-based work, being enmeshed in administrative tasks, consumed, and overwhelmed by demands – a familiar story.

Tanner (2020) takes these themes further, citing Sinclair et al.'s (2017) work with service users in a quite different context-palliative care. There, the service users saw compassion as altruistic, as action oriented, including small acts of kindness where workers demonstrated commitment, went beyond routine matters and "duty", went "above and beyond" what might be expected. These service users preferred a compassionate response to sympathy and empathy as "it was a catalyst to a deeper physical and emotional response that aimed to improve

54 Compassion

the situation" (Sinclair et al., 2017, p.444). Hay (2019) in Australia commented on how the acts of compassion through which social workers communicated with service users were valued. The same author cited practical examples similar to those noted above, simple acts – again "doing" compassion, beyond the importance of evidence-based approaches, interview techniques, counselling theories, universalised rules, principles, or ethical codes. The idea was to be with, to "sit with the discomfort of witnessing suffering and realise and value the power of subtle acts... in their rawest form" (Hay, 2019, p.370). During the recent coronavirus pandemic, Ferguson et al.'s (2021) research and Kong and Noone (2021) also drew attention to the creativity of social workers in working to remain close to service users by meeting outside, on doorsteps, in gardens, going for walks together in public spaces, and the importance of maintaining these flexible practices in future, on-going work.

A Wider Focus for Compassion in Social Work

Such acts may seem small and appear very ordinary, but they also take place in wider social and cultural contexts. As Warner (2015, p.162) argues "if compassion is only to be defined in relation to individually felt subjective experience, then it [has limits.... But defined in the...emotionally political sense, compassion becomes a very different prospect". Thus, the focus of compassion should encompass both therapeutic purpose *and* more socially active, collective effort. This links to desires to attempt and effect changes at a wider level when "moral outrage", continuing discontent, annoyance, passion, a refusal to accept the status quo, and the compassionate responses of workers to the shared sufferings of large numbers of service users can lead to motivation to work to bring to light, to translate, individual, family experiences of suffering into wider scale issues (McNay, 2008). Williams and Briskman (2015, p.1314) call this "converting outrage into action", when "compassion acts as a spur to productive actions"; it "can be used as a trigger and tool for policy change and to promote social justice" (Tanner, 2020, p.1698). Thus some of the so-called negative emotions, which may be generated in workers, such as anger, distress, frustrated desires to act, which are warned about and are criticised by some compassion writers as needing to be tolerated, to be accepted with equanimity can, in fact, also can lead to motivation, to commitment to achieving wider scale social change – with more emphasis on socially active, collective compassion. Indeed, social activists have criticised compassion, empathy, and individualised caring-based approaches as limited, because of their lack of emphasis on, insufficient attention to, the importance of the need for necessary collective, confrontational challenge in order to change long-established, well-engrained, frequently failed state, and organisational provision, policies, procedures, and practices.

Therefore, scholars argue that the disturbing, disturbed, distressing, angry feelings generated by frustrated desires of workers to enact compassion can be

Compassion **55**

used constructively; they can be productively employed when channelled, when focused upon not only individual, but collective, wider scale changes (Nussbaum, 1996; Whitebrook, 2002, 2014; Williams and Briskman, 2015). Hence, emotions of shock, annoyance, and frustration in practitioners can also be directed towards challenging structural inequalities that produce problematic social conditions. As Hoggett (2006, p.146) notes, there is a need for a "fusion of compassion towards social suffering with anger at injustices which underlie that suffering...a solidaristic notion of compassion". Warner (2015) goes on to argue that service users with whom social work comes into contact retain responsibility for their actions, but *the state* bears responsibility for often creating intolerable experiences and conditions in which, and with which, people have to live. Therefore compassion "is oriented towards the human subject as both victim of structural and institutional power and also agent of their own destiny" (Warner, 2015, p.163).

These ideas underpinning compassion-based approaches move beyond a focus on individualistic approaches (Fernando and Consedine, 2014). They highlight the importance of influencing policies at local, regional, and national levels, politics, and the structural context of social work. Compassion can be linked to radical, critical perspectives in social work, to a collective policy influencing role, as seen in local teams, the work of professional associations, unions, and the Social Workers Action Network (SWAN). Compassion-based strategies encourage practitioners to work together, to work collectively in alliances with service users against suffering, against poverty, and various aspects of social injustice and discrimination. The application of compassion-based thinking and compassion-based behaviours should be associated with a wider advocacy role and a political role for social workers, thus bringing together long-established concerns in social work about the "personal" and the "political", "private troubles" and "public issues" (Collins, 2018).

There are also ties between compassion and its associated desire to focus on suffering, with anti-discriminatory and anti-oppressive practice approaches to social work and the significance of inequality and difference, whereby people suffer as a result of discrimination and oppression related to, for instance, class, racism, sexism, disablism, ageism, sexuality, language, and religion. Compassion encourages not only sensitivity to oppression, but also the desire, the willingness to resist, to act, to challenge, to change oppressive behaviours and structures at individual, institutional and structural levels (Horsell, 2017).

Conclusion

It is important for social work students, social workers, supervisors, and managers either to discover, to learn about compassion and what it entails, or to rediscover the languages and discourses of compassion. The significance of compassion may have become obscured, clouded, threatened, even overwhelmed by a predominant focus on rational/technical approaches, on outcomes, on traditional catch words of economy, efficiency and effectiveness enacted within cash-strapped,

56 Compassion

resource limited, bureaucratic organisational contexts that can undermine and overwhelm an emphasis on compassion. In combination with social workers' existing knowledge, skills and values, a stronger focus, a stronger emphasis on compassion is likely to provide more sensitive, more responsive, more purposeful, action-oriented approaches to social work practice at all levels.

References

Armstrong, K. (2010) *Twelve Steps to a Compassionate Life*, Toronto, Alfred Knopf.

Barnes, V. (2012) "Social work and advocacy with young people: Rights and care in practice", *British Journal of Social Work,* 42.7, 1275–1292.

Batson, C. (2011) *The Altruism Question: Toward a Social-Psychological Answer*, Hillsdale, NY, Erlbaum.

Beddoe, L., Staniforth, B. and Fouche, C. (2019) "'Proud of what I do but often... I would be happier to say I drive trucks': Ambiguity in social workers' self-perception", *Qualitative Social Work*, 18.3, 530–546.

Berlant, L. (ed.) (2004) *Compassion; The Culture and Politics of an Emotion*, New York. Routledge.

Beresford, P. Croft, S. and Adshead, L. (2008) "'We don't see her as a social worker': A service user case study of the importance of the social worker's relationship and humanity", *British Journal of Social Work*, 38.7, 1388–1407.

Bilson, A. (2007) "Promoting compassionate concern in social work: Reflections on ethics, biology and love", *British Journal of Social Work,* 37, 1371–1386.

Bourdieu. P. (2012) *The Weight of the World: Social Suffering in Contemporary Society,* Cambridge, Polity Press.

Bradshaw, A. (2011) "Compassion: What history has taught us", *Nursing Times*, 107,19,1214.

Bramley, L. and Matiti, M. (2014) "How does it really feel to be in my shoes? Patients' experiences of compassion within nursing care and their perceptions of developing compassionate nurses", *Journal of Clinical Nursing,* 23, 2790–2799.

Brill, M. and Nahmani, N. (2017) "The presence of compassion in therapy", *Clinical Social Work Journal*, 45, 10–21.

British Association of Social Workers (2014) *The Code of Ethics for Social Work*, Birmingham, BASW.

British Medical Association (2011) *The Psychological and Social Needs of Patients*, London, BMA.

Brown, B., Crawford, P., Gilbert, P., Gilbert, J. and Gale, G. (2014) "Practical compassions: repertoires of practice and compassionate talk in acute mental healthcare", *Sociology of Health and Illness*, 36.3, 383–399.

Brown, R., Alderson, H., Kaner, E., McGovern, R. and Lingham, R. (2019) "'There are carers and then there are those who actually care': Conceptualisations of care among looked after children and care leavers, social workers and carers", *Child Abuse and Neglect*, 92, 2019–2029.

Canadian Nurses Association (2003) *Ethics in Practice*, Ottawa, Regulatory Policy Division of the Canadian Nurses Association.

Canda, E, Furman, L. and Canda, H-J. (2020) *Spiritual Diversity in Social Work Practice*, New York, Oxford University Press.

Charter for Compassion (2009) *The Charter for Compassion*, Bainbridge Island, WA, The Charter for Compassion.

Clark, S. and Jen, S. (2022) "' Conscious compassion": A co-created poetic representation of social workers' experiences with compassion", *Qualitative Social Work*, DOI:10.1177/14733250211070795.

Collins, M., Cooney, K. and Garlington, S. (2012) "Compassion in contemporary social policy: Applications of virtue theory", *Journal of Social Policy*, 41.2, 251–269.

Collins, M., Garlington, S. and Cooney, K. (2015) "Relieving human suffering: compassion in social policy", *Journal of Sociology and Social Welfare*, 4.2, 95–120.

Collins, S. (2018) "Ethics of care and statutory social work in the UK: Critical perspectives and strengths", *Practice: Social Work in Action*, 30.3, 31–38.

Crawford, P., Brown, B., Kvangarsnes, M. and Gilbert, P. (2014) "The design of compassionate care", *Journal of Clinical Nursing*, 25, 3589–3599.

Dalai Lama (1997) *The Heart of Compassion*, Twin Lakes, WI, Lotus Press.

Dalai Lama (2001) *An Open Heart: Practicing compassion in Everyday Life*, Boston, MA, Little Brown.

Dalai Lama (2002) "Understanding our fundamental nature", in Davidson, R. and Harrington, A. (eds.) *Visions of Compassion: Western Scientists and Tibetan Buddhists Examine Human Nature*, Oxford, Oxford University Press, pp.131–164.

Davidson, R. and Harrington, A. (eds.) (2002) *Visions of Compassion: Western Scientists and Tibetan Buddhists Examine Human Nature*, Oxford, Oxford University Press.

Department of Health (2008) *High Quality Care for All: National Health Service Next Stage Review Final Report*, London, HMSO.

Department of Health, NHS Commissioning Board (2012) *Compassion in practice: Our vision and strategy*, London, HMSO

Department of Health (2013a) *Report of the Mid-Staffordshire National Health Service Foundation Trust*, London, HMSO.

Department of Health (2013b) *Compassion in Practice: One Year On*, London, HMSO.

Dewar, B., Pullin, S. and Tocheris, E. (2011) "Valuing compassion through definition and measurement", *Nursing Management*, 17.9, 32–37.

De Zulueta, P. (2013) "Compassion in health care", *Clinical Ethics*, 8, 67–90.

Doris, J. (2010) *The Moral Psychology Handbook*, Oxford, Oxford University Press.

Dutton, J., Workman, K. and Hardin, A. (2014) "Compassion at work", *The Annual Review of Organizational Psychology and Organizational Behaviour*, 1, 277–304.

Ebbinghaus, A. (1987) *Opfer und Taterinnen*, Dusseldorf, Delphi Politik.

Egan, G. (2010) *The Skilled Helper*, Belmont, CA, Brooks Cole.

Ekman, P. (2016) "What scientists who study emotion agree about", *Perspectives on Psychological Science*, 11, 31n41.

Engen, H. and Singer, T. (2015) "Compassion-based emotion regulation up-regulates experienced positive affect and associated neural responses", *Cognitive and Affective Neuroscience*, 10.9, 1291–1301.

Epstein, M. (1988) "The deconstruction of the self: Ego and 'egolessness' in Buddhist insight meditation", *Journal of Transpersonal Therapy*, 20.1, 61–69.

Farnfield, S. and Kaszap, P. (1998) "What makes a helpful grown-up? Children's views of professionals in the mental health services", *Health Informatics Journal*, 4, 3–11.

Ferguson, H., Pink, S. and Kelly, L. (2021) "12 lessons for children's social work from practising under Covid", *Community Care*, 5 February.

Fernando, A. and Considine, N. (2014) "The transactional model of physician compassion", *Journal of Pain and Symptom Management*, 48.2, 289–298.

Firth-Cozens, J. and Cornwell, J. (2009) *The point of care: Enabling compassionate care in acute hospital settings*, London, The Kings' Fund.

58 Compassion

Flores, R. and Brown, P. (2018) "The changing place of care and compassion in the English National Health Service: An Eliasean perspective", *Social Theory of Health*, 16.2, 156–171.

Frost, L. and Hoggett, P. (2008) "Human Agency and Social Suffering", *Critical Social Policy*, 28.4, 438–460.

Gibbs, P. (2017) "Higher Education: A Compassion Business or Edifying Experience?" in Gibbs, P. (ed.), *The Pedagogy of Compassion at the Heart of Higher Education* Cham, Springer, pp.1–18.

Gilbert, P. (2005) *Compassion: Conceptualisation, Research and Use in Psychotherapy*, London, Routledge.

Gilbert, P. (2013) *The Compassionate Mind,* London, Little Brown.

Gilbert, P. and Choden (2013) *Mindful Compassion*, London, Constable and Robinson.

Gilbert, P., Catarino, F., Duarte, C., Matos, M., Kolts, R. Stubbs, J., Cerassato, L., Duarte, J., Pinto-Gouveia, J. and Bascan, J. (2017) "The development of compassion engagement and action scales for self and others", *Journal of Compassionate Health Care,* 4.4, 1–24.

Gilbert, P. (2019) "Explorations into the nature and functions of compassion", *Current Opinions in Psychology,* 26, 108–114.

Goetz, J., Kelner, D. and Simon-Thomas, G. (2010) "Compassion: An evolutionary analysis and empirical review", *Psychological Bulletin,* 136.3, 351–374.

Gregory, J. (2015) "Engineering compassion: The institutional structure of a virtue", *Journal of Social Policy*, 44.2, 339–356.

Gu, J., Baer, R., Kuyken, W. and Strauss, C. (2020) "Development and properties of the Sussex-Oxford Compassion Scales (SOCS)", *Assessment*, 27.1, 3–20.

Harris, D. (2020) "Compassion and resilience" in Thompson, N. and Cox, G. (eds.), *Promoting Resilience,* Abingdon, Routledge, pp.209–215.

Hay, J. (2019) "'Care is not a dirty word!' Enacting an ethic of care in social work practice", *European Journal of Social Work*, 22.3, 365–375.

Henshall, L., Alexander, T, Molyneaux, P., Gardiner, E. and McLellan, A. (2017) "The relationship between perceived organisational threat and compassion for others: Implications for the NHS", *Clinical Psychology and Psychotherapy*, 25.2, 231–249.

Hoggett, P. (2006) "Pity compassion and solidarity" in Clarke, S., Hoggett, P. and Thompson, S. (eds.), *Emotion, Politics and Society,* New York, Palgrave Macmillan, pp.145–161.

Horsell, C. (2017) "A politics of compassion: Informing a new social policy for homelessness?", *International Social Work*, 60.4, 966–975.

Hugman, B., Pawar, M., Anscombe, A. and Wheeler A. (2020) *Virtue Ethics in Social Work*, Abingdon, Routledge.

Ivtzan, I., Lomas, T., Hefferon, K. and Worth, P. (2016) *Second Wave Positive Psychology*, London, Routledge.

Jazaieri, H., Jinpa, K., McGonigal, K., Rosenberg, E., Finkelstein, J., Simon-Thomas, E., Cullen, M., Doty, J., Gross, J. and Goldin, P. (2014) "Enhancing compassion: A randomised control trial of a compassion cultivation programme", *Journal of Happiness Studies*, 24.14, 1113–1126.

Jinpa, T. (2016) *A Fearless Heart: How the Courage to be Compassionate Can transform Our Lives,* New York, Hudson Street.

Kanov, J., Maitlis, S. Worline, M., Dutton, J., Frost, P. and Lilius, J. (2004) "Compassion in organisational life", *American Behavioural Scientist*, 47.6, 808–827.

Kanov, J., Powley, E. and Walshe, N. (2017) "Is it o.k. to care? How compassion falters and is courageously accomplished in the midst of uncertainty", *Human Relations*, 70.6, 751–771.

Kinman, G. and Grant, L. (2020) "Emotional demands, compassion and mental health in social workers", *Occupational Medicine*, 70, 89–94.

Kirby, J. (2017) "Compassion interventions: The programmes, the evidence and implications for research and practice", *Psychology and Psychotherapy Theory, Research and Practice*, 90.3, 432–455.

Kirby, J., Tellegen, C. and Steindl, S. (2017) "A meta-analysis of compassion-based interventions: Current state of knowledge and future directions", *Behaviour Therapy*, 48, 778–792.

Kleinman, A. Das, V. and Lock, M. (eds.) (1997) *Social Suffering*, Berkeley CA, University of California Press.

Klimecki, C., Leiberg, J., Lamm, C. and Singer, T. (2012) "Different patterns of brain plasticity after compassion and empathy training", *Cerebral Context*, 23.7, 1552–1561.

Kong, S-T. and Noone, C. (2021) *Social Work During Covid-19: Learning for the Future: Challenges, Best Practice and Professional Transformation*, Birmingham, BASW.

Larkin, P. (2016) "Compassion: A conceptual reading for palliative and end of life care" in Larkin, P. (ed.) *The Essence of Palliative and End of Life Care*, Oxford, Oxford University Press, pp.1–10.

Ledoux, K. (2015) "Understanding compassion fatigue: understanding compassion", *Journal of Advanced Nursing*, 71.9, 2041–2050.

Ling, D., Olver, J. and Petrakis, M. (2020) "Investigating how viewing common humanity scenarios impacts compassion: A novel approach", *British Journal of Social Work*, 50, 1724–1742.

Lutz, A., Brefczynski-Lewis, J., Johnstone, T. and Davidson, R. (2008) "Regulation of the neural circuitry of emotion by compassion and meditation: Effects of meditative expertise", *PLoS One*, 3.3, e1897, DOI:1371/ journal.pone. 0001897.

Macbeth, A. and Gumley, A. (2012) "Exploring compassion: A meta-analysis of the association between self-compassion and psychopathology", *Clinical Psychology Review*, 32, 545–552.

Matos, M., Duarte, C., Duarte, J., Pinto-Gouvela, J., Pettrochi, N., Basran, J. and Gilbert, P. (2017) "Psychological and physiological effects of compassionate mind training: a pilot randomised controlled study", *Mindfulness*, 8, 1699–1712.

McNay, L. (2008) "The Trouble with Recognition, Subjectivity, Suffering and Agency", *Sociological Theory*, 3, 271–296.

Morgan, G. (2018) *Start*, Edinburgh, Fledgling Press.

Munro, E. (2011) *The Munro Review of Child Protection: Final Report, a Child Centred System*, London, HMSO.

Nillson, P. (2014) "Are empathy and compassion bad for the professional social worker?" *Advances in Social Work*, 15.2, 294–305.

Northern Ireland Social Care Council (2019) *Standards of Conduct and Practice for Social Workers*, Belfast, NISCC.

Nouwen, H., McNeill, D. and Morrison, D. (2002) *Compassion: A Reflection on the Christian Life*, New York, Doubleday.

Nursery and Midwifery Council (2007) *Essential skills clusters for pre-registration nursing programmes*, London, NWC.

Nussbaum, M. (1996) "Compassion: The basic social emotion", *Social Philosophy and Policy*, 13.1, 27–58.

Nussbaum, M. (2001) *Upheavals of Thought: The Intelligence of Emotions*, Edinburgh, Cambridge University Press.

O' Connell, M. (2009) *Compassion: Loving Our Neighbour in an Age of Globalisation*, Maryknoll, NY, Orbis.

60 Compassion

O'Leary, P., Tsui, M-S. and Ruch, G. (2013) "The boundaries of the social work relationship revisited: Towards a connected, inclusive and dynamic conceptualisation", *British Journal of Social Work,* 43, 135–153.

Ortego-Galan, A., Ruiz-Fernando, M. and Ortiz-Amo, R. (2021) "Compassion and empathy in community social workers: A qualitative study", *Health and Social Care in the Community*, 29.5, 1349–1358.

Ovrelid, B. (2008) "The cultivation of moral character: A Buddhist challenge to social workers", *Ethics and Social Welfare*, 2.3, 243–261.

Ozawa de Silva, B., Dodson-Lavelle, B., Ralson, C., Negi, L, Silva, B. and Phil, D. (2012) "Compassion and ethics: Scientific and practical approaches to the culturation of compassion as a foundation for ethical subjectivity and well-being", *Journal of Healthcare, Science and Humanities*, 2, 145–161.

Papadopoulos, I., Zorba, A., Koulouglioti, C. et al. (2016) "International study on nurses' views and experiences of compassion", *International Nursing Review*, 63.3, 395–405.

Pearson, A. (2006) "Powerful caring", *Nursing Standard*, 20.48, 2022.

Pommier, E., Neff, K. and Toth-Kiraly, I. (2020) "The development and validation of the compassion scale", *Assesssment*, 27.1, 21–39.

Price, J. (2010) *Sacred Scriptures of the World Religions; An Introduction*, New York, Continuum.

Radey, M. and Figley, C. (2007) "The social psychology of compassion", *Clinical Social Work Journal,* 35, 207–214.

Rhodes, M. (1986) *Ethical Dilemmas in Social Work Practice*, London, Routledge and Kegan Paul.

Roberts, L., Rees, A., Mannay, D., Bayfield, H., Corliss, C., Diaz, C. and Vaughan, R. (2021) "Corporate patenting in the pandemic: Considering the delivery and receipt of support to care leavers in Wales during COVID-19", *Children and Youth Services Review*, 10.1016/j.childyouth106155.

Rogers, C. (1967) *On Becoming a Person: A Therapist's view of Psychotherapy*, London, Constable.

Schopenhauer, A. (1995) *On the Basis of Mortality*, New York, Berghahn.

Scottish Social Services Council (2019) *Standards in Social Work Education in Scotland*, Dundee, SSSC.

Schaub, J., Hewitson, A., Haworth, S. and Miller, R. (2022) "A leadership model for social work: Drawing on health care to inform social work leadership", *British Journal of Social Work,* DOI:10.1093/bjsw/bcab185.

Sheppard, M. and Charles, M. (2015) "Head and heart: An examination of the relationship between the intellectual and interpersonal in social work", *British Journal of Social Work*, 45, 1837–1854.

Sheppard, M., Charles, M., Rees, P., Wheeler, M. and Williams, R. (2018) "Inter-personal and critical-thinking in those about to enter qualified social work: A six-centre study", *British Journal of Social Work*, 48, 1855–1873.

Simpson, A., Clegg, S. and Pitsis, T. (2014)"'I used to care but things have changed': A genealogy of compassion in organizational theory", *Journal of Management*, 23.4, 347359.

Sinclair, S., Beamer, K., Hack, T., McClement, S., Bouchal, S., Chochinov, H. and Hagen, N. (2017) "Sympathy, empathy and compassion: A grounded theory study of palliative care patients' understandings, experiences and preferences", *Palliative Medicine,* 31.5, 437–447.

Sinclair, S., Hack, T., McClemant, S., Bouchal, S., Chochinov, H. and Hagen, N. (2020) "Healthcare providers perspectives on compassion training: A grounded theory study", *BMC Medical Education*, https;/doi.org/10.1186/s12909-020-02164-8.

Sinclair, S., Kondejewski, J., Hack, T., Boss, H. and MacInnis, C. (2022) "What is the most valid and reliable compassion measure in health care? An updated comprehensive and critical review", *The Patient-Patient Centred Outcomes Research*, DOI:10.1007/s40271-022-00571-1.

Singer, T. and Klimecki, O. (2014) "Empathy and compassion", *Current Biology*, 24.18, 875–878.

Singh, P., King-Shier, K. and Sinclair, S. (2018) "The colours and contours of compassion: A systematic review of the perspectives of compassion among ethnically diverse patients and health providers", *PLoS ONE*, 13.5, e0197261, DOI:10.137/journal.pone.0197261.

Singleton, V. and Mee, S. (2017) "Critical Compassion: Affect, discretion and policy care relations", *The Sociological Review Monographs*, 65.2, 130–149.

Smith, M., Cree, V., MacRae, R., Sharp, D., Walker, S. and O' Halloran, S. (2017) "Social suffering: Changing organisational culture in children and families social work through critical reflection groups-insights from Bourdieu", *British Journal of Social Work*, 47, 973–988.

Spandler, H. and Stickley, T. (2011) "No hope without compassion: The importance of compassion in recovery focused mental health services", *Journal of Mental Health*, 20.6, 555–566.

Steffen, P. and Masters, K. (2005) "Does compassion mediate the intrinsic religion-health relation-ship?", *Annals of Behavioural Medicine*, 30.3, 217–224.

Stickle, M. (2016) "The expression of compassion in social work practice", *Journal of Religion and Spirituality in Social Work: Social Thought*, 35, 12, 120–131.

Strauss, C., Taylor, B., Gu, J., Kuyken, W., Baer, R., Jones, F. and Cavanagh, K. (2016) "What is compassion and how can we measure it? A Review of definitions and measures", *Clinical Psychology Review*, 47, 15–27.

Tanner, D. (2020) "'The love that dare not speak its name': The role of compassion in social work practice", *British Journal of Social Work*, 50.6, 1688–1705.

Tsang, N. (2017) "Otherness and empathy-implications of Levinas ethics for social work education", *Social Work Education*, 36.3, 312–322.

Van de Cingel. M. (2009) "Compassion and professional care: Exploring the domain", *Nursing Philosophy*, 10, 124–136.

Vittelone, N. (2011) "Contesting Compassion", *The Sociological Review*, 59,579596.

Von Dietze, E. and Orb, A. (2000) "Compassionate care: A moral dimension of nursing", *Nursing Inquiry*, 7.3, 168–174.

Walsh, J. (2018) "Working with complexity and ambiguity in caring relationships" in Ruch, G., Turney, D. and Ward, A. (eds.), *Relationship -Based Social Work*, London, Jessica Kingsley, pp.203–220.

Ward, A. (2006) *Working in Group Care Social Work and Social Care in Residential and Day Care Settings*, Bristol, Policy Press.

Warner, J. (2015) *The Emotional Politics of Social Work and Child Protection*, Bristol, Policy Press.

Watson, J. (2006) "Can an ethic of caring be maintained?", *Journal of Advanced Nursing*, 54.3, 257259.

Weng, H., Fox, A., Shackman, A., Stodola, D., Caldwell, J., Rogers, D. and Davidson, R. (2013) "Compassion training alters altruism and neural responses to suffering", *Psychological Science*, 24, 171–180.

Whitebrook, M. (2002) "Compassion as a political virtue", *Political Studies*, 50,529544.

Whitebrook, M. (2014) "Love and anger as political virtues" in Ure, M. and Frost, M. (eds.), *The Politics of Compassion*, London, Routledge, pp.21–36.

62 Compassion

Whiting, R. (2020) "Compassion through intercorporeality: The value of the phenomenological approach of David Michael Levin to social work education", *Social Work Education*, https://doi. org/10.1080/026515479.2020.1771299.

Williams, C. and Briskman, L. (2015) "Reviving social work through moral outrage", *Critical and Radical Social Work*, 3.1, 3–17.

Worline, M. and Dutton, J. (2022) "The courage to teach with compassion: Enriching classroom designs and practices to foster responsiveness to suffering", *Management Learning*, DOI:10.1177/13505076211044611.

Wulfekuhler, H. and Rhodes, M. (2021) "Flourishing in social work organisations", *Ethics and Social Welfare*, 15.3, 263–278.

Younas, A. and Madigan, J. (2019) "Proposing a policy framework for nursing education for fostering compassion in nursing students: A critical review", *Journal of Advanced Nursing*, 75, 621–636.

Yuill, C. (2018) "Social workers and alienation: the compassionate self and the disillusioned juggler", *Critical and Radical Social Work*, 6.3, 275–289.

Yuill, C. and Mueller-Hirth, N. (2019) "Paperwork, compassion and temporal conflicts in British social work", *Time and Society*, 28.4, 1532–1551.

Zembylas, M. (2013) "The "Crisis of Pity" and the Radicalization of Solidarity: Toward Critical Pedagogies of Compassion", *Educational Studies*, 49, 504–521.

3

COMPASSION FATIGUE

Introduction

While social workers encounter many examples of service user strengths, achievements, and resilience, they are also in contact with some service users who have experienced, or are experiencing, traumatic negative life events. In turn, social workers themselves may have experienced, or be experiencing, negative events. As we saw in chapter 1, at work they may be subject to multiple demands, be on the receiving end of aggressive and depressing outbursts and public criticism, while receiving little positive recognition for good quality work, accompanied by few financial rewards (Coffey et al., 2004). As we also saw in chapter 1, they may be employed in organisations where there are high workloads, high staff turnover rates, and frequent changes in policies and procedures (Evans and Huxley, 2009; McFadden et al., 2015; Ravalier, 2017; Ravalier et al., 2021; Schraer, 2015). They may have little control over their work, limited support from line managers and, possibly, from team members and colleagues (Ravalier, 2017; Ravalier et al., 2021). They may also be members of minority communities who experience discrimination and oppression.

Therefore, the position of social workers can sometimes be a difficult one. Concerns have been expressed in the UK and elsewhere about some social workers' low motivation and commitment to their work and the high incidences of illnesses and absences (McFadden, 2018; Stanford, 2011). Hence, one important aspect of a concept such as compassion fatigue is that it draws attention again to the demands of social work and to the negative consequences that may be linked to compassion fatigue, such as difficulties in providing effective, reliable, responsive provision for service users. Thus, there are sound reasons for exploring compassion fatigue and considering positive approaches to it, even if it can be a disputed and challenging concept.

DOI: 10.4324/9781003112532-4

64 Compassion Fatigue

In this chapter, we will examine the recent development of compassion fatigue, and consider definitions of it and its relationship to burnout, trauma, vicarious trauma, and secondary traumatic stress. We will continue with an examination of the debates about empathy and compassion fatigue, which have important implications for social workers. Then criticisms of the concept will be explored. We will explore research findings about compassion fatigue and social workers in a variety of settings before the chapter concludes with further consideration of implications for social work practice.

Burnout, Trauma, Vicarious Trauma, and Secondary Traumatic Stress

Against the backcloth described above and earlier in the first chapter, it is not surprising that many practitioners experience periods of vicarious trauma, secondary traumatic stress, compassion fatigue, and burnout. These are changing, sometimes overlapping, constructs; different definitions and measures are used to describe and to analyse the adverse physical, emotional, moral, and social aspects of professional care giving (Harr et al., 2014; Pelon, 2017; Senreich et al., 2020). As we shall see later, research about these topics comes to different conclusions, which can make it difficult to synthesise the findings to build evidence-based and evidence-informed practice (Harr et al., 2014).

This chapter will focus upon compassion fatigue, which has been described as a combination of the symptoms of vicarious trauma, secondary traumatic stress, and burnout (Newell and MacNeill, 2010; Stamm, 2010; Tanner, 2020). First of all, we will now consider these terms in a little more depth.

The use of the term burnout developed in the mid-1970s. It is seen as a state of emotional, physical, psychological, and spiritual exhaustion. It develops gradually in intensity over a prolonged period of time to the extent of a person becoming "worn out". It is said to be a cumulative build-up of working in organisations and emotionally demanding situations, not just with people experiencing trauma (Baugerud et al., 2018). For some years burnout has not been specifically linked to the helping professions; it has been more strongly related to general work-based stress and organisational elements such as excessive workloads, lack of worker control, unfair agency policies, clashes between organisational values, professional values, and limited support opportunities (Conrad and Kellar-Guenther, 2006; Harr and Moore, 2011; Senreich et al., 2020; Stamm, 2010). Maslach (for instance, 2003) whose work is often used in assessing levels of burnout describes it as comprising of three elements – emotional exhaustion, depersonalisation, and reduced feelings of accomplishment. It involves "the depletion of...compassion, [it leads to] boredom, cynicism, diminution of enthusiasm, temporary distress, and depression" (Diaconescu, 2015, p.57). It can also entail feelings of hopelessness, irritation, low levels of productivity, and limited energy allied with restricted opportunities to have satisfying work experiences (Baugerud et al., 2018). Therefore, burnout is clearly a threat to job satisfaction, which can affect job performance, commitment to service users, to the profession, the organisation, and desire to stay in a job (Hombrados-Mendieta et al., 2011; Lizano and Mor-Barak, 2015; Wagaman et al., 2015).

Although research evidence would suggest that while there are difficulties in defining the term "trauma", in distinguishing between the impact of major, significant past, present and less significant negative or adverse events, and the impact of oppression, social workers spend time dealing with trauma and it clearly does make a considerable impact upon them (Beddoe et al., 2019; Martin-Cuellar et al., 2018).

In the USA there is considerable, current interest in trauma-informed social work practice (for example, Brent-Godley, 2019). Ben-Porat et al. (2021) in a study with social work students in Israel found, according to the students' reports, they spent nearly five hours out of twelve dealing with trauma in their placement work. Butler et al. (2017) discovered just under half of the students in their sample were working "often" or "very often" with trauma.

Bride (2007) in a study of mainly mental health and substance use social workers and large-scale research by Rienks (2020) with child welfare workers suggested over a third of the practitioners addressed trauma issues at least occasionally, with over a half doing so "often" or "very often" in Bride's (2007) study.

However, debates surround the possible impact of the frequency of interviews, the percentage of time spent with, and number of, "trauma clients" in an overall workload on the risk of professional helpers developing vicarious trauma – with conflicting and varying research findings. Some suggest this is a key variable in rates of workers' vicarious traumatisation, while others suggest no significant differences (Lee, 2017; Mendez-Fernandez et al., 2021). Middleton and Potter (2015) found a significant relationship between vicarious trauma, turnover, and intention to leave among a large sample of over 1,000 child welfare professionals in the USA, a third were experiencing core aspects of vicarious traumatisation, with participants perceiving vicarious trauma symptoms in well over a half of their colleagues.

The term vicarious trauma started to be used around the early/mid-1990s, based upon Pearlman's work with survivors of sexual abuse and incest (McCann and Pearlman, 1990). It focused upon the negative effects of working with people who experience trauma and the consequences of repeatedly undertaking empathic work. Turgoose and Maddox (2017) suggest vicarious trauma involves the practitioner's indirect experiences; it may involve the assimilation, the integration of service users' experiences, and the negative memories of trauma – as if they were the worker's own. Vicarious trauma concentrates more upon the long-term, possibly permanent *cognitive* impact of such interactions, i.e. the impact upon the practitioner's sense of self, reshaping their belief systems, their views about other people, raising issues about safety, intimacy, and trust (Newell and McNeill, 2010). It has been described as

66 Compassion Fatigue

> the negative transformation in the… worker's inner experience resulting from…engagement with the client's trauma material… [it] can result in significant disruption of one's sense of meaning, connection, identity and world view… in one's affect tolerance, psychological needs…interpersonal relationships and memory
>
> *(Pearlman and Saakvitne, 1995, p.151).*

This can leave practitioners vulnerable to emotional and spiritual consequences that can become a permanent feature– which is said to be one of the distinguishing features of vicarious traumatisation in comparison to compassion fatigue (Lee et al., 2018). Practitioners may have unrealistic expectations as "rescuers" in trying to meet the long-term needs of service users when significant, extensive change is difficult to achieve; they may see their helping efforts as futile, may use negative coping strategies and lack emotional support, which increases one's risk of vicarious traumatisation (Lee et al., 2018).

Clearly, vicarious traumatisation is a serious and worrying phenomenon. Dombo and Whiting-Blome (2016), after reviewing a range of studies, suggested the prevalence rate of vicarious trauma among child welfare workers was between a quarter and a third. But others such as Lee et al. (2018) argue that smaller numbers of social workers will be, and are, affected by it – less than imagined in suggestions in the original literature. Support measures from team members, colleagues, supervisors, and from outside the workplace can be used to prevent it (Collins, 2020; Mendez-Fernandez et al., 2021). Indeed, as we shall see later in the book, theories, models, and extensive research have also emerged which emphasise post-traumatic growth, vicarious resilience, and compassion satisfaction rather than vicarious traumatisation (van Heugten, 2011).

Secondary traumatic stress also developed in the mid-1990s. It is linked to the behaviour resulting from knowing about, exposure to, and listening to, accounts of a disturbing situation or traumatic event experienced by another person. It is accompanied by the consequences of helping or wanting to help people experiencing trauma and people who are suffering (Community Care/ Unison, 2021; Figley, 1995; Senreich et al., 2020). Figley (1995) perceived secondary traumatic stress to be similar to post-traumatic stress disorder, but experienced *second hand* and also as similar to compassion fatigue.

Among social workers, Choi (2011) found that the size of caseload and time spent working with trauma issues linked to violence and sexual assault had no significant relationship to secondary traumatic stress, while those who worked with service users with higher levels of trauma actually displayed lower levels of secondary traumatic stress. This was in contrast to the findings of Armes et al. (2020). Quinn et al. (2019) also point out that, although low income is considered to be an important factor that predicts secondary traumatic stress, the relationship between it and social workers' income has been rarely investigated, as do Schrag et al. (2021) in their study of interpersonal violence and sexual assault workers. Both studies found low income did significantly predict secondary traumatic stress. This aspect would benefit from further exploration, especially as income also impacts upon social workers' self-care as we shall see in Chapter 5, while social workers generally tend to regard the pressures, the efforts to increase their salaries as perhaps being overwhelmed by their tendency towards giving priority to selfless, altruistic, caring for service users which we have seen, and will see, in other parts of this book.

Several studies have suggested low levels of secondary traumatisation among social workers. For instance, only seven per cent of hospital social workers who provided emergency treatment during war in Israel reported secondary traumatisation, while the levels of distress were significantly lower than those of the general population (Dekel et al., 2007). Low levels of secondary traumatisation were also reported among social workers in war situations and among practitioners following 9/11(Adams et al., 2006, 2008; Lev-Wiesel et al., 2009; Shamai and Ron, 2009). It does seem, however, that these studies related to the shorter-term experience of trauma, rather than the on-going, longer-term experiences of social workers in some of the other studies.

Symptoms of secondary trauma include intrusive thoughts, avoidant responses, and physiological arousal (Bride, 2007). Armes et al. (2020) point out that evidence from research in the USA suggests the prevalence of secondary trauma rates among social workers varies from 15 to 35 per cent. This figure relates to both "generic" and child welfare workers, but most research in various countries indicates higher levels of secondary trauma among child welfare workers. In Israel, Weiss-Dagan et al. (2016) reported secondary traumatic stress at high to extreme intensity among 65 per cent of child protection social workers, compared with just over a third of family workers. Furthermore, in each case the child welfare workers in Rienks' (2020) study in the USA reported much higher levels of individual symptoms and overall symptoms than those in Bride's (2007) "generic" sample. These studies tend to confirm the findings of other studies in the USA that child welfare workers there experience more secondary traumatic responses than other social workers, although this topic seems to have received less attention in the UK.

Thus, despite the varying research findings about, and some criticisms of, the trauma, vicarious trauma, secondary traumatic stress and burnout concepts, and the development of a more positive focus upon post-traumatic growth and vicarious resilience discussed in the next chapter, what is important is that there is clear evidence of the distressing, negative impact of these concepts on a significant proportion of social workers in several countries (Armes et al., 2020; Beddoe et al., 2019; Rienks, 2020; Rayner et al., 2020; Weiss-Dagan et al., 2016).

Compassion Fatigue

Turgoose and Maddox (2017) and others suggest compassion fatigue is relevant to helping *generally*; it is not specific to those who work with trauma. Compassion fatigue has also been linked to a range of other helping professionals, including

68 Compassion Fatigue

doctors, nurses, and mental health workers who are providing care for distressed people as a core task (Adams et al., 2006).

The term compassion fatigue appears to be first linked to Joinson's (1992) work focused on compassion fatigue amongst nurses. Figley (1995) developed the concept, first relating it to counsellors and therapists. Figley and Stamm (2002, p. 2–3) describe the use of the term compassion fatigue as a "more user-friendly term for secondary traumatic stress", as less stigmatising, less strongly linked to the implications of psychiatric classification and labelling. It has more appeal to social workers; it is used in the UK and international documents offering ethical guidance to social workers during the recent pandemic (Community Care/ Unison, 2021; Harr et al., 2014; IFSW, 2020).

Ledoux (2015, p. 2047) suggests compassion fatigue occurs "when the act of caring has been impeded or obstructed". Some have suggested compassion fatigue can be a "natural consequence" of caring and a "cost of caring" (Figley, 1995: Stamm, 2010). Distress comes about not only from helping people, but also from difficulties for a worker in expressing care, in being unable to respond to the desire to alleviate suffering (Tanner, 2020). Therefore, compassion fatigue involves an impediment, an obstruction, to intended acts of compassion; not necessarily just the feelings arising from being with other people when they are experiencing pain, but from the feelings associated with the inhibition, or prevention, of desires to act (Pelon, 2017; Tanner, 2020). It can occur suddenly, with little warning, sometimes either in response either to a particular traumatic event, or over a longer period of time, and normally there is a faster rate of recovery from compassion fatigue than burnout (Figley, 1995). It can involve fear, leading to distancing, to disconnection from service users (Stamm, 2010). Radey and Figley (2007) argue that four factors are associated with compassion fatigue among workers: previous experience of unresolved trauma, uncontrolled work stress, a lack of both self-care and job satisfaction.

Some scholars have argued that it also includes a "moral stress/distress" element, which involves ethical and value conflicts encountered in practice situations which also contributes to compassion fatigue (Harr et al., 2014; IFSW, 2020; Tanner, 2020). The expectations of workers, service users, their families, and social work organisations may be in conflict. What the worker considers to be "the right thing to do" in accordance with professional values and ethics may not be possible because of organisational policy and procedural constraints. Practitioners may experience feelings of guilt, distaste, disappointment, or despair. Ledoux (2015) has gone as far as to suggest that moral distress might be a more appropriate term to use than compassion fatigue, while Sinclair et al. (2017) express a preference for the term "compassion distress" and Figley (1995) talks about compassion stress developing into compassion fatigue.

However, despite these debates, compassion fatigue is said to have behavioural, cognitive, and emotional consequences. It has been associated with decreased productivity, diminished quality of care for service users, apathy, inferior quality work, absences from work, poor morale, high staff turnover rates, and physical and mental health issues (Kinman and Grant, 2020; Pelon, 2017). There may be concentration problems and pre-occupation with trauma. There may be feelings of powerlessness, sadness, depression, increased feelings of impatience, irritability, anxiety and anger, reduced self-esteem, and eating and sleeping problems (Conrad and Kellar-Guenther, 2006; Figley, 1995; Harr et al., 2014). Compassion fatigue can also be accompanied by a decrease in willingness to help other people, increased rigidity, poor judgment, feelings of detachment, isolation, a lack of trust and reluctance to seek support (Figley, 1995). In particular, compassion fatigue has been linked to difficulties in expressing and maintaining empathy, as we shall see later.

Figley (1995) first developed compassion fatigue scales, while later Figley and Stamm (1996) and Stamm (2005, 2010) developed compassion satisfaction and compassion fatigue scales which consider how one feels about helping others; they are designed for professionals who are exposed to stressful events and trauma in their work. These scales will be discussed further later in this chapter and in the next chapter. The compassion fatigue sub-scales measure both burnout and compassion fatigue and here we will focus on them. The burnout section of the sub-scales includes questions about being trapped, the exhaustion experienced by working as a helper, feelings about being bogged down or overwhelmed by the amount of work, the size of workload encountered, and losing sleep as a result of encountering the traumatic experiences of those whom one helps. The compassion fatigue section of the sub-scales includes preoccupation about experiences with service users, difficulties in separating work life from personal life, feeling depressed because of work, feeling infected by the traumatic stress of service users, feeling as if one was experiencing the trauma of a person helped, having intrusive, overwhelming, frightening thoughts about helping and avoiding activities that act as a reminder of negative experiences with service users.

Empathy, Compassion Fatigue, and Social Workers

As noted in the previous chapter for many years empathy has been a core skill that has played a key part in counselling endeavours and in social work, both in developing relationships and in on-going work. It is clearly linked to the client-centred work of Carl Rogers (1957) along with many others who have developed his ideas (for instance, Egan, 2001). Empathy is clearly very valuable and important for practitioners in communicating understanding to service users about their thoughts and feelings (Wagaman et al., 2015). While extensive use of empathy in practice can be a source of stress, it can also be a source of strength, satisfaction, energy, and fulfilment (Miller and Sprang, 2017; Newell et al., 2016; Radey and Figley, 2007; Rayner et al., 2020). For instance, empathy has been seen by many social work researchers as predicting and *increasing* compassion satisfaction rather than compassion fatigue (for instance, Thomas, 2013; Wagaman et al., 2015; Yi et al., 2019). This will be discussed further in the chapter on compassion satisfaction. Miller and Sprang (2017) argue that the idea of a

70 Compassion Fatigue

willingness to experience, to explore, to tolerate intense feelings in interviews is seen as being at the core, at the heart of effective helping. It is acknowledged that such strong feelings may include anger, anxiety, fear, frustration, sadness, and depression – feelings that may well be uncomfortable and painful. But Miller and Sprang (2017) suggest that these are not necessarily traumatic or harmful to the worker; they do not "cause" compassion fatigue, it is trying to limit or deny responses to such feelings that might be harmful. They argue strongly and comprehensively about the importance of individual, group, and organisational support for such empathic endeavours. Miller and Sprang (2017, p.155) conclude, perhaps controversially, that energy and efforts to avoid and/or inhibit intense feelings "accounts for much of what has been conceptualised as compassion fatigue".

However, an alternative view is that use of empathy, an empathic orientation or, more particularly, "excessive empathy" *is* linked to compassion fatigue (Newell et al., 2016). Some researchers while acknowledging the important and key role of empathy, tend to focus on its negative implications in developing relationships and on-going work from two perspectives (Adams et al., 2008; Figley, 1995; Figley and Stamm, 2002). Firstly, they argue empathy can lead to compassion fatigue because of the constant exposure involved when practitioners respond to deeply disturbed and disturbing feelings, demonstrate empathy in interactions with people who are suffering traumatic, emotionally damaging events, and going through distressing, difficult experiences. Secondly, that compassion fatigue *itself* can then lead to problems in maintaining empathy, emotional sensitivity, and responsiveness to service users (Turgoose and Maddox, 2017). The danger is that workers might become emotionally distant, disengaged, and detached from the feelings of those with whom they work.

Thomas (2013) and Turgoose and Maddox (2017) point out that most aspects of empathy, including the tendency to try to understand, "to fit into the shoes" of, to adopt the viewpoint of service users spontaneously in interview, were less important to the development of compassion fatigue than the tendency for some workers to feel empathic, *personal distress* in their responses. Empathic or personal distress is defined as "self-oriented feelings of personal anxiety in tense interpersonal settings" (Turgoose and Maddox, 2017, p.178). Several researchers suggest that those practitioners who expressed a great deal of empathy were more likely to experience compassion fatigue *if* they had a history of unacknowledged, unresolved trauma (Yi et al., 2019) which could be "triggered off" and "played out" in interactions with service users through "re-traumatization" experiences. Thomas (2013) sees empathic, personal distress as a self-focused, avoidant response with the worker reliving their own distress rather than empathically tuning in and helping a service user with their feelings. Higher levels of personal distress were associated with higher levels of compassion fatigue in Thomas's (2013) research with workers in the USA and in Yi et al.'s (2019) study of Korean social workers.

Therefore, research suggests many components of empathy lead to compassion satisfaction, but unregulated, unbounded, uncontrolled empathy, "spilling out" beyond immediate service user contact into a practitioner's other work, personal life, and difficulties in distinguishing one's own thoughts and emotions from those of service users can lead to personal distress. This can contribute to compassion fatigue. Hence the idea of empathy as a "double-edged" sword, with social workers apparently "walking a tightrope" between providing appropriate, responsive, sensitive empathy while not becoming "swamped" by these experiences (Badger et al., 2008; Thomas, 2013; Yi et al., 2019). Empathic concern is clearly very powerful and important in understanding other people and conveying effective understanding to them. However, as we have seen, for some practitioners the exposure to negative experiences, to traumatic events in service users' lives can lead to "uncontrolled empathy", feeling overwhelmed by service user's feelings, preoccupation with one's own distress, along with an erosion of boundaries between one's own thoughts and feelings and the thoughts and feelings of service users.

The impact of empathic interventions upon practitioners is therefore important. Social workers' skills in the use of empathy are usually established during initial social work education, which normally includes a focus on empathy as part of interview skills training. But less attention is given during qualifying education and in post-qualifying years to the *actual impact* on workers of offering empathy, either in particularly specific, fraught, traumatic situations or over prolonged periods of time during a social work career. Therefore, the compassion fatigue concept has triggered and does trigger, debates about empathy, its use, its impact upon, and the implications for workers of empathy. Pioneers in work with the compassion fatigue concept such as Figley (1995) have, rightly or wrongly, linked the use of empathy to compassion fatigue. Hence for practitioners who are often exposed to what may be the expression of intense, strong feelings from service users, the need to explore the implications of such exposure becomes more important.

Therefore, these findings have particularly prominent implications for the provision of appropriate opportunities for the emotional support of workers in establishing, maintaining, and developing empathic endeavours, in helping to maintain emotional regulation, containment and the "holding" of feelings, of detachment, separation and self-differentiation from service users' feelings. The maintenance of boundaries is a balance that can be difficult to achieve, especially if, as we saw in the previous chapter, we are looking to demonstrate real, genuine care, to "go the extra mile" and to go beyond what is normally required (Ruch et al., 2018). Therefore not only is a worker's willingness and ability to reflect upon, to discuss such reactions helpful and important, in order to ventilate feelings, to externalise them, and consider alternative approaches by putting them in a broader context, but also the need for colleagues, team members, and supervisors to be available, to be willing to listen, to respond sensitively, with support from an agency climate and culture that acknowledges a need for discussion of strong,

72 Compassion Fatigue

powerful feelings (Ruch et al., 2018). Such opportunities should be provided in frequent, extensive, intensive and emotionally responsive supervision, or through mentoring opportunities and perhaps, more particularly, in discussion of emotional reactions with colleagues in both individual, group, formal, and informal situations. These opportunities would require the organisational climate and culture, to be positively orientated to open discussion of practitioners' thoughts and feelings, particularly in response to negative interactions with service users that are emotionally demanding. Such provision could help not only to avoid the development of compassion fatigue, but also to deal with its consequences. All these elements have also perhaps come into a sharper focus during the recent COVID-19 crisis, for example, with restricted opportunities for practitioners to have face-to-face contact and discussions with their peers.

Criticisms of Compassion Fatigue

There have been criticisms of the compassion fatigue concept by a range of writers (for instance, Ledoux, 2015; Newell and MacNeill, 2010; Newell et al., 2016; Turgoose and Maddox, 2017). In this section, we will examine and attempt to evaluate some of these criticisms.

There is a danger that compassion fatigue can be perceived by professional care givers as a reflection of their own pathology, an individual lack of ability and competence. However, in fact, practitioners are subject to other strong influences, for instance, from service users, organisational policies, and structural matters such as sexism, racism, and other forms of discrimination (Ravalier, 2017; Wilkin and Hillock, 2015). Compassion fatigue and its associated concepts can lead to an over-emphasis on the individual worker, particularly at the expense of institutional factors (see, for instance, Kreitzer et al., 2020; Schrag et al., 2021; Singh et al., 2020). Some literature reflects this, falling into a trap of placing excessive emphasis on the capabilities, competencies, power, and influence of individuals. For instance, Mendez-Fernandez et al. (2021) argue that supervisors can make sure sufficient resources are available when such matters are often beyond their control. Similarly, Pearlman and Saakvitne (1995) suggest workers can make independent decisions, limit their caseloads and also, again, acquire resources when, in fact, social workers are severely restricted in these matters by national and local policies, guidance documents and financial cutbacks. Indeed, it is important to note organisational influences are more strongly emphasised in burnout theories than in compassion fatigue approaches, and this may be a legitimate criticism of the concept (for example, Maslach, 2003).

However, along with others, Sinclair et al. (2017) do highlight the importance of organisational-related factors and their impact upon compassion fatigue. These include size and type of workload, amount of assessment work, time available for on-going service user contact, quality of team relationships, frequency, amount, and type of supervision, feeling respected and valued as a worker, opportunities for appropriate information provision, professional development, administrative

Compassion Fatigue **73**

support and resources in the organisation, part-time, flexible work hours, and the physical environment of the office. For instance, Senreich et al.'s (2020) exhaustive, extensive research in the USA with about 6,000 social workers' views of their organisations indicated that 40 per cent perceived they did not receive good supervision, one third felt their caseloads were unmanageable, while two thirds did not feel valued in their professional roles; they also believed they had insufficient training opportunities. As we have already seen previously, similar concerns about organisational provision have also been found amongst some practitioners in the UK (Mickel, 2009; McFadden, 2018). Furthermore, Antonopoulu et al. (2017) also found great variation in the quality of such provision in several different local authority child-care teams in England.

From a systemic or ecological perspective, it is the interaction, the transaction between the worker's setting, and the service users' environment that is crucial in considering compassion fatigue (Fernando and Consedine, 2014). Stamm's (2010) scales about compassion fatigue and burnout do, in fact, suggest complex environments interacting together, linking to positive and negative aspects of helping others – the service user's environment, the worker's organisational context, and the personal life of the worker. However, although the burnout and compassion fatigue elements of Stamm's (2010) ProQOL measure consider some individual perceptions about work aspects, including depression and work, vicarious trauma, size of caseload, being "bogged down", and "trapped" at work, it actually seems to give limited attention to some organisational focused factors noted above. Other neglected factors include perceptions of fairness or unfairness in an organisation's policies, procedures and practices, opportunities to participate in, and to influence, organisational decision making, and to exercise control at work (Collins, 2020; Schrag et al., 2021). Similar comments could be made about another recently developed compassion fatigue scale by Eng et al. (2020) which also includes only brief consideration of workplace factors – providing only three of them – the provision of care, resources, and clear rules and regulations.

Clearly, all questionnaires have their limitations regarding length and content, but the points above seem to be important omissions. This leads to more general criticisms of compassion fatigue research; it tends to focus quite heavily on quantitative approaches at the expense of qualitative work, rarely exploring respondents' perceptions in any depth or detail. However, Bourassa's (2012) work with adult protection social workers, Kapoulitsas and Corcoran's (2015) study of Australian practitioners, Kreitzer et al.'s (2020) study with Canadian social workers, and Kim et al.'s (2021) recent sensitive, moving account of the experiences of oncology social workers in Korea are examples of studies of a qualitative nature.

Furthermore, much of the research about individually focused compassion fatigue also tends to neglect the impact of structural factors, of variables such as, class, culture, "race", ethnicity, sexuality, disability, language, and religion (Wilkin and Hillock, 2015). The impact of discrimination which can contribute

74 Compassion Fatigue

to compassion fatigue, the constant struggle of some workers against a context of large-scale oppression that permeates society's institutions is put to one side in the compassion fatigue literature which seems to under-value the impact of these significant structural influences. Research that has been undertaken about compassion fatigue and oppression has been limited. The research tends to focus more on burnout and secondary traumatic stress. Even then Cieslak et al. (2014) in their meta-analysis discovered little attention had been given to culture, while in one of the few, recent studies to consider "race", Masson and Moodey (2020) studied social workers in South Africa who, unusually, worked with the police force. Perhaps surprisingly, they found white practitioners experienced significantly higher levels of secondary traumatic stress. The authors suggested this may have been linked to white workers having previously had more privileges, better access to resources and working in more affluent areas. As a result, Masson and Moodey (2020) argued they had been less exposed to trauma, had fewer coping resources, and were less experienced in coping than Black workers who were more accustomed to in working in deprived areas, in dealing with trauma, difficulties, demands, and more limited resources.

In another study focused on black mental health professionals, a third of whom were social workers, Shell et al. (2021) found service user experiences of individual, cultural, and institutional racism were positively associated with burnout and secondary traumatic stress among practitioners. Research by Giordano et al. (2021) with predominantly white counsellors highlighted their work with Black clients who were subject to racism and racial trauma, once more the counsellors' experiences of "second hand" exposure to racial discrimination again predicted secondary traumatic stress.

In the compassion fatigue field, Schrag et al. (2021) researched practitioners who worked with victims of intimate partner violence and sexual assaults. Nearly a third of the workers had been exposed to "race" related microaggressions, the most frequently reported form of microaggression, and this was associated with compassion fatigue. Nearly a half of Black/Asian/Multi-Cultural and Native American workers had experienced microaggressions, compared with less than a third of white participants, with substantial rates of microaggressions also linked to sexuality and disability which were, in turn, associated with compassion fatigue.

These pieces of research highlight the need for minority group workers to have opportunities for formal and informal individual and group support, to discuss, to reflect upon, and consider action about the impact of discrimination and for white workers to have similar opportunities to explore the impact of work with minority group service users in order to prevent compassion fatigue.

There are also additional criticisms that the compassion fatigue approach is a negative, fatalistic one in that it omits consideration of other more positive concepts such as hope and optimism, strengths, resistance, and recovery (Collins, 2020; Lee et al., 2018; Sabo, 2011). Also, although some prominent compassion fatigue theorists and researchers do acknowledge the role and importance of

Compassion Fatigue **75**

other additional concepts such as resilience, support, coping, and self-care in mitigating compassion fatigue, these aspects are rarely actually considered in compassion fatigue research (Figley, 1995; Figley and Stamm, 2002; Kim et al. 2021; Ludick and Figley, 2017; Radey and Figley, 2007). However, some research studies have been undertaken with social workers considering more positive concepts *together* with compassion fatigue. For instance, authors have examined links with self-care (for example, Bourassa, 2012; Cuartero and Campos-Vidal, 2019). Also, although Adams et al., (2008), Bourassa (2012), and Pelon (2017) have explored the role of support, and Kapoulitsas and Corcoran (2015) considered the role of resilience in their study, more multi-faceted, interactive research work of this type is needed that combines a focus on compassion fatigue with more progressive concepts (Miller and Sprang, 2017; Newell et al., 2016).

In considering the discourse, the language used in the compassion fatigue literature is well justified, quite naturally and understandably, in view of the topic, with a focus on trauma, in using phrases such as "terrible and traumatic" recent events and "damaging and cruel" past events (Bride et al., 2007, p.155). However, equating trauma with *only* problematic, negative reactions is not always justified, as people also have resilience, along with the capacity to make a recovery (Marlowe and Adamson, 2011; Mendez-Fernandez et al., 2021). Furthermore, as some authors suggest, compassion fatigue can result from working with the general experiences of a person, rather than just their reaction to a specific event (or events); social workers also may well be caring for service users who are experiencing, who are moving through other difficulties, through other "problems of living", as well as moving through good and rewarding experiences (Baum 2016; Beddoe et al., 2019; Turgoose and Maddox, 2017).

Hence, although a service user may encounter particularly demanding, difficult, over-whelming, over-powering situations, this tends to neglect the fact that their lives may also include recent positive events and happy and harmonious past events, and experiences. Service users clearly demonstrate knowledge, survival skills, strengths, and active agency in efforts to change the present and work on the past. These positive aspects may well *co-exist* with traumatic experiences and negative experiences (Nuttman-Schwartz, 2015). So importantly, practitioners need to "acknowledge and validate experiences of trauma, while at the same time they are working with resilience, pathways to healing and ability to create meaning" (Marlowe and Adamson, (2011, p.624). Hence it is important to recognise that service users make

> responses to trauma which situate them beyond a simple victimised and damaged perspective [which] is essential if promoting health and well-being, [as] there is also an imperative for remembering that such experiences are not identity statements or automatic pathways to deleterious outcomes
>
> *(Marlowe and Adamson, 2011, p.631–632).*

76 Compassion Fatigue

Lee et al. (2018) have taken criticisms of compassion fatigue further. They draw attention to other possible limitations of the concept. These include the idea that you either "have it or you don't", the alleged lack of in-depth or detailed thought given by compassion fatigue theorists and researchers to halting its progress, and their alleged failure to consider how to stop the "run-away train". Indeed, little research has been conducted into the effectiveness of interventions to reduce compassion fatigue generally; the focus in the few existing studies is on nurses, with very few on social workers (Cocker and Joss, 2016). Fernando and Consedine (2014, p.291) also criticise the negative connotations of compassion fatigue, implying that a reservoir of compassion "dries up", with compassion fatigue as a possible "end point". This neglects the accompanying, often interlinked benefits, the rewards of compassion and compassion satisfaction, as we saw in the previous chapter and shall see in the next chapter, which involve helpers' well-being and pleasure in positive social interaction with service users, in "making a difference", in a focus on other people and mitigation of stress. In their recent qualitative study with oncology social workers, Kim et al. (2021) highlight the idea of compassion fatigue *co-existing* with, and in some cases moving on to, compassion satisfaction.

In fact, this is acknowledged in an earlier article by the prominent compassion fatigue researchers and theorists, Brian Bride, Melissa Radey and Charles Figley. They suggest workers "experience both compassion fatigue and compassion satisfaction simultaneously" as there are "some positive aspect[s] of trauma work that sustains and nourishes" practitioners (Bride et al., 2007, p.156). Figley and Stamm clearly took this to a logical conclusion in producing scales that not only evaluated burnout and compassion fatigue, but also compassion satisfaction, as seen in the work produced by Figley and Stamm (1996) and various versions of the Professional Quality of Life (ProQOL) scales by Stamm (2010). Stamm also argues clearly for a "balanced approach" between a focus on compassion fatigue and compassion satisfaction. This is eminently suited to, and congruent with, the experiences of social work professionals. It is supported by theorists such as Geoffrion et al. (2016). They argue for "a continuum" of compassion fatigue and satisfaction. This has also emerged in other research findings about social work which reveals the co-existence, the dialectic of emotional exhaustion and secondary traumatic stress with compassion satisfaction and the personal accomplishment element of burnout (for example, Stalker et al., 2007; Baldschun et al., 2019). Therefore, this also adds a cautionary note for the critics of the compassion fatigue concept – now compassion fatigue is often linked more clearly to compassion satisfaction and will be explored in more depth in the next chapter.

Social Workers, Compassion Fatigue, and other Research Findings

Research about compassion fatigue and qualified social workers seems to produce different conclusions, depending on the countries where the studies took place

Compassion Fatigue **77**

and the practice settings involved. Perhaps as one might expect, Harr et al., (2014) found social work students (in the USA) recorded lower levels of compassion fatigue than qualified workers. Younger students aged under 40 reported the highest levels of compassion fatigue and no significant differences were found in relation to ethnicity.

Thomas (2013) suggests the rates of compassion fatigue in research samples of helping professionals varies greatly, ranging up to 50 per cent. A study of social workers in Mallorca, Spain, found a third scored high in compassion fatigue, 60 per cent scored moderately, and less than one in ten scored low (Cuartero and Campos-Vidal, 2019). Alternatively, a study of social work practitioners in Montana, USA, by Caringi et al. (2017) reported that only five per cent experienced severe/high rates of compassion fatigue. Amongst Colorado, child protection social workers, Conrad and Kellar-Guenther (2006) discovered around a half experienced high or very high risk of compassion fatigue. In one of the few studies of social work professionals and compassion fatigue in the UK, Kinman and Grant (2020) reported only "moderate" compassion fatigue scores. The authors suggested that this was surprising, as nearly half of their sample was working with children and families.

In relation to adult protection work in the USA, Ghesquiere et al. (2018) found nearly a quarter of their sample were at high risk of compassion fatigue, but Bourassa's (2012) qualitative study unearthed little evidence of compassion fatigue amongst another sample of adult protection workers. Pelon's (2017) study of hospice social workers in the USA discovered nearly a quarter of the practitioners experienced high rates of compassion fatigue, around a half experienced moderate levels and nearly a quarter low levels. These studies did not tend to explore the underlying reasons as to *why* respondents had varied and different scores, but they did indicate compassion fatigue was/is a prominent problem for many workers. Pelon's (2017) research found no significant differences in compassion fatigue as regards age, marital status, type of social work qualification, frequency of supervision, and social work experience. Craig and Sprang (2010) and Yi et al. (2019) discovered those practitioners with more experience were more likely to develop compassion fatigue, but other studies have suggested contradictory findings related to more experience (Weiss-Dagan et al., 2016). In all, little research work has been done to explore the impact of compassion fatigue upon the perceptions of experienced social workers of how they undertake day-to-day tasks such as report writing, recording, assessment, and on-going work with service users. However, Denne et al. (2019) examined the relationship between compassion fatigue and hypothetical case assessments/judgements. They found the more compassion fatigued social workers "changed the lens" through which they perceived child abuse cases, with practitioners adopting a more detached, more cynical approach to working with children while having lower expectations of parents' competence.

As might be expected, Schrag et al. (2021) discovered workers who were satisfied with supervision enjoyed lower levels of compassion fatigue. Pelon

78 Compassion Fatigue

(2017) found those workers who most often had face-to-face contact with their supervisors scored lower on compassion fatigue than workers who had more telephone and e-mail contact. It does not yet appear to be clear, the extent to which supervision via Zoom or telephone contact has impacted the supervisory experience and rates of compassion fatigue during the recent pandemic.

As we saw in the first chapter, some studies have shown that being younger, female, having an early or adult "trauma history" and work-family conflict are risk factors for social workers developing compassion fatigue (such as Baugerud et al., 2018; Thomas, 2013). There is further evidence of higher rates of compassion fatigue amongst female social work practitioners in Korea (Yi et al., 2019) and amongst female mental health providers in rural settings in the USA (Sprang et al., 2007). The reasons for this may well include not only the multiple demands that many women face from both work and primary responsibility for caring roles within the family which we noted in the first chapter, but also as well, suggestions that women demonstrate greater sensitivity and empathy in their work with service users. As a result, they may be more prone to fear, rumination, and "emotional contagion", i.e. the overflow, the impact of negative feelings and difficult experiences with service users upon the workers' personal life (Baum, 2016; Baugerud et al., 2018; Thomas, 2013). Also, the impact of exposure to sexism can clearly be a contributing factor to compassion fatigue, as seen in Schrag et al.'s (2021) research with intimate personal violence and sexual assault workers, where one in five female participants experienced sexist microaggressions associated with compassion fatigue.

The evidence of the links between past traumatic events in social workers' own lives and compassion fatigue is seen in several pieces of research. These suggest that a worker with a history of trauma and anxious, avoidant, ambivalent, attachments following childhood trauma is more susceptible to experiencing compassion fatigue, especially if they have been sexually abused or experienced domestic violence and are working with a service user who has had, or is going through, such experiences (for example, Adams et al., 2006; Nelson-Gardell and Harris, 2003; Tosone et al., 2011; Thomas and Otis, 2010; Thomas, 2013). However, other studies have suggested past trauma in a worker's life is not linked to compassion fatigue, but can reinforce motivation, coping abilities, and opportunities for growth (for example, Adams et al., 2008; Bourassa, 2012; Way et al, 2004). As we also saw in the previous chapter, Thomas (2013) and Martin-Cuellar (2018) have also pointed out that in most instances the timing, the extent, the nature, and impact of past personal trauma amongst social workers linked to compassion fatigue are often unclear, and this is a controversial topic. Butler et al. (2018) highlight the most commonly related adverse childhood experiences among social work students in childhood were linked to on-going mental illness, alcohol/substance use, and the impact of parental divorce and separation, rather than traumatic events per se. Nevertheless, half of the respondents in their research reported physical, sexual, or emotional abuse, and experiencing domestic violence as potentially traumatising childhood experiences. As Butler et al.

Compassion Fatigue **79**

(2018) point out, it was the combination, the interplay, and the co-occurrence of several adverse childhood experiences which was likely to make more impact, with a third of students noting four or more adverse childhood experiences. In addition, Schrag et al. (2021) found *recent* trauma, such as the loss of a loved one and health challenges, was significantly associated with compassion fatigue among workers, while past traumas experienced as children and adults were not.

Other researchers highlight high demands from social work service users on occasions as an important influence upon practitioners' compassion fatigue. There are clear conclusions from the research of high incidences of post-traumatic stress disorder experienced by some service users in child welfare, mental health, and medical settings, with them presenting with particularly difficult and troubling situations, experiencing the most severe reactions and long-term demands, which predicted workers' levels of compassion fatigue (Sprang et al., 2007; Van Hook and Rothenberg, 2009; Yi et al., 2019). One particularly notable, perhaps obvious example, was Boscarino, et al.'s (2004) study of social workers assisting survivors of the 9/11 terrorist attacks in New York. Practitioners who worked with traumatised survivors, perhaps not surprisingly, were more at risk for developing compassion fatigue than those who did not work with survivors. Although, as yet, there is only limited evidence available, it would appear that compassion fatigue rates amongst social workers are likely to have increased during and following, the global COVID pandemic, in view of increased, prolonged pressures, stressors amongst service users and workers related to anxiety and depression rates, increases in drug and alcohol problems and restrictions on available resources, as noted previously.

Further Implications of Compassion Fatigue for Social Workers

Despite the intricacies, reservations, contradictions, and criticisms surrounding compassion fatigue, one of the benefits is that it draws attention to the demands, and the distress faced by social workers in undertaking their day-to-day tasks, especially those practitioners who are at the highest risk of compassion fatigue. Furthermore, all authors and researchers agree that, despite limitations, it is a profoundly serious and especially important topic (for example, Fox et al., 2021; Ledoux, 2015). Also, clearly, social workers may sometimes undertake routinised tasks which neither require nor provoke strong emotional responses. But at the same time practitioners do obviously encounter, both in the past and in the present lives of service users, the impact of upsetting, disturbing, and problematic events such as abuse, neglect, unexpected losses and deaths, sudden transitions, accidents, serious illnesses, violence, and worldwide crises such as the COVID-19 pandemic. Workers may then also move through emotionally upsetting responses. All of this takes place in a well-established context of inequality, poverty, poor health, difficult housing conditions, and limited educational expectations and opportunities for many service users. This can clearly and obviously be very disturbing for the practitioner.

Compassion fatigue is one aspect of negative elements in the experiences of a social worker, but it co-exists with and is also accompanied by, positive elements. Compassion fatigue, in part, helps to explain the high incidence of illnesses amongst social workers, absences from work, and departures from the profession. Part of its value is that it draws attention to consideration of what actions might be taken, and what might be done either to prevent or alleviate compassion fatigue. In a series of articles Knight (for example, 2019) has pointed out the importance, the significance of trauma-informed practice and trauma-informed care, linked to compassion fatigue, for both individual workers and their organisations. Hence, some of the "answers" lie within individual social workers, but they also lie more prominently in the organisational and structural context of social work (for instance, Ashley -Binge and Cousins, 2020; Kreitzer et al., 2020). Compassion fatigue highlights the importance of organisational support systems which we will discuss further in the next and in the final chapter. These systems should recognise and respond to the fatigue of social workers who are likely to be subject to demands from service users, the organisation, oppression, and discrimination, as well as possible pressures from their own family circumstances. Schrag et al. (2021) note how important it is to give attention to the interaction of compassion fatigue with oppression, culture, and intersecting identities in order to address bias and discrimination in organisations, while establishing and developing policies and practices which acknowledge and aim to mitigate the effects of traumas (where relevant) and to combat compassion fatigue.

Therefore, to re-emphasise the point again, the concept of compassion fatigue helps us to consider and raise social workers' own awareness of the demands made upon them. Practitioners have feelings and needs which should be met, with "in-put" to themselves rather than continuously "giving out" practical and emotional support to service users and in trying to meet their professional standards and requirements, when they need practical and emotional support. The compassion fatigue concept can help sensitise practitioners to their *own* needs, amidst the demands of their on-going work, as well as to particular emotionally exhausting, specific situations and events, such as the global pandemic, being sometimes on the receiving end of verbal threats, physical assaults, and angry, negative, emotional out-bursts, which can leave the worker drained and exhausted.

Research studies from the USA indicate specific, specialised education and training in developing particular understanding and skills in trauma-informed work can significantly increase learning about the effect of trauma upon service users as well as upon oneself as a worker, thus reducing the risk of compassion fatigue (Butler et al., 2017; Craig and Sprang, 2010; Sprang et al., 2007). For example, in Sprang et al.'s (2007) work with mental health providers, amongst those who had undertaken such specialised training only one in 20 workers scored as a high risk for compassion fatigue. A few social work courses already give considerable attention to trauma and trauma-informed content linked to compassion fatigue, such as the University of Buffalo in the USA (Butler et al., 2017).

Several writers have argued for a module or workshops starting with consideration of concepts such as pressure, stress, trauma, secondary traumatic stress, vicarious trauma, burnout, and compassion fatigue, before moving on to explore various positive aspects of well-being on social work qualifying courses and as a part of on-going professional development opportunities (see, for instance, Harr and Moore, 2011; van Heugten, 2011). However, it is also helpful to highlight the connections with important transferable knowledge and skills likely to be learned in most social work courses related to, for example, values, mental health, loss, transition, crisis intervention work, and organisations (Marlowe and Adamson, 2011).

Also, at an individual level, practitioners, practice educators, and line managers may wish to make use of the various scales we considered earlier in the chapter in order to develop their awareness of the presence of possible compassion fatigue. This may be preferably undertaken as a voluntary exercise rather than being a part of any required professional development plan or organisational requirement. However, recent COVID-19 events would suggest this matter could be an organisational priority to be undertaken in a sensitive, thoughtful, "non-blaming" manner that recognises the "normalisation" of compassion fatigue experiences (Community Care/Unison, 2021).

Conclusion

The provision of learning experiences can raise consciousness about compassion fatigue, about means for coping with it in the future through appropriate formal, informal, individual and group support, along with exploration of organisational provision, and the impact of structural matters, such as oppression and discrimination that can contribute to compassion fatigue. Clearly learning opportunities should also be available to practice educators and line managers, who may need either to develop or to refresh their capabilities in this specific area. They have particularly important roles in sensitively exploring, supporting, modelling, and reinforcing workers' appropriate reactions to compassion fatigue.

Knowledge and understanding of, and skills related to, compassion fatigue are helpful for practitioners. They help to raise our awareness, and develop our sensitivity and responsiveness to particular events or to protracted, predominantly negative experiences and what actions might be taken to alleviate them. Nevertheless, compassion fatigue alone clearly does not, and cannot, provide exclusive answers; it is but one part of a well-being continuum. Compassion fatigue is also linked to more positive concepts which can help to alleviate it. These important concepts will be discussed in the next and later chapters.

References

Adams, R., Figley, C. and Boscarino, J. (2006) "Compassion fatigue and psychological distress among social workers: A validation study", *American Journal of Orthopsychiatry*, 76.1, 103–108.

82 Compassion Fatigue

Adams, R., Figley, C. and Boscarino, J. (2008) "The compassion fatigue scale: Its use with social workers following urban disasters", *Research on Social Work Practice*, 18.3, 238–250.

Antonopoulu, P., Killian, M. and Forrester, D. (2017) "Levels of stress and anxiety in children and families social work: Workers' perceptions of organisational structure, professional support and workplace opportunities in Children's Services", *Children and Youth Services Review*, 96, 42–50.

Armes, S., Lee, J., Bride, B. and Seponski, D. (2020) "Secondary trauma and impairment in clinical social workers", *Child Abuse and Neglect*, doi.org/10.1016/j.chiau.2020.14540.

Ashley-Binge, S. and Cousins, C. (2020) "Individual and organisational practices addressing social workers experiences of vicarious trauma", *Practice: Social Work in Action*, 32.3, 191–207.

Badger, K., Royse, D. and Craig, C. (2008) "Hospital social workers and indirect trauma exposure: An exploratory study of contributing factors", *Health and Social Work*, 33.1, 63–71.

Baldschun, A, Hamalainen, J., Toto, P., Rantonen, O. and Salo, P. (2019) "Job-strain and well-being among Finnish social workers: Exploring the differences in occupational well-being between child protection workers and social workers without duties in child protection", *European Journal of Social Work*, 22.1, 43–58.

Baum, N. (2016) "Secondary traumatisation in mental health professionals: A systematic review of gender findings", *Trauma, Violence and Abuse*, 17.2, 221–235.

Baugerud, G., Vangbaek, S. and Melinder, A. (2018) "Secondary traumatic stress, burnout and compassion satisfaction among Norwegian child protection workers: Protective and risk factors", *British Journal of Social Work*, 48, 215–235.

Beddoe, L., Ballantyne, N., Maidment, J., Hay, K. and Walker, S. (2019) "Troubling trauma-informed policy in social work education: Reflections of educators and students in Aotearoa New Zealand", *British Journal of Social Work*, 49, 1563–1581.

Ben-Porat, A., Shemesh, S., Zahav, R., Gottleib, S. and Refaeli, T. (2021) "Secondary traumatization among social work students-the contribution of personal, professional and environmental factors", *British Journal of Social Work*, 51.3, 982–998.

Boscarino, J., Figley, C. and Adams, R. (2004) "Compassion fatigue following the September 11 terrorist attacks: A study of secondary traumatic stress among New York city social workers", *International Journal of Emergency Mental Health*, 6.2, 57–66.

Bourassa, D. (2012) "Examining self-protection measures guarding adult protection social workers against compassion fatigue", *Journal of Interpersonal Violence*, 27.9, 1699–1715.

Brent-Godley, T. (2019) "The necessity of trauma-informed practice in contemporary social work", *Social Work*, 64.1, 5–8.

Bride, B. (2007) "Prevalence of secondary traumatic stress among social workers", *Social Work*, 52, 63–70.

Bride, B., Radey, M. and Figley, C. (2007) "Measuring compassion fatigue", *Clinical Social Work Journal*, 35, 155–163.

Butler, L., Carello, J. and Maguin, E. (2017) "Trauma, stress and self-care in clinical training: Predictors of burnout, decline in health status, secondary traumatic stress symptoms and compassion satisfaction", *Psychological Trauma: Theory, Research, Practice and Policy*, 9.4, 416424.

Butler, L., Maguin, E. and Carello, J. (2018) "Retraumatization mediates the effect of adverse childhood experiences on clinical training-related secondary traumatic stress symptoms", *Journal of Trauma and Dissociation*, 19.1, 25–38.

Caringi, J., Hardiman, E., Weldon, P., Fletcher, S., Devlin, M. and Stanick, C. (2017) "Secondary traumatic stress and licensed clinical social workers", *Traumatology*, 23.2, 186–195.

Choi, G. (2011) "Organizational impacts on the secondary traumatic stress of social workers assisting family violence or sexual assault survivors", *Administration in Social Work*, 35.2, 225–246.

Cieslak, R., Shoji, K., Douglas, A., Melville, E., Luszcznska, A. and Benight, C. (2014) "A meta-analysis of the relationship between job burnout and secondary traumatic stress among workers with indirect exposure to trauma", *Psychological Services*, 11.1, 75–86.

Cocker, F. and Joss, N. (2016) "Compassion fatigue among health care, emergency and community-service workers: A systematic review", *International Journal of Environmental Research and Public Health,* 13,618, 2–18.

Coffey, M., Dudgill, L. and Tattersall, A. (2004) "Stress in social services: Mental well-being, constraints and job satisfaction", *British Journal of Social Work*, 34.5, 735–746.

Collins, S. (2020) *The Positive Social Worker,* London, Routledge.

Community Care/ Unison (2021) *Supporting social workers in 2021,* London, Community Care/ Unison.

Conrad, D. and Kellar-Guenther, Y. (2006) "Compassion fatigue, burnout and compassion satisfaction among Colorado child protection workers", *Child Abuse and Neglect*, 30.10, 1071–1080.

Craig, C. and Sprang, G. (2010) "Compassion satisfaction, compassion fatigue and burnout in a national sample of trauma treatment therapists", *Anxiety, Stress and Coping: An International Journal*, 23, 319–339.

Cuartero, M. and Campos-Vidal, J. (2019) "Self-care behaviours and their relationship with satisfaction and compassion fatigue levels among social workers", *Social Work in Health Care*, 58.3, 274–290.

Dekel, R., Hantman, S., Ginzburg, K. and Solomon, Z. (2007) "The cost of caring: Social workers in hospital confront on-going terrorism", *British Journal of Social Work*, 37.7, 1247–1261.

Denne, E., Stevenson, M. and Petty, T. (2019) "Understanding how social work compassion fatigue and years of experience shape custodial decisions", *Child Abuse and Neglect*, DOI:10.1016. j.chiabu, 2019, 104036.

Diaconescu, M. (2015) "Burnout, secondary traumatic stress and compassion fatigue in social work", *Revista De Assienta Sociale (Social Work Review),* 14.3, 57–63.

Dombo, A. and Whiting-Blome, W. (2016) "Vicarious trauma in child welfare workers: A study of organisational responses", *Journal of Public Child Welfare,* 10.5, 505–523.

Egan, G. (2001) *The Skilled Helper,* Pacific Grove, Brooks- Cole.

Eng, l., Nordstrom, J. and Schad, E. (2020) "Incorporating compassion into compassion fatigue: The development of a new scale", *Journal of Clinical Psychology*, DOI:10.1002/ jclp23113.

Evans, S. and Huxley, P. (2009) "Factors associated with the recruitment and retention of social workers in Wales: Employer and employee perspectives", *Health and Social Care in the Community*, 17.3, 254–266.

Fernando, A. and Consedine, N. (2014) "Beyond compassion fatigue: The transtheoretical model of physician compassion", *Journal of Pain and Symptom Management*, 48.2, 289–298.

Figley, C. (1995) *Compassion fatigue: Coping with secondary traumatic stress disorder in those who treat the traumatized,* New York, Brunner Mazel.

Figley, C. and Stamm, B. (1996) "Psychometric review of the compassion fatigue self-test" in Stamm, B. (ed.) *Measurement of Stress, Trauma and Adaptation*, Lutherville, MD, Sidran Press, pp.127–130.

Figley, C. and Stamm, B. (2002) *Treating Compassion Fatigue*, New York, Brunner Mazel.

Fox, M., Hopkins, D., Graves, J., Crehan, S., Cull, P., Birrell, B., Dunn, P., Murphy, E., Harrison, A., Hayes, M. and Yeomans, P. (2021) "Hospital social workers and

84 Compassion Fatigue

their understanding of compassion fatigue and vicarious trauma", *Asian Journal of Interdisciplinary Studies,* DOI:10.34256/ajir2113.

Geoffrion, S., Morselli, S. and Guay, S. (2016) "Rethinking compassion fatigue through the lens of professional identity: The case of child protection workers", *Trauma, Violence and Abuse,* 17.3, 270–283.

Ghesquiere, A., Plichta, S., McAfee, C. and Rogers, G. (2018) "Professional quality of life of adult protection workers", *Journal of Elder Abuse and Neglect,* 30.1, 1–19.

Giordano, A., Gorritz, F., Kilpatrick, E., Scoffone, C. and Lundeen, L. (2021) "Explaining secondary trauma as a result of clients' reports of discrimination", *Journal for the Advancement of Counselling,* 43, 19–30.

Harr, C. and Moore, B. (2011) "Compassion fatigue among social work students in field placements", *Journal of Teaching in Social Work,* 31, 350–365.

Harr, C., Brice, T., Riley, K. and Moore, B. (2014) "The impact of compassion fatigue and compassion satisfaction on social work students", *Journal of the Society for Social Work Research,* 5.2, 233–250.

Hombrados-Mendieta, I. and Costano-Rivas, F. (2011) "Burnout, workplace support, job satisfaction and life satisfaction among social workers in Spain: A structural equation model", *International Social Work,* 56.2, 228–246.

IFSW (2020) *Practising During Pandemic Condition: Ethical Guidance for Social Workers,* Rheinfelden, IFSW.

Joinson, C. (1992) "Coping with compassion fatigue", *Nursing,* 22.4, 116–120.

Kapoulitsas, M. and Corcoran, T. (2015) "Compassion fatigue and resilience: A qualitative analysis of social work practice", *Qualitative Social Work,* 14.1, 84–101.

Kim, M., Jaehee, Y., Molloy, J. and Choi, K. (2021) "The impact of compassion fatigue on the well-being of oncology social workers in Korea", *Journal of Social Service Research,* 47.5, 634–648.

Kinman, G. and Grant, L. (2020) "Emotional demands, compassion and mental health in social workers", *Occupational Medicine,* 70, 89–94.

Knight, C. (2019) "Trauma informed practice and care: Implications for field instruction", *Clinical Social Work Journal,* 47, 79–80.

Kreitzer, L., Brintnell, S. and Austin, L. (2020) "Institutional barriers to healthy workplace environments: From the voices of social workers experiencing compassion fatigue", *British Journal of Social Work,* 50, 1942–1960.

Ledoux, K. (2015) "Understanding compassion fatigue: understanding compassion", *Journal of Advanced Nursing,* 9.2, 2041–2050.

Lee, R. (2017) "The impact of engaging with clients' trauma stories: Personal and organizational strategies to manage probation practitioners' risk of developing vicarious traumatization", *Probation Journal,* 44.4, 379–387.

Lee, J., Gottfried, R. and Bride, B. (2018) "Exposure to client trauma, secondary traumatic stress and the health of the clinical social worker: A mediation analysis", *Clinical Social Work Journal,* 46.3, 223–235.

Lev-Wiesel, R., Eisikovits, Z. and Admi, H. (2009) "Growth in the shadow of war: The case of social workers and nurses working in a shared war reality", *British Journal of Social Work,* 39.6, 1154–1174.

Lizano, E. and Mor-Barak, M. (2015) "Job burnout and affective well-being: A longitudinal study of burnout and job satisfaction among public child welfare workers", *Children and Youth Services Review,* 55, 18–128.

Ludick, M. and Figley, C. (2017) "Towards a mechanism for secondary trauma induction and reduction: Reimagining a theory of secondary traumatic stress", *Traumatology,* 23.1, 112–121.

Marlowe, J. and Adamson, C. (2011) "Teaching trauma: Critically engaging a troublesome term", *Social Work Education*, 30.6, 623–634.

Martin-Cuellar, A., Atencio, D., Kelly, R. and Lardier Jr., D. (2018) "Mindfulness as a moderator of clinician history of trauma on compassion satisfaction", *The Family Journal: Counselling and Therapy for Couples and Families*, 26.3, 358–368.

Maslach, C. (2003) *Burnout: The Cost of Caring*, Los Alto, ISHK.

Masson, F. and Moodey, J. (2020) "Secondary traumatic stress: The experiences of social workers in the South African police service", *Practice: Social Work in Action*, 32.3, 169–189.

McCann, I. and Pearlman, L. (1990) "Vicarious traumatisation: A framework for understanding the psychological effects of working with victims", *Journal of Traumatic Stress*, 3, 131–149.

McFadden, P., Campbell, J. and Taylor, B. (2015) "Resilience and Burnout in Child Protection Social Workers: Individual and Organisational Themes from a Systematic Literature Review", *British Journal of Social Work*, 45.3, 1546–1563.

McFadden, P. (2018) "Two sides of one coin? Relationships build resilience or contribute to burnout in child protection social work: Shared perspectives from leavers and stayers in Northern Ireland", *International Social Work*, 1–13, DOI: 0.11710208872818788393.

Mendez-Fernandez, A., Aguiar-Fernandez, F., Lombardero-Posada, X., Murcia-Alvarez, E. and Gonzalo-Fernandez, A. (2021) "Vicariously resilient or traumatised social workers: Exploring some risk and protective factors", *British Journal of Social Work*, DOI:10.1093/bjsw/bca085.

Middleton, J. and Potter, C. (2015) "Relationship between vicarious traumatisation and turnover among social work professionals", *Journal of Public and Child Welfare*, 9.2, 195–216.

Mickel, A. (2009) "Survey reveals social workers' poor working conditions", *Community Care*, 29 July.

Miller, B. and Sprang, G. (2017) "A components-based practice and supervision model for reducing compassion fatigue by affecting clinical experience", *Tramatology*, 23.2, 153–164.

Nelson-Gardell, D. and Harris, D. (2003) "Childhood abuse history, secondary traumatic stress and child welfare workers", *Child Welfare*, 82, 5–26

Newell, J. and MacNeill, G. (2010) "Professional burnout, vicarious trauma, secondary traumatic stress and compassion fatigue: A review of theoretical terms, risk and preventative methods for clinicians and researchers", *Best Practices in Mental Health*, 6.2, 257–268.

Newell, J., Gardell, J. and MacNeill, G. (2016) "Clinician response to client trauma; A chronological review", *Trauma, Violence and Abuse*, 17, 306–313.

Nuttman-Schwartz, O. (2015) "Shared resilience in a traumatic reality: A new concept for trauma workers exposed personally and professionally to collective disaster", *Trauma, Violence and Abuse*, 16.4, 466–475.

Pearlman, L. and Saakvitne, K. (1995) *Trauma and the Therapist: Countertransference and Vicarious Trauma in Psychotherapy with Incest Survivors*, New York, Norton.

Pelon, S. (2017) "Compassion fatigue and compassion satisfaction in hospice social work", *Journal of Social Work in End-of- Life and Palliative Care*, 13, 2–3, 134–150.

Quinn, A., Ji, P. and Nackerud, L. (2019) "Predictors of secondary traumatic stress among social workers: Supervision, income, and caseload size", *Journal of Social Work*, 19.4, 504–528.

Radey, M. and Figley, C. (2007) "The social psychology of compassion", *Clinical Social Work Journal*, 35, 207–214.

86 Compassion Fatigue

Ravalier, J. (2017) *U K Social Workers: Working Conditions and Well Being*, London, BASW.

Ravalier, J., McFadden, P., Boichat, C., Claburn, O. and Moriarity, J. (2021) "Wellbeing: A large mixed methods study*", British Journal of Social Work*, 51.1, 297–317.

Rayner, S., Davis, C., Moore, M. and Cadet, T. (2020) "Secondary traumatic stress and related factors in Australian social workers and psychologists", *Health and Social Work*, 45.2, 122–130.

Rienks, S. (2020) "An exploration of child welfare caseworkers' experience of secondary trauma and strategies for coping", *Child Abuse and Neglect*, doi.org/10.1016/j.chiabu.2020.104355.

Rogers, C. (1957) "The necessary and sufficient conditions of therapeutic personality change", *Journal of Consulting Psychology*, 21, 95–103.

Ruch, G., Turney, D. and Ward, A. (2018) *Relationship-based Social Work*, London, Jessica Kingsley.

Sabo, B. (2011) "Reflecting on the concept of compassion fatigue", *On -line Journal of Issues in Nursing*, 16.1. Manuscript1.

Schraer, R. (2015) "Social workers too stressed to do their job according to survey", *Community Care*, 15 January.

Schrag, R., Wood, L., Wachter, K. and Kulkarni, S. (2021) "Compassion fatigue among the intimate partner violence and sexual assault workforce: Enhancing organizational practice", *Violence Against Women*, 28.1, 277–297.

Senreich, E., Straussner, S. and Steen, J. (2020) "The work experiences of social workers: Factors impacting compassion satisfaction in the workplace", *Journal of Social Science Research*, 46.1, 93–109.

Shamai, M. and Ron, P. (2009) "Helping direct and indirect victims of national terror: Experiences of Israeli social workers", *Qualitative Health Research*, 19.1, 42–54.

Shell, E., Teodorescu, D. and Williams, L. (2021) "Investigating race-related stress, burnout and secondary traumatic stress for black mental health therapists", *Journal of Black Psychology*, 47.8, 669–694.

Sinclair, S., Raffin-Bouchel, S., Venturato, L., Mijovic-Kondewski, J. and Smith-Macdonald, L. (2017) "Compassion fatigue: A meta narrative review of the health care literature", *International Journal of Nursing Studies*, 69, 9–24.

Singh, J., Karanika-Murray, M., Baguley, T. and Hudson, J. (2020) "A systematic review of job demands and resources associated with compassion fatigue in mental health professionals", *International Journal of Environmental Research and Public Health*, 17,6987, DOI:10.3390/ijerph 17196987.need?

Sprang, G. Clark, J. and Whitt-Woosley, A. (2007) "Compassion fatigue, compassion satisfaction and burnout: Factors implicating a professional's quality of life", *Journal of Loss and Trauma*, 12, 259–280.

Stalker, C., Mandell, D., Frensch, K., Harvey, C. and Wright, M. (2007) "Child welfare workers who are exhausted yet satisfied with their jobs", *Child and Family Social Work*, 12.2, 182–191.

Stamm, B. (2005) *The Pro QOL Scale: The Professional Quality of Life Scale: Compassion Satisfaction, Burnout and Compassion Fatigue/Secondary Traumatic Stress Scales*, Baltimore, Sidran Press.

Stamm, B. (2010) *The Concise Pro QOL Manual (Professional Quality of Life Scale: Compassion Satisfaction and Compassion Fatigue)*, Pocatello ID, Pro QOL org.

Stanford, S. (2011) "Constructing moral responses to risk: A framework for hopeful social work practice", *British Journal of Social Work*, 41, 1514–1531.

Tanner, D. (2020) "'The love that dare not speak its name': The role of compassion in social work", *British Journal of Social Work*, 50.6, 1688–1705.

Thomas, J. and Otis, M. (2010) "Intrapsychic correlates of professional quality of life: Mindfulness, empathy and emotional separation", *Journal of the Society for Social Work and Research*, 1, 83–98.

Thomas, J. (2013) "Association of personal distress with burnout, compassion fatigue and compassion satisfaction among clinical social workers", *Journal of Social Service Research*, 39, 365–379.

Tosone, C., McTighe, J., Bauwens, J. and Naturale, A. (2011) "Shared traumatic stress and the long-term impact of 9/11 on Manhattan clinicians", *Traumatic Stress*, 24.5, 546–552.

Turgoose, D. and Maddox, L. (2017) "Predictors of compassion fatigue in mental health professionals: A narrative review", *Traumatology*, 23.2, 172–185.

van Heugten, K. (2011) *Social Work Under Pressure*, London, Jessica Kingsley.

Van Hook, M. and Rothenberg, M. (2009) "Quality of life and compassion satisfaction / fatigue and burnout in child welfare workers: A study of the child welfare workers in community -based organizations in Florida", *Social Work and Christianity*, 36.1, 36–54.

Wagaman, M., Geiger, J., Shockley, C. and Segal, E. (2015) "The role of empathy in burnout, compassion satisfaction and secondary traumatic stress among social workers", *Social Work,* 60.3, 201–209.

Way, I., Van Deusen, K., Martin, G., Applegate, B. and Yandle, D. (2004) "Vicarious trauma; A comparison of clinicians who treat survivors of sexual abuse and sexual offenders", *Journal of Interpersonal Violence*, 19.1, 49–71.

Weiss-Dagan, S., Ben-Porat, A. and Itzaky, H. (2016) "Child protection workers dealing with child abuse: The contribution of personal, social and organizational resources to secondary traumatization", *Child Abuse and Neglect*, 51, 203–211.

Wilkin, L. and Hillock, S (2015) "Enhancing MSW students' efficacy in working with trauma, violence, and oppression: An integrated feminist-trauma framework for social work education", *Feminist Teacher*, 24.3, 184–205.

Yi, J., Kim, M., Choi, K., Droubay, B. and Kim, S. (2019) "Compassion satisfaction and compassion fatigue among medical social workers in Korea: The role of empathy", *Social Work in Health Care*, 58.10, 970–987.

4

COMPASSION SATISFACTION

Introduction

As we have seen in the previous chapter, social work is a demanding profession with pressure, stress, and compassion fatigue involving vicarious trauma, secondary trauma, and burnout. There has been a tendency to focus on the difficulties and problematic aspects of social work. Yet social workers also derive considerable satisfaction from their work. Therefore, as noted in the previous chapter, compassion fatigue and compassion satisfaction exist together. In this chapter, the focus will be on compassion satisfaction. Compassion satisfaction is defined; its strengths are considered, and relevant research findings are explored. Some limitations of the research are discussed. Attention is also given to the individual and organisational aspects of compassion satisfaction. Critical perspectives on compassion satisfaction are considered, such as the heavy focus on the individual social worker. Ways forward to further develop compassion satisfaction are proposed.

Social work is a profession with high ambitions, committed to addressing poverty, social change, social justice, human rights, respect for diversity, oppression and discrimination while intervening at various, wide-ranging levels (IFSW, 2014). However, research in the USA and the UK indicates that social work is one of the most stressful occupations when compared with other professions such as medicine and nursing, while different concepts have been used to describe the negative social, emotional, and physical aspects of care giving in social work, which we discussed in the previous chapter (Grant and Kinman, 2014; Senreich et al., 2020a).

Vicarious Post-Traumatic Growth and Vicarious Resilience

Alternative, fairly recently developed, more strength-based concepts are also evident, such as vicarious post-traumatic growth, and vicarious resilience, which

DOI: 10.4324/9781003112532-5

highlight that social workers enjoy their work; they can grow and develop following difficult experiences. Several researchers and writers have emphasised the role of post-traumatic *growth* in experiences with, and reactions to, stressful and traumatic events, leading to positive changes in self-perception, interpersonal relationships, and philosophy of life (for instance, Samios et al., 2013; Tedeshci and Calhoun, 2004).

Arnold et al. (2005) presented inspired, and inspiring, qualitative research about vicarious post-traumatic growth among helpers. They pointed out that while there are negative consequences of working with service users experiencing trauma, there are also positive, life changing consequences. These include increased self-confidence, self-worth, optimism, resilience, independence, acceptance, insight, sensitivity, empathy, and a deeper, wider sense of spirituality, with increased awareness of, in particular, a greater sense of meaning and possibilities.

Amongst social workers and social work students, in Israel, Ben-Porat (2015) and Ben-Porat et al. (2020) discovered "moderate", and "medium" levels of vicarious post-traumatic growth. In research focused upon the same topic and social workers working with abused children, also in Israel, Weiss-Dagan et al. (2020) noted the lack of research in this area. However, they found that although practitioners experienced secondary traumatic stress, the more experience social workers had, and the higher degree of exposure to work with abused children, the greater their vicarious growth. Other studies have emphasised vicarious growth among child welfare and child protection workers (for instance, Molnar et al., 2020; Tavormina and Clossley, 2015). Regehr et al. (2004) in their earlier research with child welfare workers also found that as levels of distress *increased*, so did levels of vicarious post-traumatic growth and positive change. Therefore, these studies again tend to reinforce the point that stress and compassion fatigue tends to go hand-in-hand with positive and rewarding aspects of social work.

Lev-Wiesel et al. (2009) found that although practitioners working in circumstances of war in Israel could find the work to be stressful and traumatic, they also found it to be challenging, reinforcing a sense of being needed, a source of personal and professional value, worth and growth, as did Shamai and Ron (2009). The latter researchers discovered that, over time, distress diminished, and growth increased. But a study of social workers also in Israel during war conditions highlighted restraints and limits to professional growth for minority workers, as Arab social work practitioners indicated no perceptions of experience of professional growth, in contrast to the growth experienced by two thirds of the Jewish workers (Baum and Ramon, 2010).

In addition to post-traumatic vicarious growth, the concept of vicarious resilience has been described as "the positive impact… [of the] personal growth… resulting from [workers] exposure to clients' resilience" (Hernandez-Wolfe, 2018, p.9). Pack (2014) and Hernandez-Wolfe et al., (2007, 2015) explored vicarious resilience, the idea of reciprocity in helping relationships, whereby working with service users successfully dealing with, recovering from, and overcoming

90 Compassion Satisfaction

trauma and adversity, then healing after facing heavy, negative odds, positively influenced, and significantly changed workers' attitudes to life, to their own resourcefulness and resilience. This led, in particular, to greater valuing of their contribution to the helping process. Other studies discovered child protection social workers were inspired and were strengthened by service users' experiences in coping with adverse situations and achieving change in their lives (Hurley et al., 2013, 2015). This reinforced the practitioners' feelings of doing positive work. Sharing a sense of effective meaning in life and a sense of purpose in growth-producing experiences were seen as significant, with social workers feeling privileged, and honoured to share in service users' experiences while placing their own demands and difficulties into a much wider perspective (Beddoe et al., 2019; Collins, 2020). Additional studies of helpers have reinforced this point about the privilege of being able to be involved with service users' stories and to "walk in sacred places" with service users (Hunter, 2012, p.129).

Satisfaction in Social Work

Along with these positive concepts – vicarious post-traumatic growth and vicarious resilience – there is also evidence from large-scale and small-scale research studies over the past 20 to 30 years in the UK that social work practitioners generally enjoy high levels of satisfaction in their work. For instance, although it was 20 years ago, Rose (2003) undertook a wide-ranging survey of a large number of occupational groups in the UK. Social work was placed just within the top twenty groups that experience high job satisfaction. However, research studies also tend to emphasise the negative aspects of social work. For instance, Collins (2008) cites Coffey et al.'s (2004) study of stress which highlighted the four per cent of social work staff in the UK who were absent through illness, although 96 per cent were not off work.

Much research has been undertaken about a general tendency to concentrate upon negative rather than positive experiences. Myers (2000) and Robertson and Cooper (2011) pointed out that psychology research contained at least 15 times as many articles focused upon negative rather than positive topics. Cooper et al. (2013) also note that around 20 times more research material has been produced about negative emotions rather than positive emotions. Furthermore, negative experiences and emotions tend "to have a stronger effect on our information processing systems, memory, self-concept and relationships, while outcomes of positive events tend to be underestimated, under-emphasised and under-valued" (Collins, 2020, p.4). This also applies to helping professionals, who tend to prioritise "problem saturated conversations"; they experience difficulties in considering, exploring and discussing good, rewarding and positive aspects of their work, accompanied by a tendency to take them for granted (Moorhouse, 2011; Wheeler and McElvaney, 2018).

However, surveys in the UK in Community Care also consistently indicate social work has rewards and satisfactions. For example, Mickel (2009) noted that three quarters of social workers were very or fairly satisfied with their jobs. Also, Baginski et al. (2009) found nearly three quarters of 1,000 respondents to be satisfied with their work. Evans and Huxley (2009) discovered two thirds of social workers in Wales were at least satisfied with their work. Another Community Care survey (Cooper, 2015) and McFadden's (2016) study of burnout and social workers clarified that, despite high levels of emotional exhaustion and feelings of depersonalisation, almost all respondents also experienced high levels of personal accomplishment – feelings of competence and success. A large-scale Guardian survey (2017) indicated over 80 per cent of workers were proud of what they did. Three quarters enjoyed their jobs, and got real satisfaction from their work, believing they were "making a difference". In fact, 17 per cent did say they wanted to leave social work, but reduced caseloads and better support would have changed their minds. Ravalier (2017, p.14) found workers to be "relatively to highly positive and fulfilled", despite poor working conditions. Recent research in Wales and Ireland discovered most social work practitioners looked forward to going to work and were satisfied with the quality of their endeavours (Burns et al., 2019; Pithouse et al., 2018).

Also, as we have already seen in an earlier chapter, even during the strains and pressures of the COVID-19 pandemic, social work professionals enjoyed good levels of well-being and decent quality of working life (McFadden et al., 2021). Johnson et al. (2021) found that three quarters of 2,000 practitioners in the UK were satisfied with their work, and their sense of achievement, with higher levels of satisfaction linked to work with particular service user groups in settings such as youth justice, adoption and fostering and leaving care compared with more general children and family work and "duty" teams. Levels of satisfaction were also linked to OFSTED ratings of local authorities, the frequency of reflective supervision, and continuing professional development opportunities.

In particular, numerous surveys and a multiplicity of research studies over many years have emphasised the fact that social workers derive a great deal of satisfaction from their face-to-face interactions with service users (see, for instance, Antonopoulu et al., 2017; Evans and Huxley, 2009; McFadden et al., 2015). As Collins (2020) points out, a key, central, possibly obvious point to be taken from the research studies cited, is the exhaustive, extensive evidence that, although social work is demanding and stressful, it is also rewarding. Furthermore, many international studies over the past 25 years to the present time also reveal prominent levels of satisfaction for social work practitioners in countries such as Canada, the USA, and Greece, the latter a country which has experienced massive economic upheavals in recent years (Hermon and Chablah, 2019; Karpetis, 2015; Stalker et al., 2007).

As Collins (2020) points out, little research has been conducted that directly focuses on pride in, and the joys, pleasures, and enjoyment of, social work. Pooler et al.'s (2014a, b) work is an exception. They specifically asked practitioners about the *joys* of social work – a surprisingly unusual perspective. Workers particularly enjoyed "making connections" with people, and making relationships with both

92 Compassion Satisfaction

service users and colleagues. They believed they were effective in advocating for active change for service users in their own organisations and in service users' communities. Again, the social work task provided a sense of meaning, of purpose, of pride in serving and helping others, which "fitted" with the workers' ideals and with their beliefs, giving them a powerful sense of professional identity. Finally, social work was not seen as "just a job", but as a part of life, involving both personal and professional learning and growth, with satisfaction obtained from seeing small changes (Collins, 2020).

Pride amongst social workers has received particular attention recently. In Beddoe et al.'s (2019) study, almost all respondents did feel proud to be a social worker. Interestingly, there was evidence of resistance to, and questioning of, the use of the term "pride", with some workers putting forward views concentrated upon focusing upon the importance of *humility*, in contrast to pride. Pride was particularly associated with a collective identity linked to shared values about social work, along with opportunities to collaborate with marginalised people, who were often placed in the role of "underdog". In Savaya's (2022) research with practitioners in Israel among "clusters" related to pride, that of being a force for change was rated highest – a similar finding to Pooler et al.'s (2014a, b) and Beddoe et al.'s (2019) studies. Pride in achieving service users' desired goals was prominent, as was mobilising external resources for positive change. Practitioners felt pride in their sense of accomplishment and goal attainment in interactions with service users, rather than pride related to beliefs in their own abilities. Both Beddoe et al. (2019) and Savaya (2022) found associations between pride, well-being, and satisfaction.

By examining satisfaction in social work, the narrative shifts from a deficit-based to a strengths-based focus (Bae et al., 2020). This concentrates on why practitioners remain in social work, with more particular emphasis placed on continuing professional development and organisational policies and practices to help increase the retention of social workers. Bae et al. (2020) go on to point out that a focus on satisfaction and protective factors not only improves the well-being of social workers and morale in social work agencies but also, importantly, contributes to the quality of service that service users receive.

In concluding this section, it is helpful to note that satisfaction amongst social workers has perhaps been approached from three different perspectives. Firstly, from the more traditional approach to job satisfaction (for instance, Stalker et al., 2007); secondly, the concept of life satisfaction as part of subjective well-being (for example, Diener et al., 1999; Graham and Shier, 2010) and thirdly, in more recent years, the concept of compassion satisfaction – which is the focus of this chapter. Researchers such as McFadden et al. (2015) have tended to see compassion satisfaction as having a more individualistic, service user-focused approach. In contrast, other scholars such as Holmes et al. (2021), Senreich et al. (2020a), and Baugerud et al. (2018) link compassion satisfaction much more closely to the influence of social work agency perspectives. Hence there may be tension between approaches which focus compassion satisfaction more on face-to-face work with service users in and of itself, and those which locate compassion satisfaction much more firmly in organisational contexts.

Compassion Satisfaction

Compassion satisfaction has been defined as "the level of satisfaction helping professionals find in their job and the degree to which they feel successful" (Conrad and Kellar-Guenther, 2006, p.1074). It presents as "pleasure and... fulfilment [derived] from doing work well and from contributing to the well-being of others" (Pelon, 2017, p.137). It provides "motivation, stamina, interest, and sense of accomplishment in aiding clients" (Wagaman et al., 2015, p.203). Therefore, compassion satisfaction focuses on the benefits of emotional engagement with service users and compassionate helping, despite the complex, contradictory risks and costs of caring (Pelon, 2017; Stamm, 2010). It can also involve feeling positive about relationships with one's colleagues and sustaining beliefs about "making a difference", and making a contribution towards the greater good of society through one's career choice in working with people who may need care (Stamm, 2010). According to Figley and Stamm (1996) and Stamm (2002), compassion satisfaction is strongly impacted upon by "internal" motivational factors, such as perceptions of self-confidence, competency and control, and "external" factors, such as demands made by an organisation and support/feedback from colleagues, supervisors, and others (see Collins, 2020). Earlier, Collins and Long (2003) put forward the view that compassion satisfaction can serve as a protective factor by strengthening practitioners' sense of worth, by contributing to workers' optimism and a deep belief in the general good of humanity. Compassion satisfaction is also seen in positive attitudes to work, and improved performance with more hope for positive outcomes (Wagaman et al., 2015). It also "assists the professional in overcoming the assault on belief systems and assumptions that occurs in the course of interventions with difficult clients or traumatic situations" (Harr, 2013, p.83).

As we saw in the previous chapter, measures of compassion satisfaction are often derived from the work of Figley (1995, 2002), initially focused on compassion fatigue. The measure most often used is a version of Stamm's Professional Quality of Life scale (Pro QOL, Stamm, 2010). It is a 30-item questionnaire designed for professionals who are exposed to primary or secondary trauma in their work. It measures both compassion fatigue (secondary traumatic stress and burnout) and compassion satisfaction – both the negative and positive aspects of helping. The satisfaction element, the focus of this chapter, assesses the pleasures practitioners experience when they carry out their work. Example questions include, I feel satisfaction from being able to help people; I feel invigorated after working with those I help; I believe I can make a difference through my work.

94 Compassion Satisfaction

Research Findings and Compassion Satisfaction

Much extensive, and recent, research has suggested compassion satisfaction is associated with lower levels of burnout and compassion fatigue in social work. It can also mitigate the undesired effects of burnout and compassion fatigue (for example, Bae et al., 2020; Baugerud et al., 2018; Butler et al., 2017; Conrad and Kellar-Guenther, 2006; Harr et al., 2014; Pelon, 2017; Senreich et al., 2020a; Van Hook and Rothenberg, 2009; Wagaman et al., 2015;).

Harr and Moore (2011) undertook research with about 250 social work students in the USA based on the ProQOL measure. They found that out of the 30 statements overall, including secondary traumatic stress and burnout, the statements relating to compassion satisfaction were ranked the highest. In a study of social work students from one programme by Butler et al. (2017), well over a half were in the average range for compassion satisfaction and over 40 per cent in the high range. Perhaps surprisingly, the same researchers discovered those students who worked on practice placements with "traumatised" service users and whose work "addressed trauma", reported *higher* levels of compassion satisfaction. However, this may have been partly accounted for by the fact that their social work programme specifically included well-established learning opportunities about trauma-related work.

Another study by Harr et al. (2014) discovered no statistical differences between social work students and qualified workers in relation to compassion satisfaction although, as might be expected, the qualified workers had higher levels of burnout and compassion fatigue.

In research with psychologists and social workers undertaking trauma work, Craig and Sprang (2010) found nearly a half of respondents scored in the high range for compassion satisfaction. In a pioneering study of compassion satisfaction in the UK amongst over 250 therapists employed by the NHS, Sodeke-Gregson et al. (2013) discovered over 50 per cent scored within the average range for compassion satisfaction, while nearly 40 per cent had higher potential. "Maturity", time spent in research and development activities and perhaps as might be expected, higher perceptions of supportive management and good quality supervision predicted higher scores for compassion satisfaction.

Research with social workers in Mallorca, Spain indicated over a quarter of participants enjoyed high levels of compassion satisfaction with only about a fifth experiencing low levels (Cuartero and Campos-Vidal, 2019). In Senreich et al.'s (2020a) impressive, extensive, large-scale study of 6,000 social workers in various settings in the USA, nearly 60 per cent of participants reported high levels of compassion satisfaction, with strikingly, *less than one per cent* reporting low levels. Hence an extremely large majority of practitioners experienced considerable rewards and satisfaction, once again despite negative experiences in their work. Another striking research finding emerged from a recent study of over 180 social workers during the pressures and demands of the recent COVID-19 pandemic in

Compassion Satisfaction **95**

the USA, where almost all the practitioners enjoyed average-to-high compassion satisfaction (Holmes et al., 2021).

In Conrad and Kellar- Guenther's (2006) earlier research with 365 child protection workers in Colorado, USA, nearly three quarters of the respondents expressed high or good potential for compassion satisfaction. Baldschun et al. (2020) in a large-scale study of Finnish social workers and child protection workers discovered well over three quarters of both groups experienced moderate levels of compassion satisfaction. In another study of child protection workers in Norway, Baugerud et al. (2018) also found well over three quarters of respondents experienced moderate levels of compassion satisfaction, with 14 per cent reporting high levels and just one per cent low levels. None of the participants were at risk for high levels of secondary traumatic stress or burnout. Experiencing positive challenges at work, feeling well motivated to undertake tasks, a sense of "mastery" and competence in the work were associated with high levels of compassion satisfaction. These researchers suggest the findings may have been partly the result of social workers in Norway enjoying good working conditions linked to generous benefits such as extensive time for leave and supportive supervision accompanied by an emphasis on autonomy. These researchers also perhaps present a rather cynical, negative interpretation about the levels of compassion satisfaction found in their study, linking these to the possible difficulties of seeing changes in service users in child protection work, while discussing the "limited pleasures" experienced by social workers.

Alternatively, Bae et al. (2020) in their study of 120 workers highlight the pleasures, the rewards practitioners see from experiencing positive growth and changes in service users' behaviours, with the workers sharing service users' good feelings about these changes. Wagaman et al. (2015) also point out that practitioners vicariously benefit from the improved functioning of service users and the heightened emotions surrounding the sharing of successes.

In research with around 50 hospice social workers, Pelon (2017) found the majority of respondents scored average and high ratings for compassion satisfaction, while a fifth scored in the low range. Ghesquiere et al. (2018) in a rare study of adult protection workers also discovered a fifth of participants experienced low scores for compassion satisfaction and a similar proportion experienced high scores.

In one of the few UK studies to examine compassion satisfaction among social work professionals, Kinman and Grant's (2020) research with just over 300 social workers reported that compassion satisfaction scores were above the mid-point of the scale. Compassion satisfaction was seen as being beneficial for well-being while buffering the negative effects of emotional demands on workers' mental health. In a study of independent residential childcare workers in the UK, three quarters of the respondents experienced average-to-high compassion satisfaction, around a quarter experienced high levels, and a quarter low levels. Work engagement and compassion satisfaction were strongly and positively correlated (Audin et al., 2018).

96 Compassion Satisfaction

As regards age and ethnicity, in research with social work students, Harr and Moore (2011) did not find any statistical differences related to compassion satisfaction. In another study with social work students, Butler et al. (2017) discovered ethnicity and gender were not significantly associated with compassion satisfaction, but age was, i.e. older students experienced more compassion satisfaction.

Pelon's (2017) research with social workers did not find any significant differences in compassion satisfaction scores related to gender, age, social work experience, marital status, and type of social work qualification. However, Salloum et al. (2015) and Prost and Middleton (2020) noted significantly higher compassion satisfaction scores among female child welfare workers. The latter authors argued female practitioners may obtain more intrinsic rather than extrinsic rewards from the work than men; they may see more value in, and rely more on, co-worker support, all of which may contribute to higher levels of compassion satisfaction. Also, females may be more likely to be employed on a part-time basis which enables work to be placed more readily into a wider, broader context.

Xu et al.'s (2019) research concluded Bachelor level workers had lower levels of satisfaction compared to Masters' level workers, suggesting the reason for this was that the latter usually are more experienced. Audin et al. (2018) in the UK and Senreich et al.'s. (2020a) large-scale study in the USA found no significant differences in relation to social work experience, in contrast to the findings of several studies where more experienced social workers enjoyed more compassion satisfaction (Craig and Sprang, 2010; Thomas, 2013; Wagaman et al., 2015). It is difficult to ascertain the reasons for the differences in these findings – most of which were located in research studies in the USA. They may be related to the different social and organisational contexts in which workers were located. Nevertheless, Thomas (2013), Howard et al. (2015), and Senreich et al. (2020a) did find being older and having children was associated with higher levels of compassion satisfaction.

Senreich et al.'s (2020a) extensive study pointed out that while Asian practitioners did not manifest differences in compassion satisfaction scores, Black and Latino workers had higher levels of compassion satisfaction with lower levels of work-related stress, compared to white workers. The researchers suggested this was perhaps the result of experiencing "racial bias" accompanied by perceptions and experiences of their own marginalisation that might enhance their satisfaction in helping a very diverse range of service users. Practitioners who were identified as Buddhist experienced higher levels of compassion satisfaction, while those identified as atheist or agnostic experienced lower levels Those with current mental health and physical health problems experienced lower levels of compassion satisfaction (Senreich et al., 2020a). Using the same large-scale sample, a later study by Senreich et al. (2020b) explored compassion satisfaction among heterosexual, lesbian, gay, and bisexual social workers, finding no significant differences between the groups and with scores in the high range, suggesting lesbian, gay, and bisexual workers were resilient and enjoyed their work, despite personal and structural pressures.

Limitations of the Research

Much of the research into compassion satisfaction is of a quantitative nature. Little qualitative research seems to exist where social workers are asked about their perceptions of compassion satisfaction, using less structured and more open-ended, semi-structured questions. Also, quantitative research tends to focus on particular, and sometimes narrow, aspects of the topic, while neglecting others, depending on the nature and content of the quantitative instruments used. For example, Yi et al. (2019) pointed out in their research they did not consider resilience and coping mechanisms, which are important, additional concepts linking to compassion satisfaction. On the other hand, Wachter et al. (2020) in a study of intimate partner violence and sexual assault workers specifically focused on resilience and coping related to compassion satisfaction. Researchers in the compassion satisfaction field have tended to consider other, various, but different concepts, in addition to compassion fatigue/satisfaction scales. For instance, Bae et al. (2020) considered emotional intelligence. Some researchers considered mindfulness (for example, Decker et al., 2015; Martin-Cuellar et al., 2018). Some concentrated more on social workers' individual self-care (for instance, Butler et al., 2017; Cuartero and Campos–Vidal, 2019), while others emphasised the role of practitioners' empathy (such as, Thomas, 2013; Wagaman et al., 2015; Yi et al., 2019) or positive emotions (Samios et al., 2013). Yet others focused on the significance of the interaction of the individual with the organisational context (Bae et al., 2020; Baugerud et al., 2018; Senreich et al. 2020a). Hence, as Wagaman et al. (2015, p.203) bluntly and succinctly put it, "No formula or simplified approach to compassion satisfaction is known"; the above findings reinforce that point.

Empathy, an Individual Focus, and Compassion Satisfaction

As regards empathy Wagaman et al. (2015) found a significant relationship between expressions of empathy and compassion satisfaction. They established that some components of empathy predicted increased compassion satisfaction, i.e. self–other awareness and affective responses. Affective response was defined as "the automatic and unconscious response of affect sharing or the mirroring of another person's actions". Self-other awareness consisted of "the ability to recognise and understand one's emotions and thoughts, as well as distinguish the self from others" (Wagaman et al., 2015, p.203)

As we saw in the extensive discussion in the previous chapter, Thomas (2013) and Yi et al. (2019) went on to describe empathy as a "double edged" sword, with *empathic concern* clearly seen as valuable, especially important for effective

98 Compassion Satisfaction

understanding, and excellent communication when working with service users, and as positively associated with, and a predictor of compassion satisfaction. Nevertheless, it also placed workers at risk of compassion fatigue and burnout. As we saw in an earlier chapter, Thomas (2013) argues that continued, on-going, frequent empathic efforts and making persistent empathic responses can lead to *personal distress* being experienced by some practitioners when working with service users' suffering. Personal distress is, perhaps unsurprisingly, associated with lower compassion satisfaction. In a study of medical social workers in Korea, Yi et al. (2019) noted empathic concern was positively associated with compassion satisfaction, while personal distress was associated with secondary traumatic stress, compassion fatigue, and burnout. Religious affiliation, higher levels of empathic concern, and lower levels of personal distress were significantly associated with higher levels of compassion satisfaction. Yi et al. (2019, p.981) helpfully point out that it is clearly valuable to have a balance between "having empathic concern and minimising personal distress", aided by effective affect regulation and self–other awareness in order to maximise compassion satisfaction. As we saw in the previous chapter, ideas about containment, "holding", self-differentiation, and reflection on workers' feelings through supervision and discussions with colleagues have been long established in social work as particularly important contributors to the healthy functioning of social workers, with the provision of emotional support essential to endeavours in maintaining compassion satisfaction (Ruch et al. 2018).

The contribution of individual workers "characteristics" or traits to compassion satisfaction should be treated with caution. There is a danger in seeking to emphasise personality *traits* when perhaps the emphasis should be on fluid and changeable personality *states*, i.e. individual worker characteristics are influenced by changing personal, organisational, service user environments and situations, along with differing demands from work at any particular time. For example, as we saw in the previous chapter, attention has been given to the impact of traumatic events in the early life histories upon practitioners, such as several adverse childhood experiences (ACEs), leading to increased possibilities of vulnerability to secondary traumatic stress/vicarious traumatisation and the possible reawakening of childhood traumas in workers by the traumas experienced by service users. However, this may well *not* impact upon compassion satisfaction. Indeed, while Howard et al.'s (2015) study of nearly 200 U.S. social workers revealed they had significantly more ACEs than "the norm", but those with a higher number of ACEs actually had *higher* levels of compassion satisfaction. Also, in research with therapists, including social workers, Martin-Cuellar et al. (2018) found past and recent experiences of trauma had no impact on levels of compassion satisfaction, as did Killian (2008) and Thomas and Otis (2010). Furthermore, Frey et al.'s (2017) research with sexual assault and domestic violence workers found personal trauma experiences predicted *increased* compassion satisfaction.

Other studies have highlighted that positive personality traits or states have developed in helpers following interactions with service users experiencing

Compassion Satisfaction **99**

traumatic events, such as resilience, hopefulness, optimism, and resourcefulness – all of which contribute to compassion satisfaction (Hernandez-Wolfe, 2018; Moorhouse, 2011; Wheeler and McElvaney, 2018).

A Wider Focus on Compassion Satisfaction

As we saw in the previous chapter, compassion satisfaction is linked to social workers' personal and work environments and service users' environments (Stamm, 2010). These environments interact together in a complex manner. Apart from the organisational context itself, for social workers, the interaction between work-life balance is significant. Several researchers highlight this aspect. For instance, a study with social workers in Israel indicated those who experienced high levels of compassion satisfaction perceived improved quality in their marital relationships (Finzi-Dottan and Kormosh, 2016). Bae et al. (2020) found practitioners who had better work-life balance, with minimum conflict between home life and work demands, experienced greater compassion satisfaction. Another element is the extent to which a worker feels committed to the social work profession, to the values of social work, a feeling of belonging in the profession, of making a difference, and a sense of social work as a "calling" or "mission" (Harr, 2013; Johnson et al., 2021; McFadden et al., 2015; Stalker et al., 2007). This may well be a more important determinant of compassion satisfaction than organisational commitment. However, organisational elements themselves clearly have a particularly important part to play. In the UK, as we have already seen, Antonopoulu et al.'s (2017) study pointed out the many differences in social work organisational provision in relation to team, colleague, supervision, and administrative support, not only between organisations, but *within* local authority organisations.

Also, according to Senreich et al. (2020a, p.104) "The social work workplace was the most robust... in predicting levels of compassion satisfaction" and feeling valued as a professional was " by far the largest...value of all the variables... in regard to the impact on compassion satisfaction". Thus, as in many other studies, this research highlighted, firstly, the significant impact of the organisational context upon social workers' compassion satisfaction and, secondly, the importance of practitioners feeling recognised, appreciated, emotionally rewarded and valued for their work by their employing agency (also, Evans and Huxley, 2009; Huxley et al., 2005; Johnson et al., 2021). In addition, Senreich et al. (2020a) in the USA found having sufficient training opportunities, good quality individual and group supervision, and feeling safe from physical harm at work all predicted greater compassion satisfaction.

Furthermore, Baugerud et al. (2018, p.231) noted in their research that "organisational factors might be critical precursors to... compassion satisfaction", in highlighting workload, appropriate levels of challenge in work undertaken, with a sense of commitment, identification with, and belonging to, the organisation as predictors of compassion satisfaction. Bae et al. (2020, p.105) were

100 Compassion Satisfaction

yet other researchers who found that the workplace had "a major impact on compassion satisfaction" while observing that control over work and professional autonomy was positively associated with it. Bae et al. (2020) and Xu et al. (2019) also reported social workers who had the opportunity to undertake "indirect practice" and to be involved in other roles, such as education and training, rather than focusing entirely on "direct practice" were amongst those who enjoyed greater compassion satisfaction. This is an interesting, perhaps somewhat unexpected, yet unexplained finding, that is at odds with the findings of many other research studies, which emphasise the particular importance for social workers of face-to-face interactions with service users. An implication of this finding is that it can perhaps be helpful to have the opportunity to undertake a variety of work tasks, roles, and professional development opportunities, beyond direct work with service users, in order to acquire new learning, different experiences and to refresh existing learning and experiences – all of which facilitate compassion satisfaction.

As a wide range of researchers have pointed out, there are also many and varied organisational variables that can impact compassion satisfaction. Some researchers have noted important limitations to their endeavours because they did not consider particular elements. For example, both Bae et al. (2020) and Senreich et al. (2020a) acknowledged they did not consider the role of support from workers' colleagues. This was seen as especially important in Frey et al.'s (2017) study of sexual assault and domestic violence workers. Many people would consider support to be a very significant concept in helping maintain compassion satisfaction, especially as compassion satisfaction also emphasises relationships with supervisors, colleagues, and the importance of team building, as well as service user relationships. (Stamm, 2010: Collins, 2020). Furthermore, there is an aspect of worker/environment "fit" that is important, i.e. the extent to which a practitioner feels "at home", appropriately located, settled, secure and rewarded in work with a particular agency, service user group or groups (Wachter et al., 2020). While many workers select and chose the service user groups with whom they wish to work, others may be allocated by their agencies to work in settings where there is a shortage of staff – often in settings involving children and families – which might not be the worker's initial, first-choice preference. However, commitment to, and working with a particular service user group and compassion satisfaction may well change; research has demonstrated that it may develop positively over time about work with a particular service user group, about which one had reservations – such as working with children and families (Burns et al., 2019).

Some Further Criticisms of Compassion Satisfaction

In considering ways forward, a systems, or ecological perspective helps us to locate compassion satisfaction within a wide range of different levels of intervention, possibly ranging from the political to the individual (Edwards and

Goussios, 2021). In the UK, compassion satisfaction also exists and persists despite a context of the negative impact of neoliberalism and prolonged austerity upon social workers' functioning and service users' environments, along with the accompanying corrosive and extensive erosion of local authority resources by one third over the past ten years (Collins, 2020). As we have already seen, "New Managerialism" has dominated policy thinking. This has been at the expense of participative democracy, cooperation, quality of process, and social work values linked to trust, justice, fairness, and equality (Astvik et al., 2019; Wachter et al., 2020). This obviously makes it harder for practitioners to experience compassion satisfaction when their helping endeavours are likely to be dominated by rationing, gatekeeping, assessment requirements, rules, and excessive procedural guidance. Singleton and Mee (2017) while pointing out the "good" aspects of compassion satisfaction, have also highlighted possible difficulties in maintaining it and the danger of possible "harms", when set against a problematic background of multiple, negative social, environmental, and economic factors, which means it is difficult for practitioners who are struggling to make an impact when confronted with extensive hardship and difficulties. Therefore, compassion satisfaction perhaps tends to focus on the reactions of the individual worker to particular service users, at the expense of, to the neglect of, the broader, wider inequalities of the social, cultural, and organisational context (Singleton and Mee, 2017).

Further Ways Forward

As noted previously, organisational working conditions and restrictions obviously and clearly impact upon social work students and workers. There are many elements in social work agencies that influence feelings of compassion satisfaction (Ravalier, 2019). Workloads that blend and balance, high demand, complex work with more moderate demands are likely to increase compassion satisfaction, as is a reduction in administrative demands (see, for instance, Thomas, 2013). It is also helpful if practitioners feel they have good, genuine opportunities to influence organisational policies, procedures, and practices thus empowering workers to feel they have an effective influence, "say" and "voice" and that the organisation has mechanisms that are open to hearing their voices (Pack, 2014; Wachter et al., 2020). This is likely to enhance compassion satisfaction. Having to implement policies, procedures, and practices that professionals feel have been imposed upon them "top down", that are unfair and with which they disagree, is clearly likely to decrease compassion satisfaction. However, opportunities to resist, to adjust, to work to modify policies and practices in face-to-face contact with service users, to avoid implementing what workers consider to be unjust and inappropriate procedures, also provide chances to enhance compassion satisfaction (Collins, 2020). Therefore, greater freedom of action, to work in a flexible manner with service users is also thought to make a positive contribution to compassion satisfaction (Bae et al., 2020; Collins, 2020).

102 Compassion Satisfaction

Furthermore, because compassion satisfaction in social work can be thought to be a somewhat elusive concept that may not be well understood, there is clearly a need for further education and training about it at both qualifying and post-qualifying levels, in universities and in social work organisations to either establish or develop, more knowledge and understanding of the concept (for example, Wagaman et al., 2015). There is evidence that compassion satisfaction can be taught and effectively learned about. For instance, Kinman and Grant (2017) demonstrated in the UK that an eight-week-long training programme, partly linked to compassion satisfaction led to increased levels of compassion satisfaction in early career social workers.

It is also important for social work lecturers, practice teachers, mentors, and line managers to have capabilities related to the compassion satisfaction concept. They can then reinforce learning about the topic through giving more positive, strengths-based feedback to students and qualified social workers, while also presenting behaviours that emphasise and that model the core elements of compassion satisfaction. Compassion satisfaction scales might also be used as a guide by individuals for themselves working alone, or as a basis for reflective discussion in supervision, or with colleagues, rather than using the scales as an attempt to either negatively categorise or label.

Both students and workers can also share together learning about compassion satisfaction in a group, collective discussions on either initial education courses/programmes or in agency-based "good practice" groups, possibly facilitated by a knowledgeable and skilled so-called "champion" or "expert" in compassion satisfaction-based approaches. Collective discussion groups have a valuable, prominent part to play in raising awareness of, feelings about, and in responding to, compassion satisfaction (Harris, 2020). Such groups could be focused upon realistic but optimistic expectations, sharing, discussing, and celebrating strengths, positive experiences, positive movement, small- and large-scale achievements in working with service users in easing suffering and preventing harm, within a wider context of coping with experiences of negative events, trauma, and compassion fatigue (Butler et al., 2017; Harr et al., 2014).

Links can be made here to the ideas underpinning Appreciative Inquiry, developed in the 1980s in the research, organisational analysis and development and change fields (Cooperrider and Whitney, 2005; Whitney, 2004). The emphasis is on transformational capabilities, the power of assets, hopes, possibilities, and opportunities (Whitney and Trosten-Bloom, 2010). This involves exploring what is working well, "best practices", "successes", and what people really care about in working towards a positive future (Cooper et al., 2013; Letson et al., 2020). Appreciative Inquiry can follow distinct phases of Discovery, Dream, Design, and Destiny.

Work is done by sharing workers' experiences together, with an emphasis on participating in co-operative discussion and debate (Collins, 2020). This should arouse, energise, and excite people without a need for provocation, persuasion, or coercion (Cooper et al., 2013). Practitioners are supported to come together

Compassion Satisfaction **103**

to share stories of encouraging developments; the positive narratives that can be built upon in the future.

In the UK, studies have been undertaken which examine social work and Appreciative Inquiry. These link to work with small numbers of students (Hughes, 2012), practice learning managers (Bellinger and Elliott, 2011), experienced social workers (Wendt et al., 2011), workers in social work pilot projects (Teater and Carpenter, 2017) and in criminal justice (for instance, Robinson et al., 2012).

However, in fact, despite Appreciative Inquiry's heavy emphasis on positives, Grant and Humphries (2006), Bellinger and Elliott (2011), and Robinson et al. (2012) all recognise the need to explore workers' negative experiences. For instance, Carter (2006) acknowledges a place for "stories of the worst", as well as "stories of the best", because practitioners need to ventilate, to express negative experiences and emotions, to have them heard, to be listened to, and understood, as well as focusing on present and future positives. The ideal might well be "to integrate, to synthesise both negative and positive experiences as interdependent, interacting aspects of human behaviour functioning in a dialectical relationship" (Collins, 2020, p.6), but with more emphasis on reframing, on encouraging, growth-promoting aspects of compassion satisfaction.

Robinson et al.'s (2012) work is a good example of what can be achieved through Appreciative Inquiry. Probation workers shared their good, their best experiences of working with service users, which is perhaps unusual, as discussion groups can often tend to focus on particularly difficult, demanding problematic situations (Carter, 2006). Criminal justice workers were asked about their "best times", their overall experiences of good quality work with service users, their "best case scenario" illustrating good quality practice in a particular, individual instance, and good quality practices in their teams or office location. Many workers were reluctant, modest, and self-effacing, preferring to talk about the work of colleagues rather than their own interventions. Nevertheless, for most practitioners, the most significant, important theme was discussing their best work, to think about it from a positive angle, which tended "to elicit and expose achievements and success stories that are otherwise hidden from view" (Robinson et al., 2012, p.12). Usually, practitioners had neither the opportunity, the setting or forum, to consider these positive aspects of their work, nor to experience support, encouragement, and recognition for their efforts and achievements. Monitoring or surveillance matters had often tended to overwhelm the consideration and the discussion of good practices and achievements in individual supervision (Collins, 2020). Participants also valued the initial dreaming phase of Appreciative Inquiry which helped to enable the inevitable, frequent frustrations, and common complaints to be eventually reframed in more positive terms, as aspirations for the future. By moving away from negatives, concentrating more on achievements, and what had been done well, recognising, acknowledging, discussing, and reinforcing these aspects was experienced as empowering.

104 Compassion Satisfaction

Similar to some of the ideas underpinning Appreciative Inquiry, some years ago Parton and O'Byrne (2000) also commented about the need for more reflective discussion of "good work" by social workers, linked to solution-focused approaches and achievement of difficult tasks. This entailed remembering, recalling, and celebrating active demonstrations of "successes", occasions when social work intervention had "made a positive impact". Parton and O'Byrne (2000) emphasised the importance of positive discourse and inspiring talk, with more focus placed on encouraging language, for instance, linked to, for example, hope, control, and agency, rather than despair, hopelessness, and helplessness, with less emphasis on social workers internalising "problems", with more focus on "externalising" them, locating them in wider perspectives, in wider perspectives in structural, national, policy, and workplace contexts (also see Collins, 2020).

By considering the points noted above, a developing emphasis on compassion satisfaction can build up, help to maintain optimism, confidence, a sense of purpose and meaning, set against what is often a bleak and barren backdrop (Harr et al., 2014). Focusing upon, and sharing experiences of, compassion satisfaction also helps both students and workers to be more in touch with good feelings about themselves, their own good work, and the significance of their contributions to the well-being of others (Harr et al., 2014). "Buddy" and/or mentor provision, whereby more experienced colleagues provide supportive, "non assessed", consultation opportunities, and guidance to new students or workers, partly linked to and based upon, compassion satisfaction ideals, is another way of providing an appropriate focus on the topic. Group discussions, shared supervision and mentoring experiences can all help to locate, to reframe, what may appear to be immediate, pressing, overwhelming, individualised problems and difficulties into a shared, collective, commonly experienced, more positively orientated, longer-term, wider professional context.

Conclusion

A focus on compassion satisfaction has real, genuine strengths, with its emphasis on the enjoyment, the positives, and the good aspects of relationships with service users and colleagues. Dangers lie in what could be interpreted as its rather narrow focus on the individual social worker and interactions with service users, their families, and colleagues, at the expense of its location within a wider setting. Hence compassion satisfaction should embrace these matters more intensely through an ecological, systems-based lens, which recognises the significance of collective influences and endeavours. Furthermore, while compassion satisfaction has much to offer as a concept concerned with highlighting the rewards of social worker, service user, and colleague interactions, more needs to be said about *how* compassion satisfaction can be achieved, the means by which it can be attained and maintained, which again links to structural, ecological, and systems thinking. In conclusion, compassion satisfaction is a complex, multi-layered concept. Hence social workers should be prepared to continue to struggle, not only

Compassion Satisfaction **105**

with the concept of compassion satisfaction itself, but also with the many-sided contexts in which it is located.

References

Antonopoulu, R., Killian, M. and Forrester, D. (2017) "Levels of stress and anxiety in children and family social work: Workers' perceptions of organisational structure, professional support and workplace opportunities in Children's Services", *Children and Youth Services Review*, 96, 42–50.

Arnold, D., Calhoun, L., Tedeschi, R. and Cann, A. (2005) "Vicarious post-traumatic growth in psychotherapy", *Journal of Humanistic Psychology*, 45.2, 239–263.

Astvik, W. Welander, J. and Larsson, R. (2019) "Reasons for staying: A longitudinal study of work conditions predicting social workers' willingness to stay in their organisation", *British Journal of Social Work*, DOI:10.1093/bjsw/bcz103.

Audin, K., Burke, J and Ivtzan, I. (2018) "Compassion fatigue, compassion satisfaction and work engagement in residential childcare", *Scottish Journal of Residential Child Care*, 17.3, 1–25.

Bae J., Jennings, P., Hardeman, C., Kim, E., Lee, M., Littleton, T. and Sasa, S. (2020) "Compassion satisfaction among social work practitioners: The role of work-life balance", *Journal of Social Science Research*, 46.3, 320–330.

Baginski, M., Moriarity, J., Manthorpe, J., Stevens, M., MacInnes, T. and Nagendran, T. (2009) *Social Workers' Workload Survey*, London, Social Work Task Force.

Baldschun, A., Hamalainen, J., Totto, P., Rantonen, O. and Salo, P. (2020) "Job-strain, and well-being among Finnish social workers: Exploring the differences in occupational well-being between child protection social workers and social workers without duties in child protection", *European Journal of Social Work*, 22, 1, 43–58.

Baugerud, G., Vangbaek, S. and Melinder. A. (2018) "Secondary traumatic stress, burnout and compassion satisfaction among norwegian child protection workers: Protective and risk factors", *British Journal of Social Work*, 48, 215–235.

Baum, N. and Ramon, S. (2010) "Professional growth in turbulent times: An impact of political violence on social work practice in Israel", *Journal of Social Work*, 10.2, 119–157.

Beddoe, L., Staniforth, B. and Fouche, C. (2019) "'Proud of what I do but often...I would be happier to say I drive trucks': Ambiguity in social workers' self-perception", *Qualitative Social Work*, 18.3, 530–546.

Bellinger, A. and Elliott, T. (2011) "What are you looking at? The potential of appreciative inquiry as a research approach for social work", *British Journal of Social Work*, 41.4, 708–725.

Ben-Porat, A. (2015) "Vicarious posttraumatic growth: domestic violence therapists versus social service department therapists in Israel", *Journal of Family Violence*, 30, 023–933.

Ben-Porat, A., Gottlieb, S., Raphael, T., Shemesh, S. and Zahav, R. (2020) "Vicarious growth among social work students: What makes the difference?", *Health and Social Care in the Community*, 28, 662–669.

Burns, C., Christie, A. and O'Sullivan, S. (2019) "Findings from a longitudinal qualitative study of child protection social workers' retention, job embeddedness, professional confidence and staying narratives", *British Journal of Social Work*, DOI:10.1093/bjsw/bcz083.

Butler, L. Carello, J. and Maguin, E. (2017) "Trauma, stress and self-care in clinical training: Predictions of burnout, decline in health status, secondary traumatic stress symptoms and compassion satisfaction" *Psychological Trauma*, 9.4, 416–424.

106 Compassion Satisfaction

Carter, B. (2006) "One expertise among many-working appreciatively to make miracles instead of finding problems: Using appreciative inquiry as a way of reframing research", *Journal of Research in Nursing*, 11, 48–63.

Coffey, M., Dudgill, L. and Tattersall, A. (2004) "Stress in social services: Mental well-being, stress and job satisfaction", *British Journal of Social Work*, 34.5, 735–746.

Collins, S. and Long, A. (2003) "Working with the psychological effects of trauma: Consequences for mental health-care workers: A Literature Review", *Journal of Psychiatric and Mental Health Nursing*, 10, 417–424.

Collins, S. (2008) "Statutory social workers: Stress, job satisfaction, coping, social support and individual differences", *British Journal of Social Work*, 38.6, 1173–1193.

Collins, S. (2020) *The Positive Social Worker,* London, Routledge.

Conrad, D. and Kellar-Guenther, Y. (2006) "Compassion fatigue, burnout and compassion satisfaction among Colorado child protection workers", *Child Abuse and Neglect*, 30.10, 1071–1080.

Cooper, J. (2015) "Exhausted social workers on the edge of burnout, but still achieving positive change", *Community Care*, 15 July.

Cooper, C. Flint-Taylor, J. and Pearn, M. (2013) *Building Resilience for Success*, London, Palgrave.

Cooperrider, D. and Whitney, D. (2005) *Appreciative Inquiry Handbook: A Positive Revolution in Change*, Williston, VT, Berrett-Koehler.

Craig, C. and Sprang, G. (2010) "Compassion satisfaction, compassion fatigue and burnout in a national sample of trauma treatment therapists", *Anxiety, Stress and Coping*, 23.3, 319–332.

Cuartero, M. and Campos-Vidal, J. (2019) "Self-care behaviours and their relationship with satisfaction and compassion fatigue levels among social workers", *Social Work in Health Care*, 58.3, 274–290.

Decker, J., Brown, J., Ong, J. and Stiney-Ziskind C. (2015) "Mindfulness, Compassion Fatigue and compassion satisfaction among social work interns", *Social Work and Christianity*, 42.1, 28–42.

Diener, E., Suh, E., Lucas, R. and Smith, H. (1999) "Subjective well-being: Three decades of progress", *Psychological Bulletin*, 125.2, 276–302.

Edwards, K. and Goussios, A. (2021) "Who is responsible for compassion satisfaction? Shifting ethical responsibility for compassion fatigue from the individual to the ecological", *Ethics and Social Welfare*, 16.3, 246–262.

Evans, S. and Huxley, P. (2009) "Factors associated with the recruitment and retention of social workers in Wales: Employer and employee perspectives", *Health and Social Care in the Community*, 173, 254–266.

Figley, C. (1995) *Compassion Fatigue: Coping with Secondary Traumatic Stress Disorder in those Who Treat the Traumatised*, New York, Brunner Routledge.

Figley, C. (2002) "Compassion fatigue: Psychotherapists' chronic lack of self-care", *Journal of Clinical Psychology*, 58.1, 1433–1441.

Figley, C. and Stamm, B. (1996) "Psychometric review of compassion fatigue self-test" in Stamm, B. (ed.), *Measurement of Stress, Trauma and Adaptation,* Derwood, MD, Sidran Press, pp.127–130.

Finzi-Dottan, R. and Kormosh, M. (2016) "Social workers in Israel: compassion fatigue, and spill-over into married life", *Journal of Social Service Research*, 42.5, 703–717.

Frey, L., Beesley, D., Abbott, D. and Kendrick, E. (2017) "Vicarious resilience in sexual assault and domestic violence advocates", *Psychological Trauma, Theory, Research Practice and Policy*, 9.1, 44–51.

Ghesquiere, A., Plichta, S., McAfee, C. and Rogers, G. (2018) "Professional quality of life of adult protective service workers", *Journal of Elder Abuse and Neglect*, 30.1, 1–19.

Graham, J. and Shier, M. (2010) "The social work profession and subjective well-being: The impact of a profession on overall well-being", *British Journal of Social Work*, 40.5, 1553–1572.

Grant, S and Humphries, M. (2006) "Critical evaluation of appreciative inquiry", *Action Research*, 4.4, 401–418.

Grant, L. and Kinman, G. (2014) *Developing Resilience for Social Work Practice*, London, Palgrave.

Harr, C. (2013) "Promoting workplace health by diminishing the negative impact of compassion fatigue and increasing compassion satisfaction", *Social Work and Christianity*, 40.1, 71–88.

Harr, C. and Moore, B. (2011) "Compassion fatigue among social work students in field placements", *Journal of Teaching in Social Work*, 31, 350–363.

Harr, C. Brice, T., Riley, K. and Moore, B. (2014) "The impact of compassion satisfaction and compassion fatigue on social work students", *Journal for the Society for Social Work and Research*, 5.2, 233–251.

Harris, D. (2020) "Compassion and resilience" in Thompson, N. and Cox, G. (eds.), *Promoting Resilience: Responding to Adversity, Loss and Vulnerability*, London, Routledge, pp.209–215.

Hermon, S. and Chablah, R (2019) "A longitudinal study of stress and satisfaction among child welfare workers", *Journal of Social Work*, 19.2, 192–215.

Hernandez-Wolfe, P., Gangsei, D. and Engstrom, D. (2007) "Vicarious resilience: A new concept in work with those who survive trauma", *Family Process*, 46.2, 239–241.

Hernandez-Wolfe, P., Killian, K., Engstrom, D. and Gangsei, D. (2015) "Vicarious resilience, vicarious trauma and awareness of equity in trauma work", *Journal of Humanistic Psychology,* 55.2, 153–172.

Hernandez-Wolfe, P. (2018) "Vicarious resilience: A comprehensive review", *Revista Estudios Sociales*, 66, 9–17.

Holmes, M., Rentrope, C., Korsch-Williams, A. and King, J. (2021) "Impact of COVID-19 pandemic on posttraumatic stress, grief, burnout and secondary trauma of social workers in the United States", *Clinical Social Work*, 49, 495–504.

Howard, A., Parris, S., Hall, J., Call, C., Razuri, E., Purvis, K. and Cross, D. (2015) "An examination of the relationships between professional quality of life, adverse childhood experiences, resilience, and work environment in a sample of human service providers", *Children and Youth Services Review*, 57, 141–148.

Hughes, M. (2012) "Unitary appreciative inquiry: a new approach for researching social work education and practice", *British Journal of Social Work*, 42.7, 1358–1388.

Hunter, S. (2012) "Walking in sacred spaces in the therapeutic bond: Therapists experiences of compassion satisfaction coupled with the potential for vicarious traumatization", *Family Process,* 51.2, 179–192.

Hurley, D., Martin, L. and Halberg, R. (2013) "Resilience in child welfare: A social work perspective", *International Journal of Child, Youth and Family Studies*, 2, 259–273.

Hurley, D., Alvarez, L. and Buckley, H. (2015) "From the zone of risk to the zone of resilience: Protecting the resilience of children and practitioners in Argentina, Canada and Ireland", *International Journal of Child, Youth and Family Studies*, 6, 17–51.

Huxley, P., Evans, S., Gately, C. Webber, M., Mears, A., Pajak, S., Kendall, T., Medina, J. and Katona, C. (2005) "Stress and pressure in mental health social work: The worker speaks", *British Journal of Social Work*, 35.7, 1063–1079.

108 Compassion Satisfaction

International Federation of Social Workers (2014) *Global Definition of the Social Work Profession,* Rheinfelden, International Federation of Social Workers.

Johnson, C., Sanders-Earley, A., Shannon, E., Winterbotham, M., Mclaughlin, H., Pollock, S., Scholar, H. and McCaughan, S. (2021) *Longitudinal Study of Local Authority Child and Family Social Workers (Wave3),* London, Department of Education.

Karpetis, G. (2015) "Psychological distress among mental health social workers", *European Journal of Social Work,* 18.5, 745–755.

Killian, K. (2008) "Helping till it hurts? A multi-method study of compassion fatigue, burnout and self-care in clinicians working with trauma survivors", *Traumatology,* 14.2, 32–44.

Kinman, G. and Grant, L. (2017) "Building resilience in early career social workers: Evaluating a multi-model intervention", *British Journal of Social Work,* 47, 1979–1988.

Kinman, G. and Grant, L. (2020) "Emotional demands, compassion and mental health in social workers", *Occupational Medicine,* 70, 89–94.

Letson, M., Davis, C., Sherfield, J., Beer, C. Philips, R. and Wolf, K. (2020) "Identifying compassion satisfaction, burnout & traumatic stress in Children's Advocacy Centres", *Child Abuse and Neglect,* 110(Part3), 104240, DOI:10.1016/jchiabu 2019, 104240.

Lev-Wiesel, R., Goldblatt, H., Eisikovits, Z. and Admi, H. (2009) "Growth in the shadow of war: The case of social workers and nurses working in a shared war reality", *British Journal of Social Work,* 39, 1154–1174.

Martin-Cuellar, A., Atencio, D., Kelly, R. and Lardier Jr., D. (2018) "Mindfulness as a moderator of clinical history of trauma on compassion satisfaction", *The Family Journal: Counselling and Therapy for Couples and Families,* 26.3, 358–368.

McFadden, P., Campbell, A. and Taylor, B. (2015) "Resilience and burnout in child protection social workers: Individual and organisational themes from a systematic literature review", *British Journal of Social Work,* 54, 1546–1563.

McFadden, P. (2016) *Measuring Burnout among UK Social Workers,* Belfast QUB, Community Care.

McFadden, P., Neill, R., Mallett, J., Manthorpe, J., Gillen, P., Moriarty, J., Currie, D., Schroder, H., Ravalier, J., Nicholl, P. and Ross, J. (2021) "Mental wellbeing and quality of working life in UK social workers before and during the COVID-19 pandemic: A propensity score matching study", *British Journal of Social Work,* DOI:10.1093/bjsw/bcab108.

Mickel. A. (2009) "Survey reveals social workers' poor working conditions", *Community Care,* 29 July.

Molnar, B., Meeker, S., Manners, K., Tieszen, L., Kalergis, K., Fine, J., Hallinan, S., Wolfe, J. and Wells, M. (2020) "Vicarious traumatization among child welfare and child protection professionals: A systematic review", *Child Abuse and Neglect,* https//doi.org/10.1016/jchiabu2020, 104679.

Moorhouse, A. (2011) "Sparks in the dark-various resilience: A qualitative exploration of the lived experience of a group of professionals working in the area of sexual abuse", *Feedback-the Journal of the Family Therapy Association of Ireland,* 13, 63–78.

Myers, D. (2000) "The funds, friends and faith of happy people", *American Psychologist,* 55, 56–67.

Pack. M. (2014) "Vicarious resilience: A multi-layered model of stress and trauma", *Affilia: Journal of Women and Social Work,* 29, 18–29.

Parton, N. and O'Byrne, P. (2000) *Constructive Social Work,* Houndmills and London, Macmillan.

Pelon, C. (2017) "Compassion fatigue and compassion satisfaction in hospice social workers", *Journal of Social Work in End-of -Life and Palliative Care,* 13, 2–3, 134–150.

Pithouse, A., Brookfield, C. and Rees, A. (2018) "Why are social workers in Wales the 'Happiest'? A Conundrum Explored", *British Journal of Social Work*, doi10.1093/bjsw/bcy119.

Pooler, D., Wolfer, T. and Freeman, M. (2014a) "Finding joy in social work: Interpersonal resources", *Families in Society*, 95.1, 34–42.

Pooler, D., Wolfer, T. and Freeman, M, (2014b) "Finding joy in social work: Intrapersonal resources", *Social Work*, 59.3.1, 213–221.

Prost, S. and Middleton, J. (2020) "Professional quality of life and intention to leave the workforce: Gender disparities in child welfare", *Child Abuse and Neglect*, doi.org/10.1016/jcniabu.2020.104535.

Ravalier, J. (2017) *Social Workers: Working Conditions and Well Being*, London, BASW.

Ravalier, J. (2019) "Psychosocial working conditions and stress in UK social workers", *British Journal of Social Work*, 49, 371-390.

Regehr, C., Hemsworth, D., Leslie, B., Howe, P. and Chau, S. (2004) "Prediction of post-traumatic stress in child welfare workers: A linear structural equation model", *Children and Youth Services Review*, 26.4, 331–346.

Robertson, I. and Cooper, C. (2011) *Wellbeing, Productivity and Happiness at Work*, London, Palgrave

Robinson, G., Priede, C., Farrall, C., Shapland, J. and McNeill, F. (2012) "Doing strengths-based research: Appreciative Inquiry in a probation setting", *Criminology and Criminal Justice*, 13.1, 3–20.

Rose, M. (2003) "Good deal, bad deal? Job satisfaction in occupations", *Work, Employment and Society*, 17.3, 503–530.

Ruch, G., Turney, G. and Ward, A. (2018) *Relationship- Based Social Work*, London, Jessica Kingsley.

Salloum, A., Kondrat, D., Johnco, C. and Olson, K (2015) "The role of self-care on compassion satisfaction, burnout and secondary traumatic stress among child welfare workers", *Children and Youth Services Review*, 19, 54–61.

Samios, C., Abel, 1. and Rodzik, A. (2013) "The protective role of compassion satisfaction for therapists who work with sexual violence survivors: an application of the broaden-and-build theory of positive emotions", *Anxiety, Stress and Coping*, 21.6, 610–623.

Savaya, S. (2022) "Shame and pride among social workers in Israel: A concept map", *British Journal of Social Work*, DOI:10.1093/bjsw/bcacf026.

Senreich, E., Straussner, S. and Steen, J. (2020a) "The work experiences of social workers: Factors impacting compassion satisfaction and workplace stress", *Journal of Social Service Research*, DOI:10.1080/014883762018.1528491.

Senreich, E., Straussner, S. and Cooper, C. (2020b) "Health, wellness and workplace experiences of lesbian, gay and bi-sexual social workers", *Journal of Gay and Lesbian Social Services*, 32.2, 209–239.

Shamai, M. and Ron, P. (2009) "Helping direct and indirect victims of national terror: Experiences of Israeli social workers", *Qualitative Health Research*, 19, 42–54.

Singleton, V. and Mee, S. (2017) "Critical compassion: Affect, discretion and policy-care relations", *The Sociological Review Monographs*, 65.2, 130–149.

Sodeke-Gregson, E., Holttum, S. and Billings, J. (2013) "Compassion satisfaction, burnout and secondary traumatic stress in UK therapists who work with adult trauma clients", *European Journal of Psychotraumatology*, 4.1, 1–10.

Stalker, C., Mandell, D., Frensch, K., Harvey, C. and Wright, M. (2007) "Child welfare workers who are exhausted yet satisfied with their jobs: How do they do it?", *Child and Family Social Work*, 12.2, 182–191.

110 Compassion Satisfaction

Stamm, B. (2002) "Measuring compassion satisfaction as well as compassion fatigue: Developmental history of the fatigue and satisfaction test" in Figley, C. (ed.) *Treating Compassion Fatigue*, New York, Brunner Mazel, pp.107–119.

Stamm, B. (2010) *The Concise ProQOL Manual* (second edition), Pocatello, ID, ProQOL.org.

Tavormina, M. and Clossley, L. (2015) "Exploring crisis and its effects on workers in child protective services work", *Child and Family Social Work*, 22.1, 126–136.

Tedeshci, R. and Calhoun, S. (2004) "A clinical approach to posttraumatic growth" in Linley, P. and Joseph, S. (eds.) *Positive Psychology in Practice,* Hoboken, NY: John Wiley, pp.503–518.

Teater, B. and Carpenter, J. (2017) "Independent social work practice with adults in England: An appreciative inquiry of a pilot programme", *Journal of Social Work*, 17.1, 34–51.

The Guardian (2017) "A ray of hope for social workers", 29 March.

Thomas, J. (2013) "Association of personal distress with burnout, compassion fatigue, and compassion satisfaction among clinical social workers" *Journal of Social Service Research*, 39, 365–379.

Thomas, J. and Otis, M. (2010) "Intra psychic correlates of professional quality of life: Mindfulness, empathy and emotional separation", *Journal of the Society for Social Work and Research*, 1, 83–98.

Van Hook, M. and Rothenberg, M. (2009) "Quality of life and compassion satisfaction/fatigue and burnout in child welfare workers in community based care organisations in central Florida", *Social Work and Christianity*, 36.136–154.

Wachter, K., Schrag, R. and Wood, L. (2020) "Coping behaviours mediate associations between occupational factors and compassion satisfaction among the intimate partner violence and sexual assault workforce", *Journal of Family Violence*, 35, 143–154.

Wagaman, M., Geiger, J., Shockley, C. and Segal, A. (2015) "The role of empathy in burnout, compassion satisfaction and secondary traumatic stress among social workers", *Social Work*, 60.3, 201–209.

Weiss-Dagan, S., Ben-Porat, A. and Itzhaky, H. (2020) "Secondary traumatic stress and vicarious post-traumatic growth among social workers who have worked with abused children", *Journal of Social Work*, DOI:10.1177/1468017320981363.

Wendt, S. Tuckey, M. and Prosser, B. (2011) "Thriving, not just surviving, in emotionally demanding fields of practice", *Health and Social Care in the Community*, 19.3, 317–325.

Wheeler, A. and McElvaney, R. (2018) "'Why would you want to do that work?' The positive impact on therapists of working with child victims of sexual abuse in Ireland: a thematic analysis", *Counselling Psychology Quarterly*, 1.4, 513–527.

Whitney, D. (2004) "Appreciative Inquiry and the elevation of organisational consciousness" in Cooperrider, D. and Avital, M. (eds.) *Constructive Discourse in Human Organisation*, Oxford, Elsevier, pp.125–146.

Whitney, D. and Trosten-Bloom, A. (2010) *The Power of Appreciative Inquiry,* Berkeley, CA, Berrett Koehler.

Xu, Y., Harmon-Darrow, C. and Frey, J. (2019) "Rethinking professional quality of life for social workers: Inclusion of ecological self-care barriers", *Journal of Human Behaviour in the Social Environment*, 29.1, 11–25.

Yi, J., Kim, M., Choi, K. and Droubay, B. (2019) "Compassion satisfaction and compassion fatigue among medical social workers in Korea: The role of empathy" *Social Work In Health Care*, doi:10.1080/00981389.2019.1686678.

5

SELF-CARE TO PROMOTE SELF-COMPASSION

Introduction

Self-care has recently become part of the "official" discourse of social work; it is endorsed and emphasised in professional documents in various countries, including the UK, where it figures prominently in the Professional Capabilities Framework in England (BASW, 2018) and, to a lesser extent, in the Standards for Employers of Social Workers (Local Government Association, 2020). It has also received more attention following the recent coronavirus pandemic from BASW (2020a, b) and from the International Federation of Social Workers (2020). Books have been published on self-care in the USA (such as Cox and Steiner, 2013; Grise-Owens et al., 2016; Smullens, 2015). Research has also started to proliferate in the USA about self-care and social work. But surprisingly, until recently, the concept has been the subject of little research or literature produced in the UK, perhaps apart from a general text that touches on self-care professional practices going beyond social work (Parry, 2017) and a self-care handbook, written by social workers, but also aimed at a wider professional audience (Mordue et al., 2020).

In this chapter, we will explore self-care in more depth. We will consider definitions of self-care, explore ideas that underpin the concept, discuss its application in practice, examining recent research findings about social work students and social workers drawn mainly from the USA. We will debate strengths, weaknesses, and critical perspectives surrounding self-care. Suggestions will be made for further development of the self-care concept in the UK within the context of other theories, social work education, and on-going professional development.

DOI: 10.4324/9781003112532-6

112 Self-Care to Promote Self-Compassion

Caring and Self-Care

Social work has an exceptionally long history of caring for, and of working with, people as unique individuals, set within interactions in wider society. Social workers are expected to care about, and to be committed to their work, with many practitioners seeing social work as a vocation and a calling (Collins, 2016, 2021). Yet social workers do not seem to be expected to give much attention to caring for their own needs, although as we saw in a previous chapter, attention has been given to various aspects of the stress that practitioners experience in their day-to-day work (Coffey et al., 2009; Lloyd et al., 2002; Ravalier, 2017). Research studies have also pointed out consequences of stressful and traumatic experiences for some social workers, which can include physical and mental health problems (for instance, Griffiths et al., 2018). Pyles (2020) draws attention to the neglect of social workers' needs. Pyles (2020, p.185) trenchantly suggests that

> social work is a social justice profession concerned with the wellbeing of individuals, groups, organisations, and communities and seeks to enable access to wellness and justice for marginalised populations…However, it has failed to advocate for the wellbeing of social workers themselves.

Willis and Molina (2019, p 83) reinforce this point, arguing that social workers' "responsibility to ourselves-our wellness is as important as responsibilities to clients, colleagues, practice settings, broader society" (Willis and Molina, 2019, p.83).

To counteract the impact of the demands made upon workers, as we have already seen, the professional needs of practitioners are intended to be met, in part, by the support available from team members, colleagues, mentoring possibilities, professional associations and unions, professional development opportunities and, in particular, the potential contribution of good quality, reflective supervision that is sensitive to workers' emotional and practical needs (Ashley-Binge and Cousins, 2020 Collins, 2020, 2021; Lee, 2017). It is also acknowledged that practitioners may simultaneously benefit from support and functioning in a variety of personal roles outside those that are work-based, through interactions with family members, friends, and by undertaking personal leisure interests and hobbies (for example, Lee and Miller, 2013).

It has perhaps been assumed that self-care practices are "taken for granted", take place "naturally" amongst social workers, without them being considered as such, without them needing to receive much attention, or being subject to discussion, debate, or analysis (Newcomb et al., 2017). Nevertheless, the importance of self-care is supported from several perspectives. These include, firstly, the likelihood of effective self-care practices encouraging reduced turnover and increased retention rates of social workers in their organisations, accompanied by the provision of more consistent, longer-lasting, on-going relationships with service users (Griffiths and Royse, 2017). Secondly, self-care holds promise for maintaining, and in improving, the physical, psychological, and emotional well-being of practitioners (Salloum et al., 2015).

Self-Care

Similar to the other core concepts discussed in this book, self-care is located in an ecological, systems context; also, it clearly cannot and does not stand alone as a theoretical concept; it interacts with others; it overlaps with some of them (Salloum et al., 2018). For instance, elements of self-care link closely with other psychological concepts such as, in particular, coping (Lee, 2017; Mette et al., 2020; Owens-King, 2019; Rienks, 2020), as well as resilience (Beddoe et al., 2013; Grant et al., 2015; La Mott and Martin, 2019), support, personal control, and agency (Jeffrey, 2011; Lee and Miller, 2013). Indeed, the self-care literature itself contains several direct references to these topics (Bressi and Vaden, 2017; McGarrigle and Walsh, 2011). For a more detailed discussion of coping, control and agency, resilience and support in social work, see Collins (2020).

Self-care involves taking action. It should mean undertaking multi-dimensional practices and activities to try to alter one's personal and professional behaviours, structures, and to change working patterns and work conditions, while continually bearing in mind the responsibilities of the social work agency to support and to facilitate such endeavours (Bloomquist et al., 2015; Salloum et al., 2015). Hence, knowledge and understanding of self-care are inextricably interwoven with interactions at micro, mezzo, and macro levels (Dombo and Gray, 2013).

It is only in relatively recent times that the concept of self-care has started to become a focus in professional and international social work (CASW, 2005; BASW, 2018, 2020a, b; IFSW, 2019, 2020; NASW, 2008, 2021). In Canada, the CASW (2005) requires attention to be given to self-care. Also, self-care practices are recommended in the USA. The National Association of Social Workers (NASW, 2008, pp.268–269) asserted the value of self-care "as under-pinning to best practice in the profession … [and that a] key to prevention and management of adverse conditions…is the practice of self-care…which is vital ". Self-care is seen as "an essential component in competent, compassionate and ethical...practice...[which]reflects a choice and commitment to become actively involved in maintaining one's effectiveness as a social worker" and "a means of maintaining… competence, strengthening the profession and preserving the integrity of…work with clients" (NASW, 2008, pp.269–270). Furthermore, just recently, the NASW Code of Ethics (2021) has been revised; it now includes explicit reference to the need for social workers to care for themselves both pro-fessionally and personally, as well as, very importantly, the role of social work organisations and educational institutions in promoting appropriate policies, practices, and materials to support self-care, but it still does not feature in the core competences for social work education in the USA (Miller et al., 2021).

114 Self-Care to Promote Self-Compassion

In England, The Professional Capabilities Framework (BASW, 2018) consistently and persistently refers to self-care for social work students and social workers throughout the various stages of their careers, ranging from the very earliest beginnings at the point of entry to initial qualifying education through to work as very experienced practitioners. Social workers are said "to demonstrate professional commitment by taking responsibility for...self-care", as part of their identity and behaviours as practitioners committed to professional development (BASW, 2018, p.1), while the IFSW (2019, para. 9.6) states social workers "have a duty... to care for themselves professionally and personally". However, both these self-care statements pay little attention to the role of the practitioner's workplace.

Self-care has also figured prominently in recent guides to social workers' well-being in the UK linked to COVID-19 (BASW, 2020a, b). In a recent Community Care guide, Grant and Kinman (2020, p.5) comment "it is crucial to practise self-care...you need to be as understanding and caring towards yourself as you are to other people". Yet there has been surprisingly little research or literature based in Europe, and particularly in the UK, about self-care and social work. However, in the USA explorations of the topic have developed rapidly in recent years, as seen, for example, in the work of Karl Bloomquist, Alison Salloum, and, particularly, the prolific research by Jay Miller and colleagues.

Definitions of Self-Care

There are various definitions of self-care. They tend to focus on "a range of activities an individual may engage in with the purpose of managing their physical and emotional health" (Salloum et al., 2015, p.55). There is no right or wrong approach to self-care (Dalphon, 2019; Dorociak et al., 2017). It is seen as fluid and changing over time and space; it may well vary at different points in one's life and professional career (Dombo and Gray, 2013; Griffiths et al., 2019).

A distinction is made between personal and professional self-care (NASW, 2008, 2021). Lee and Miller (2013, p.98) define personal self-care as "a process of purposeful engagement in practices that promote holistic health and well-being", while professional self-care involves "engagement in practices that promote effective and appropriate use of the self in the professional role", also to promote health and well-being. However, not all theorists agree with this separation.

According to Bloomquist et al. (2015), the domains of self-care involve various practices. They include:

- Physical self-care linked to actions to promote physical well-being such as a healthy diet, regular sleep, and exercise. This has perhaps been the traditional, long-established, "common sense", health focus for self-care activity.
- Psychological self-care linked to actions taken to develop self-awareness and sound decision making. Psychological self-care can include mindfulness, keeping a journal and, if necessary, possible involvement in receiving

counselling. It could also include undertaking reflective activities and self-care planning, although it could be argued that these could, or should, be seen as elements of professional self-care.

- Emotional self-care which refers to actions to promote emotional well-being such as effective use of humour, positive self-talk, and spending time with people whose company you enjoy, such as some family members and friends.
- Spiritual self-care which concerns finding meaning and purpose in life. This might be linked to spending time in religious or spiritual activities, praying, or meditating.
- Professional self-care, which involves, for example, participating in discussions with team members and other colleagues, setting limits in work with service users, setting appropriate boundaries between work and home life, obtaining regular, good quality supervision, attending continuing professional development events, and advocating for one's needs in, or outside the social work organisation, through professional organisations and/or unions.

Research about Self-Care, Other Helping Professionals, and Social Work

There is evidence that self-care activities can ameliorate distress among counsellors, therapists, and social workers (for example, La Mott and Martin, 2019; Miller et al., 2019a, b, 2021; Owens-King, 2019). As noted above, there are also suggestions from research that self-care activities can play a prominent part in reducing the turnover of social work staff (Miller et al., 2018, 2019a, b). For example, Griffiths and Royse's (2017) work with social workers who had resigned, discovered more time for self-care would have been an important element in helping them to remain in their jobs. Several researchers have pointed out that effective social worker self-care practices can encourage the adaptation of more appropriate coping strategies and more use of support (Butler et al., 2017; Dombo and Gray, 2013; Owens-King, 2019; Salloum et al., 2015, 2018), while Xu et al. (2019) discovered *barriers* to self-care significantly increased risk of secondary trauma symptoms and burnout. Acker (2018) also found that self-care strategies are associated with job satisfaction for social workers.

Several studies indicate that those who undertook more self-care practices experienced higher levels of compassion satisfaction. Alkema et al. (2008) researching the activities of hospice professionals indicated a relationship between self-care strategies and higher levels of compassion satisfaction. They discussed the importance of supportive networks, getting adequate sleep, eating healthily, and addressing social and vocational needs. This research highlighted the role of emotional and spiritual self-care and the idea of a balance between personal and professional activities. La Mott and Martin's (2019) study of mental health providers also found significant relationships between those who engaged in higher levels of self-care related to physical, emotional, spiritual, and professional well-being, and higher levels of compassion satisfaction. Salloum et al.'s

116 Self-Care to Promote Self-Compassion

(2015, 2018) work with child welfare workers, Cuartero and Campos-Vidal's (2019) and Shepperd and Newell's (2020) studies of social workers, found those who undertook more self-care practices experienced higher levels of compassion satisfaction. Bloomquist et al. (2015) also discovered that both professional and emotional self-care practices by social workers and social work students were associated with greater compassion satisfaction.

Nevertheless, on the other hand, not all findings from self-care research have been positive. For example, Bober and Regehr (2006) failed to find any protective effects of self-care against secondary stress in therapists, while there was no relationship between self-care practices, compassion satisfaction, compassion fatigue, or burnout in a study of therapists working with children (Killian, 2008). In studies of social workers, Xu et al. (2019) did not find support for a hypothesis that self-care behaviours were negatively related to compassion satisfaction, while barriers to self-care did not decrease the potential for compassion satisfaction. Salloum et al. (2015) and Bloomquist et al. (2015) found no relationship between self-care and secondary traumatic stress. From the latter study, surprisingly, it emerged that "psychological" self-care (defined as including, for example, taking time for reflection, keeping a journal, practising mindfulness, having a self-care plan, and participating in counselling for oneself) was associated with *higher* levels of burnout and secondary traumatic stress. The reasons for this were unclear, although it could be argued that workers with higher levels of stress and burnout are more likely to make more attempts to use self-care strategies, which may not be successful.

Social Workers, Social Work Students, and Use of Self-Care Practices

Findings from Bloomquist et al.'s (2015) and Martin et al.'s (2020) work highlighted that social work practitioners' *perceptions* of self-care, their attitudes, and beliefs towards it were positive. These researchers found respondents valued self-care, perceiving it to be important, and to be effective in combating stress. But a particularly notable problem revealed by research findings is the limited *actual use* of self-care activities. For instance, large-scale study of practitioners in the USA by Bloomquist et al. (2015) and numerous studies by Jay Miller and colleagues found social workers engaged neither frequently nor routinely in self-care behaviours, but only on a limited basis, in only "moderate", modest amounts. In several studies, similar findings also were evident in research with social work students (Diebold et al., 2018; Grise-Owens et al., 2018; O'Neill et al., 2019). Thus, self-care is clearly seen as, perceived to be, a "good thing", an important "way to be", but there are problems in following up beliefs in self-care, in matching intentions with *actual* activities and practices.

Interestingly, Butler et al., (2017) reported considerable variations in what they called "self-care effort" amongst the social work students in their research, discovering a quarter reported increasing self-care effort during their course, a quarter reported maintaining the same self-care effort, but a half recorded *decreased* self-care effort. Unfortunately, the explanations and the reasons for this were not explored. But all these findings would seem to reinforce the understandable point that self-care was, and is, seen by workers and students as secondary to their wider responsibilities, to obligations to service users and institutional requirements. Furthermore, in a large-scale study of health–care social workers undertaken in the USA before and during the recent coronavirus pandemic by Miller and Cassar (2021), significant pre/post *decreases* were found in *all* self-care practices across multiple domains.

Although it might be argued that professional socialisation as a social worker is, in part, a self-interested process linked to a rewarding career and increasing remuneration, as we noted earlier in the book, practitioners may feel professional, moral, and ethical pressure to perceive and experience social work as a commitment, an opportunity to offer altruistic, selfless service and care, putting the needs of service users ahead of their own – "you before me" (Fox et al., 2021). As we have already seen, social workers may feel demands and they may experience pressure and expectations, to "go the extra mile" for service users; the requirements and commitment to care for service users may clash with professional requirements and ethical desires to care for one-self, amidst a sea of constantly shifting, fluid and changing tensions (Weinberg, 2014). Therefore, there is a danger that self-care could become a marginal-ised, peripheral activity, especially during times of particular crises, such as the recent COVID-19 epidemic, as an adjunct, extra, or add on to "core" concerns surrounding the professional functioning of workers, with self-care seen and experienced as some kind of luxury, "selfishness", or self-indulgence rather than an important element – "you instead of me" (Miller et al., 2018; Miller and Cassar, 2021). Hence, if self-care is largely seen by practitioners as valuable, beneficial and helpful, in view of its limited *actual* use in day-to-day practice, there is a need for social work trainees, lecturers, social workers, and super-visors to develop further understanding of the self-care concept, while being more aware of, sensitive to, and committed to, actually *implementing* and inte-grating self-care practices on a regular basis into their personal and working lives (Collins, 2021).

Researchers, including Alkema et al. (2008) and Miller et al. (2017, 2018, 2019a, b), have found more experienced practitioners engaged in more self-care. However, a cause for worry is that the more hours a practitioner worked, the less self-care was actually practised (Miller et al., 2019a, b; Miller and Cassar, 2021). These researchers along with Shepperd and Newell (2020), also found the healthier a worker reported themselves to be, the more likely they were to involve themselves in self-care. Practitioners who were members of a professional association or union, who were married or living with a partner also reported greater use of self-care practices. Finally, Miller et al. (2018, 2019a, b, 2020, 2021) concluded that workers who perceived themselves to be more financially stable engaged more in personal self-care, the suggestion being that they had

118 Self-Care to Promote Self-Compassion

more money and time for such activities; they were more able to pay for help and assistance around the home and with other tasks.

In looking at self-care activities *actually used* often or frequently by workers, in studies of child welfare workers and social work students, it was found time with family and friends, hobbies, exercise, "healthy habits", discussions with work colleagues, and use of humour were most frequently used (Fox et al., 2021; Moore et al., 2011; O'Neil et al., 2019; Shannon et al., 2014; Van Hook and Rothenberg, 2009). According to Bloomquist et al.'s (2015) findings, practitioners engaged in physical self-care most frequently, followed by professional, emotional, and psychological self-care. The least frequently practiced activities were writing a journal, practising yoga, participating in stress management training and, surprisingly and of particular importance, negotiating one's own needs at work. Cuartero and Campos-Vidal (2019) in Spain also found attention to spiritual growth, meditation, mindfulness, and yoga to be the least frequently used activities. These findings are a further indication of social workers' difficulty and reluctance to actually consider, concentrate upon, and work on their own needs in their day-to-day personal and professional lives.

The role of spiritual self-care perhaps requires further exploration, as Bloomquist et al. (2015) explained that while respondents indicated being engaged less frequently in spiritual self-care, it was negatively predictive of burnout, while Collins (2005) has drawn attention to the use of spiritual self-care to assist social workers with their feelings of compassion fatigue, excessive commitment to the job, and sometimes traumatic work demands.

In researching what they termed trauma-informed self-care practices, Salloum et al. (2018) focused more specifically on social workers' emotional responses to service users who had experienced trauma, alongside the workers' use of professional self-care. These researchers suggested the most commonly used self-care practices were requesting and expecting regular, good-quality supervision, utilising peer support from team and agency colleagues, setting realistic work goals, requesting, and accepting feedback from others. The least commonly used trauma-informed self-care activities included, interestingly, aspects which neglected organisational matters, such as attempts to obtain a balanced caseload involving less emphasis on work with traumatised service users, making use of other resources within the agency and training related to stress management or secondary trauma. This raises a critical question noted earlier which we will consider again later. Social workers' self-care work obviously takes place not only outside work but also within agency contexts which have a significant impact (Newcomb, 2021).

The Impact of Culture, "Race", and Gender

Similar to resilience, self-care definitions and research in social work appear to be based on white, Western, Eurocentric, able-bodied populations, which do not fully acknowledge the different perspectives, the different meanings

Self-Care to Promote Self-Compassion **119**

ascribed to self-care by people from diverse cultures and various minority groups (Collins, 2020, 2021). Additional pressures from discrimination, marginalisation, and inequality possibly lead to particularly strong external and internal, self-imposed pressures on minority group practitioners to provide high-quality services to service users at the expense of further consideration of their personal and professional needs, including self-care.

When considering gender, Xu et al. (2019) and Cuartero and Campos-Vidal (2019) highlighted that females aged from around thirty to the fifties, undertaking major responsibilities for family care were likely to be experiencing competing demands from caring for young, adolescent, or adult children, or grandchildren, in addition to possibly meeting the needs of ageing parents. Hence these pressures from personal life, added to professional demands from employing bodies and the likelihood of engaging with the needs of many service users, could lead to a lack of time, energy, and space for self-care – particularly for females, who comprise the vast majority of social workers.

Miller et al. (2019a, 2020c) pointed out that white/Caucasian social workers engaged in significantly higher levels of self-care than practitioners from other ethnic groups. However, there is only limited research which highlights the significance of structural influences such as gender, culture, and "race" upon self-care endeavours in social work, along with the need for further exploration of these matters. But Nyak (2020) does so in a very powerful, inspirational, and thought-provoking article. She draws attention to a model of Black feminist self-care practice set within a context of power relations to safeguard women of colour from intersectional racism. As Nyak (2020, p.7) puts it:

> Black feminist self-care practice...invokes an...anti-racist political imperative that radically challenges traditional social work theories...In a situation of chronic racist denigration the concept and practice of self-care for women of colour is political... apolitical models of self-care ... are woefully inadequate to deal with the trauma and loss produced by intersectional racism. [Therefore] models of self-care for women of colour in social work must address... intersectional racist 'entrapments' and herein lies the rationale for a Black feminist model of self-care for women of colour developed by women of colour.

Nyak (2020) goes on to emphasise self-care practices as a positive response by Black, female social workers to fear, tiredness, exhaustion, and pressures to be silent, to internalise negative experiences of racism and sexism, along with a climate of ignoring, of negating the power of their feelings of guilt and anger. The response to this means putting silence into words, having a voice, talking back, becoming energised, acknowledging the power of angry feelings, and turning them into action and achievement. This leads us to consideration of other critical issues associated with self-care.

Dangers of an Excessive Focus on the Individual and the Neglect of Structures and the Workplace

In addition to culture, "race", and gender, other structural divisions, oppressions linked to, for instance, religion, sexuality, physical and learning (dis)abilities, and those whose first language is not English could impact upon workers' perceptions of their ability, means, and ways to self-care. These aspects have also been neglected in the literature and research; they require further exploration (Collins, 2021). Furthermore, self-care for minorities should involve opportunities to share experiences with other members of minority groups, either in person or virtually, in order to offer mutual support (Wyatt and Ampadu, 2021). Such experiences could take place in local, regional, national, or wider contexts. In order to truly facilitate self-care, this really should involve breaking out of local boundaries which, important though they may be, may also be parochial and restrictive. In other words, self-care possibilities for minority groups should be wide ranging and not geographically restricted activities.

Self-care can be criticised for its lack of attention to the wider structural context in which it is located; not only in relation to the social divisions noted above, but also from the workplace, political, and policy perspectives (Bressi and Vaden, 2017; Hendrix et al., 2020; Newcomb, 2021; Stuart, 2021). Too much emphasis on narrow stereotypes of self-care can divert attention away from structural matters and the social work agency to an excessive focus on the "self-improvement" of the individual worker. The spotlight falls on individual behaviours; as with self-compassion, the individual practitioner can be seen as responsible, who then can be blamed for allegedly poor self-care practices, poor responses to pressure and stress when, in fact, structural, political, policy and institutional contexts impose enormous pressures and stress that would make heavy demands upon, and tax, the capabilities of any social worker (BASW, 2018; Hendrix et al., 2020; Lee, 2017; Stuart, 2021).

The danger is that a culture of self-care can dominate that is based on individualism, consumerism, and capitalism (Wyatt and Ampadu, 2021). Therefore, the social worker can be encouraged and be expected to focus excessively on individual self-care, coping, adjustment, acceptance of existing arrangements and survival rather than resisting, challenging, and working to change organisational practices, wider policy, political and structural imperatives (Kinman and Grant, 2011; Stuart, 2021). Self-care research has explored such matters briefly, i.e., consideration of social workers taking social action as a part of self-care approaches, but such action was not rated highly by practitioners in one particular large sample in the USA (Bloomquist et al., 2015).

This finding reinforces the argument that self-care must include connectivity through collective elements (Wyatt and Ampadu, 2021). Nyak (2020, p.1) strongly emphasises this point about Black feminist self-care and social work when affirming "the power of collective dialogue as a primary strategy". Pyles (2020) also supports collective perspectives and justice approaches to self-care.

Self-Care to Promote Self-Compassion **121**

In an engaging, stimulating, challenging and wide-ranging article, she, and Stuart (2021), raise critical questions about the dominant role of self-care as a tool of managerialism in encouraging, and in reinforcing adaptation to the status quo and existing power structures rather than, alternatively, acting as a part of collective endeavours for transformative change in structural practices, working against intersectional oppression. Pyles (2020, p.184) concludes "there are limits to the ability of individual self-care interventions because there must be systemic interventions to address structural and cultural causes". In their recent panoramic, visionary work, this is reinforced by Powers and Engstrom (2020, p.30); they go further in promoting, in linking "the dire need for *radical* self-care", to solidarity in political activism, which challenges social injustice and works through social justice in advocating collective action surrounding the global political climate and the environmental climate crisis. These are examples of social work writers who see the potential of self-care as a launching pad for much wider-scale social change.

Therefore, in considering *self*-care, we should strive also to maintain and to develop a focus on *group and collective elements* (Frost et al., 2017; Newcomb, 2021; Stuart, 2021; Wyatt and Ampadu, 2021), adopting a critically questioning attitude to the use of the term *self*-care, which implies a heavy focus on the individual, i.e. "care by the self and for the self", as part of a discourse once embedded in individualistic, traditional, medical model thinking (Bressi and Vaden, 2017, p.34). Indeed, this is the setting, the location in which the roots and origins of the term self-care in the 1960s and 1970s are to be found, i.e. related to patient health and physical practices related to illness (Miller et al., 2020a, c). In fact, Bressi and Vaden (2017) have also suggested alternative aims and goals for self-care; those which are *less* concerned with practitioners' physical health. They encourage social workers to persist, to persevere, and to stick with the vulnerability, oppression, discrimination, difficult feelings, and uncertainty evident in social work relationships. This emphasises ways in which practitioners can be positively encouraged and be actively changed, as a result of interactions with service users, with a reinforcement of the role of working with service users in bringing meaning and purpose to workers' lives. As we saw in the previous chapter on compassion satisfaction, there are links here with associated thinking about the rewards of social work, with ideas about post-traumatic growth and vicarious resilience, i.e. the positives associated with sometimes inspiring interactions and experiences with the strengths of service users. This can function as an aid to positive forms of psychological, emotional, and professional self-care for practitioners, helping them to maintain their well-being (Hernandez-Wolfe, 2018; Hurley et al., 2015; Pack, 2014).

Education and Training

As regards initial qualifying education and training, research in the USA, China, and Australia suggests social workers do not feel well prepared by

122 Self-Care to Promote Self-Compassion

their programmes/courses for engagement in the use of professional self-care techniques to support themselves (Bloomquist et al., 2015; Newcomb et al., 2017; Wang et al., 2020). The same researchers comment on a gap between social workers' and students' apparent *perceptions* of the value, and the importance of learning about self-care in social work programmes compared to the *actual* learning opportunities available – a parallel to the situation in social work practice. In Shannon et al. (2014) and Diebold et al.'s (2018) studies, students were also cynical about attempting self-care within the context of their perceptions of the excessive demands of their social work programmes. Kinman and Grant (2011) also noted that students in the UK tended to focus on self-care as an intrapersonal, individualistic phenomena rather than associating it with interpersonal, organisational, or structural elements.

Nevertheless, self-care literature has pointed out the need for social work education and social work agencies to take a more prominent role in developing learning about the concept, alongside relevant skills development, as self-care can obviously be learned about (see, Diebold et al., 2018; Newell and Nelson-Gardell, 2014; Xu et al., 2019). For example, Miller (2020b) described and analysed a short, voluntary, online module about self-care for social work students which revealed significant growth and improvements linked to that area. Miller et al. (2021) also emphasise the role of compulsory, obligatory written assignments about self-care in helping to establish and develop these aspects.

However, a word of caution should be added about social work students' self-care activities, which reinforces earlier points about self-care, allied to the lack of attention to structural divisions. Much of the research about self-care and social work students, as we have seen in the case of social workers, has focused upon Caucasians, with a lack of attention to diversity matters (Griffiths et al., 2019). Therefore, there is a clear need for more research, debate, and action on this topic.

Various suggestions have also been made to improve teaching and learning opportunities about self-care in social work programmes/courses (for example, Adamson et al., 2014; Beddoe et al., 2013; Miller et al., 2021). As seen in the previous chapter, one suggested starting point is a focus on various aspects of stress, vicarious trauma, compassion fatigue, and burnout, before moving on to consider post-traumatic growth, vicarious resilience, compassion satisfaction, self-care, coping, and other more positive topics (Grant et al., 2015; Newell and Nelson-Gardell, 2014; Xu et al., 2019). Where possible, self-care could be learned about either as part of a specific module or workshops, or could be integrated throughout various modules and practice experiences, assisted by social work educators and practice teachers who have a commitment to, and have positive experiences of, self-care (Grant, Kinman and Baker, 2015; Grise-Owens et al., 2018; Lewis and King, 2019).

Several authors have pointed out the importance of educators effectively modelling self-care practices (see Myers et al., 2020). Promisingly, in the USA, Miller et al. (2018b) found a sample of social work educators "frequently" engaged in self-care activities – more often than practitioners. Grant et al. (2015) found social work educators in the UK had positive attitudes towards developing learning experiences on social work programmes linked to self-care, yet they also expressed reservations about time, workload demands, and a need for them to develop more understanding in that area. Furthermore, a third of Myers et al.'s (2020) social work educator respondents in the USA highlighted a lack of institutional support for their self-care endeavours. Hence reservations about the lack of organisational support for self-care from some social work practice-based agencies seem to be mirrored by similar situations in several academic institutions where social work courses are located.

Studies have found that social work students and social workers' overall well-being, including elements of self-care, was enhanced through reflective supervision (see, for instance, Pack, 2012). The importance of reflective supervision, with an emphasis on emotional responses, has been a long-established approach in social work (Ruch, 2002; Schon, 1983). However, here our focus will be on just one aspect of reflection – its link to self-care. Two recent articles have concentrated on this area (Curry and Epley, 2020; Glassburn et al., 2019). These authors argue that critical reflection (or reflexivity) encourages students to concentrate more on professional self-care, to consider more carefully the challenges to their own well-being, to examine action strategies to work on the causes of such challenges, along with the general and specific challenges of social work practice with service users. Particular emphasis is given to the significance of critical reflection on the impact of political, structural, and social forces on self-care. The importance of such discussion about self-care with trusted supervisors and peer colleagues is highlighted, suggesting that these opportunities not only enable students (and workers) to think about, and identify, self-care interventions, but these activities can also act as an intervention in, and of themselves, in providing care and concern to participants which, in turn, encourages self-care (Newcomb, 2021). Hence self-care and reflection appear to be a "natural fit" that could be developed further.

Curry and Epley's (2020) research is based on a higher education establishment which emphasises reflective practices, with weekly one-to-one reflective supervision and reflective practice seminars. They argue (p.14) that a "learning environment and institutional culture that intentionally supports students' self-care seems important...[it] helps students take better care of themselves" in relation to physical, psychological, and emotional demands. Emphasis is placed on the importance of institutional and workplace provision for, and support of, self-care. Participants found reflective individual supervision and reflective group sessions had a positive, meaningful impact in enhancing both practice with service users and self-care. Participants reported being better able to care for themselves personally and professionally. They enjoyed improved emotional health; they were more aware, and more accepting of their emotions, with good opportunities to explore, to "revisit" emotions and integrate them with practice. They could "sustain" themselves more in social work, as self-care made the work

124 Self-Care to Promote Self-Compassion

more "bearable" and less "overwhelming". They felt more empathic and less judgmental. Furthermore, participants developed a firm commitment to, and high expectations of, sound standards and appropriate provision of self-care in present and future practice settings.

In addition to the development of reflective self-care practices in individual and group discussions, research evidence also notes the influence of reflective writing on self-care. For example, Moore et al. (2011) describe the use of self-care assessment in the form of reflective bi-weekly journals with first-year MSW students, which resulted in reduced stress levels, accompanied by improved ability to focus and to concentrate on class work. Lewis and King (2019, p.98) asked students to "operationalise specific workplace self-care strategies within... practice settings". These included individual self-care assessments, a personalised self-care plan, and a written critical, reflective assignment emphasising self-care strategies for the present and for development in future professional work. Students valued these learning experiences, gained new knowledge, and new insights into the use of self-care strategies to help alleviate stress. This enhanced a "balanced" approach to their personal and professional lives.

The use of a self-care plan, involving a range of self-care activities, including a journal, is also advocated by other researchers (for instance, Grise-Owens et al., 2018; Shannon et al., 2014). Care plans could be reviewed regularly both online, individually and in group discussions. Recently, increasing emphasis has been placed on establishing and on maintaining individual self-care plans for both students and practitioners (also see, Armes et al., 2020; Brown, 2020; Lee et al., 2020). A self-care plan should set out intentions, potential goals, and activities, test out possibilities, assess them, provide a structure for regular reviews to revise plans and importantly to clarify external and internal resources to fall back upon in tough times, endorsing the acquisition of self-care behaviours as continuing, sustainable habits over a longer time span. Various suggestions have been made for the content of the self-care plans. For example, Rienks (2020) advocates a focus on physical health, emotional health, and social support both within and external to the social work agency as key aspects to provide a foundation for future self-care work. However, a great deal depends on the individual's motivation and commitment to establish and follow through with these plans, as well as active, committed institutional facilitation from supervisors and colleagues.

At present, learning/working agreements are an established, common place requirement in student practice placements; they are used to clarify and to review mutual expectations, goals, learning opportunities, assessment procedures and practices, supervision, and other aspects of plans for social work student placements in the UK. A case could be made for including self-care plans within such agreements, or as a separate document. Again, there are questions about whether such plans should be obligatory and mandatory, or of a more flexible, permissive nature.

It is important to help lay the foundations to help development of good practices in self-care during a social work programme/course. There is considerable evidence that social work programmes can be stressful experiences for some social work students – maybe just as stressful as experiences as a qualified worker (for instance, Collins et al., 2010). Also, at degree level many students may be young, may lack practice experience, perhaps may have limited self-awareness, along with the likelihood of them being at an early stage of development in relation to reflection and reflective skills (Newcomb et al., 2017). The latter also explored the impact of adverse childhood experiences (ACEs) upon the self-care of a group of undergraduate social work students. The students with larger numbers of ACEs had to offer a lot of care to other family members when moving through childhood, did not have positive models for self-care in their formative years, with little experience of self-care when young. Newcomb et al. (2017) suggested they might particularly benefit from more opportunities to learn about self-care and self-care strategies during their programmes. However, it seems unfair, inappropriate, discriminatory, and stigmatising to focus only on some students in this way The main point is that establishing effective self-care practices for *all* students during qualifying education can lay the foundations for effective self-care practices in the future as a qualified worker (Miller et al., 2021).

The Social Work Organisation and the Individual

Bloomquist et al. (2015) and Kinman and Grant's (2017) research clearly endorsed that self-care should continue to be learned about, practised, and reinforced in the early and subsequent years of one's career in social work after initial qualification. However, they concluded social workers believed their employing organisations did not either teach or help them, learn about self-care practices. At present, it is also unclear which qualified social workers might benefit most from giving more time and attention to self-care matters. Self-care might have more meaning for particular workers in particular settings with particular service user groups, in urban or rural areas and at particular times in their careers (Downing et al., 2021). Research would suggest young, single, inexperienced, female, early career stage workers might particularly benefit from self-care activities (Collins, 2020, 2021). Clearly self-care is also impacted upon by variations in the local workplace context in which a practitioner is located. Therefore, the setting, and the location for social work, will impact heavily on the need for, and actual practices of, self-care (Newcomb, 2021). Self-care might also have particular meaning for social workers working in local authority settings in the most deprived areas, with high workloads, the most limited resources, and restricted support provision from colleagues and supervisors. This raises again an interesting question about whether it should be mandatory to undertake initial or further self-care education and training in a social work organisation, and if any follow-ups to such training should be mandatory, imposed on all practitioners, as suggested by Miller (2020a), or if it should be undertaken on a voluntary basis with workers choosing, electing to undertake such experiences.

126 Self-Care to Promote Self-Compassion

There are also debates about the nature of such training – should the focus be on face-to-face learning, online experiences, or a hybrid combination of the two? Miller (2020a) describes and analyses short-term face-to-face training interventions about self-care for qualified workers. This revealed significant increases in knowledge, accompanied by the development of confidence to initially engage with relevant values and skills in self-care practices. Nevertheless, the same author also noted that participants were not fully confident in their ability to demonstrate *on-going* relevant skills, to continue to maintain, to consistently consolidate, and to carry out self-care practices within their agencies. He and Kinman and Grant (2017) highlighted the need for continuing "refresher" education and training opportunities, accompanied by a commitment from supervisors and colleagues to regularly support on-going self-care endeavours over a longer period. This also raises questions again about the value of, the need for, self-care plans with regular reviews for qualified social workers similar to, but developed from, self-care plans for social work students noted above.

It is possible, if one wished, to become closer to, to be more aware of, one's need for, and use of, self-care activities (or lack of them) by using one or more of the various scales available. Dorociak et al. (2017) have produced a general Professional Self-Care Scale linked originally to psychologists, while Bloomquist et al. (2015), Salloum et al. (2015, 2018), and Lee, Miller and Bride (2020) have provided sets of measures of self-care specifically for social work. Such scales might also be used in supervision and as part of professional development plans. However, the use of scales in this manner could then possibly become linked to organisational surveillance and control measures. This point raises again the question of, and issues about, mandatory, or voluntary use of scales, similar to the debate about mandatory or voluntary self-care education and training opportunities for qualified social workers. Also, as is the case with most of the scales mentioned in this book, the scales noted above clearly tend to focus more on the individual rather than the workplace context. This again can lead to an under-emphasis of the role of the workplace in self-care, as was seen in a small-scale study of social workers in the USA by Hendrix et al. (2020) when, surprisingly, no participant commented on the fact that their organisations should take some responsibility for self-care. Alternatively, in Fox et al.'s (2021) research with hospital social workers in Australia, almost all participants saw self-care as a joint responsibility between individual workers and the organisation. Workers in Newcomb's (2021) qualitative research in the same country went even further, placing more emphasis on general caring provision from workplaces and their staff, rather than on self-care in and of itself.

Bressi and Vaden (2017) and Xu et al. (2019, p.21) argue that social work organisations should value self-care, and should give it a higher priority, as it is "a critical component in social workers' professional lives". McGarrigle and Walsh's (2011) research emphasised the need for *a balance* between a worker's own accountability to themselves for self-care, alongside the organisation's accountability. Hence self-care should clearly be a shared, joint enterprise. The social work agency has a responsibility to facilitate staff self-care endeavours by providing important, essential, vital elements such as *permission, time, space, and place* for relevant self-care activities (Cuartero and Campos-Vidal, 2019; McGarrigle and Walsh, 2011; Stuart, 2021). Other research has pointed out lack of time, high, unmanageable caseloads, and unsupportive supervision ill-informed about self-care concepts, as common barriers to self-care activities of social workers (Lee et al., 2017; Newcomb, 2021). These, and other aspects require the development of appropriate policies, procedures, practices, and further attention from social work agencies to support self-care endeavours. Ashley-Binge and Cousins (2020, p.204) put this provocatively, concisely, and bluntly: "all the exercise[and] yoga... in the world will not ameliorate a culture of bullying, poor quality supervision or unrealistic caseloads". Hence the idea is that if a public building is burning, if you happen to be in there and get burnt, the problem lies in the burning building, not the individual.

In the UK, social work organisations already have a duty to care (Lee, 2017), while the Standards for Employers of Social Workers in England (Local Government Association, 2020) comment on the need for employers to create and encourage a culture of self-care. Therefore, supportive resources and enabling structures should be available to facilitate increased learning opportunities about, and reduction of, barriers to self-care practices (Fox et al., 2021). These could include the provision of workshops to enhance learning related to self-care concepts, to review use of them, the provision of more effective, consistently used workload management systems, supervision that is based on critical reflection, which is both practically and emotionally supportive, and is also well informed about, and provides an appropriate model for, self-care. This should be allied to good opportunities for formal and informal interactive discussions between staff about self-care (Fox et al., 2021; Frost et al., 2017).

As we have seen earlier, these elements should be underpinned by an approach whereby the social work agency appreciates, recognises, and actively conveys to staff a feeling that they are wanted, valued, and respected, as seen in the findings of a host of research studies (for instance, Evans and Huxley, 2009; Huxley et al., 2005; Newcomb, 2021). In other words, social workers should feel they are cared for and cared about, in order to facilitate self-care, just as they in turn are expected to care for, and care about, service users (Collins, 2016, 2021). As Powers and Engstrom (2020, p.31) succinctly state, self-care "is not merely about being better equipped for professional roles and responsibilities as...each social worker has their own intrinsic value and deserves to be cared for (by self and others)... as "human beings" and not just as " human doings".

This also involves recognition by the workplace of the interplay between social workers' personal lives and their professional lives, for instance, understanding of, and acting upon, demands from family (where relevant), ensuring there is a flexible approach to working hours, job sharing, part-time work, agile and home-based working, family commitments, and illnesses (Grant and Kinman, 2014; Kalliath et al., 2015; Lee et al., 2017). Self-care for workers also involves

128 Self-Care to Promote Self-Compassion

the social work agency providing good on-going professional development opportunities and opportunities for practitioners to have, and to use, external counselling for emotional difficulties if required. Of course, such suggestions are by no means new. They have been highlighted in extensive research and literature outside the self-care field.

Conclusion

We have considered the development of the self-care concept, discussed definitions, considered various research findings, and positive and negative elements. We have seen that there has been limited research, with little evaluation of self-care and social work in the UK. Nevertheless, self-care has now started to assume considerable prominence in the "official" literature of social work education, in the professional development of social workers internationally and in the UK. It is also clear that while self-care has been advocated in the UK, it has been at the expense of exploring, writing about, and researching its validity (Collins, 2021).

Nevertheless, a great strength of the focus on the concept is that, like compassion fatigue, it recognises the need for "replenishment and renewal" amongst social workers (Harr, 2013, p.83). Self-care should be more clearly located, integrated, and consolidated within the educational and organisational contexts of social work to encourage students, practice teachers, educators, workers, and managers to develop their awareness of practices linked to self-care. This has major implications for professional well-being, job satisfaction, retention, and turnover in social work. There also is a need to maintain a balance between social work developing a pragmatic, practical commitment to self-care, appreciating, valuing, and enacting it, while simultaneously retaining an ethical critical, questioning approach to its strengths, limitations, and weaknesses (Pyles, 2020; Stuart, 2021).

Structural contexts for self-care tend to have been neglected. For instance, although writers and researchers in the field of self-care and social work have started to consider the implications of culture, "race" and gender, these are only beginnings (Nyak, 2020; Pyles, 2020). The implications of other social divisions such as sexuality, (dis)ability, and language have yet to be explored.

Furthermore, the most powerful links to the self-care concept involve the contributions of self-compassion and mindfulness. These are the topics that will be explored in the next two chapters.

Finally, it remains to be seen if self-care becomes a more established, core feature of social work theory, social work education, social work agencies, social work practice, and on-going professional development in the UK. Certainly, at present, a great deal more work is needed to develop the literature, the research bases of self-care in the UK. It is to be hoped that such work will continue at some pace, in order to facilitate appropriate growth and positive developmental opportunities, both for the present and future generations of social work students, practitioners, and service users.

References

Acker, G. (2018) "Self-care practices among social workers: Do they predict job satisfaction and turnover intentions?", *Social Work in Mental Health,* 16.6, 713–727.

Adamson, C. Beddoe, L. and Davys, A. (2014) "Building resilient practitioners: Definitions and practitioner understandings", *British Journal of Social Work*, 44.3, 522–541.

Alkema, K., Linton, J. and Davies, R. (2008) "A study of the relationship between self-care, compassion satisfaction and burn out among hospice professionals", *Journal of Social Work in End-of-Life and Palliative Care*, 4.2, 101–119.

Armes, S., Lee, J., Bride, B. and Seponski, D. (2020) "Secondary trauma and impairment in clinical social workers", *Child Abuse and Neglect,* doi.org/10.1016/j.chiabu 2020.14540.

Ashley-Binge, S. and Cousins, C. (2020) "Individual and organisational practices addressing social workers' experiences of vicarious trauma". *Practice: Social Work in Action,* 32.3, 191–207.

BASW (2018) *The Professional Capabilities Framework*, Birmingham, BASW.

BASW (2020a) *Social Worker Wellbeing and Working Conditions: Good Practice Toolkit*, Birmingham, BASW, Bath Spa University and Social Workers Union.

BASW (2020b) *Quick Guide: Self-Care for Social Workers during COVID-19,* Birmingham, BASW.

Beddoe, L., Davys, A. and Adamson, C. (2013) "Educating resilient practitioners", *Social Work Education*, 32.1, 100–117.

Bloomquist, K., Wood, L., Friedmeyer-Trainor, K. and Kim, H. (2015) "Self-care and professional quality of life: Predictive factors among MSW practitioners", *Advances in Social Work*, 16.6, 292–311.

Bober, T. and Regehr, C. (2006) "Strategies for reducing secondary or vicarious trauma: Do they work?", *Brief Treatment and Crisis Intervention*, 6.1, 1–9.

Bressi, S. and Vaden, E. (2017) "Reconsidering self care", *Clinical Social Work Journal*, 45, 33–38.

Brown, M-E. (2020) "Hazards of our helping profession: A practical self-care model for social work practice", *Social Work*, 65.1, 38–44.

Butler, l., Carello, J. and Maguin, E. (2017) "Trauma, stress and self-care in clinical training: Predictors of burnout, decline in health status, secondary traumatic stress symptoms and compassion satisfaction", *Psychological Trauma, Theory, Research, Practice and Policy*, 9.4, 416–424.

Canadian Association of Social Workers (2005) *Code of Ethics*, Ottawa, CASW.

Coffey, M., Dudgill, L. and Tattersall, A. (2009) "Working in the public sector: A case study of social services", *Journal of Social Work,* 9.4, 420–442.

Collins, W. (2005) "Embracing spirituality as an element of professional self-care", *Social Work and Christianity*, 32, 263–274.

Collins, S., Coffey, M. and Morris, L. (2010) "Social work students: Stress, support and well-being", *British Journal of Social Work*, 40.3, 963–982.

Collins, S. (2016) "The commitment of social workers in the UK: Committed to the profession, the organisation and service users?", *Practice: Social Work in Action*, 28.3, 159–179.

Collins, S. (2020) *The Positive Social Worker*, London, Routledge.

130 Self-Care to Promote Self-Compassion

Collins, S. (2021) "Social workers and self-care: A promoted yet unexamined concept?", *Practice: Social Work in Action*, 33.2, 87–102.

Cox, K. and Steiner, S. (2013) *Self-Care in Social Work: A Guide for Practitioners, Supervisors and Administrators*, Washington, NASW.

Cuartero, M. and Campos-Vidal, J. (2019) "Self-care behaviours and their relationship with Satisfaction and Compassion Fatigue levels among social workers", *Social Work in Health Care*, 58.3, 274–290.

Curry, A. and Epley, P. (2020) "It makes you a healthier professional': The impact of reflective practice on emerging clinicians' self-care", *Journal of Social Work Education*, DOI:10.1080/10437797.2020.1817825.

Dalphon, H. (2019) "Self-care techniques for social workers: Achieving an ethical harmony between work and well being", *Journal of Human Behaviour in the Environment*, 29.1, 8–95.

Diebold, Kim, W. and Elze, D. (2018) "Perceptions of self-care among MSW students: implications for social work education", *Journal of Social Work Education*, 54.4, 657–667.

Dombo, E. and Gray, R. (2013) "Engaging spirituality in addressing vicarious trauma in clinical social workers: A self-care model", *Social Work and Christianity*, 40.1, 89–104.

Dorociak, K., Rupert, P., Bryant, F. and Zahniser, E. (2017) "Development of the professional self-care scale", *Journal of Counselling Psychlogy*, 64.3, 325–334.

Downing, K., Brackett, M. and Riddick, D. (2021) "Self-care management101: Strategies for social workers and other frontline responders during the COVID-19 pandemic in rural communities", *Journal of Human Behaviour in the Social Environment*, 31, 353–361.

Evans, S. and Huxley, P. (2009) "Factors associated with the recruitment and retention of social workers in Wales: Employer and employee perspectives", *Health and Social Care in the Community*, 173, 254–266.

Fox, M., Hopkins, D., Graves, J., Crehan, S., Cull, P., Birrell, B., Dunn, P., Murphy, E., Harrison, A. Hayes, M. and Yeomans, P. (2021) "Hospital social workers and their understanding of compassion fatigue and vicarious trauma", *Asian Journal of Interdisciplinary Research*, DOI:https;// doi.org/10.34256/ajir2113.

Frost, L., Hojer, S. Campanini, A., Sicora, A. and Kullberg, K. (2017) "Why do they stay? A study of resilient child protection workers in three European countries", *European Journal of Social Work*, 21.4, 485–497.

Glassburn, S., McGuire, L. and Lay, K. (2019) "Reflection as self-care: Models for facilitative supervision", *Reflective Practice*, 20.6, 692–704.

Grant, L. and Kinman, G. (eds.) (2014) *Developing Resilience for Social Work Practice*, London, Palgrave.

Grant, L. and Kinman, G. (2020) *Developing Emotional Resilience and Wellbeing: A Practical Guide for Social Workers,* London, Community Care.

Grant, L., Kinman, G. and Baker, S. (2015) "'Put on your own oxygen mask before assisting others': Social work educators' perspectives on the 'emotional curriculum'", *British Journal of Social Work*, 45.8, 2351–2367.

Griffiths, A. and Royse, D. (2017) "Unheard voices: Why former child welfare officers left their posts", *Journal of Public Child Welfare*, 11.1, 73–90.

Griffiths, A., Royse, D. and Walker, R. (2018) "Stress among child protective service workers: Self reported health consequences", *Children and Youth Services Review*, 90, 46–53.

Griffiths, A., Royse, D., Murphy, A. and Starks, S. (2019) "Self-care practice in social work education: A systematic review of interventions", *Journal of Social Work Education*, DOI:10.10801/10437797.2018.1491358.

Grise-Owens, E., Miller, J. and Eaves, M. (eds.) (2016) *A-Z Self-Care Handbook for Social Workers and Other Helping Professionals,* Philadelphia, New Social Worker Press/White Hat Communications.

Grise-Owens, E., Miller, J., Escobar-Radcliff, l. and George, N. (2018) "Teaching note - teaching self-care and wellness as a professional practice skill: A curricular case example", *Journal of Social Work Education,* 54.1, 180–186.

Harr, C. (2013) "Promoting workplace health by diminishing the negative impact of compassion fatigue and increasing compassion satisfaction", *Social Work and Christianity,* 40.1, 71–88.

Hendrix, E., Barusch, A. and Gringeri, C. (2020) "Eats me alive!: Social workers reflect on practice in neoliberal contexts", *Social Work Education,* doi.org/10.1080/02615479 .2020.1718635.

Hernandez-Wolfe, P. (2018) "Vicarious resilience: A comprehensive review", *Revisita Estudios Socailes,* 66, 9–17.

Hurley, D., Alvarez, L. and Buckley, H. (2015) "From the zone of risk to the zone of resilience: Protecting the resilience of children and practitioners in Argentina, Canada and Ireland", *International Journal of Child, Youth and Family Studies,* 6.1, 17–51.

Huxley, P., Evans, S., Gately, C., Webber, M., Mears, A., Pajak, S., Kendall, T., Medina, J. and Katona, C. (2005) "Stress and pressure in mental health social work: The worker speaks", *British Journal of Social Work,* 35.7, 1063–1079.

International Federation of Social Workers (2019) *Global Social Work Statement of Ethical Principles,* Rheinfelden, IFSW.

International Federation of Social Workers (2020) *Practising During Pandemic Conditions: Ethical Guidance for Social Workers,* Rheinfelden, IFSW.

Jeffrey, L. (2011) *Understanding Agency,* Bristol, Policy Press.

Kalliath, P., Kalliath, T. and Chan, C. (2015) "Work and family conflict as predictors of psychological strain: Does social support matter?", *British Journal of Social Work,* 45.8, 2387–2403.

Killian, K. (2008) "Helping till it hurts? A multi-method study of compassion fatigue, burn out and self-care in clinicians working with trauma survivors", *Traumatology,* 14.2, 32–44.

Kinman, G. and Grant, L. (2011) "Exploring stress resilience in trainee social workers: The role of emotional and social competences", *British Journal of Social Work,* 41.2, 261–278.

Kinman, G. and Grant, L. (2017) "Building Resilience in early-career social workers: Evaluating a multi-model intervention", *British Journal of Social Work,* 47.7, 1979–1998.

La Mott, J. and Martin, L. (2019) "Adverse childhood experiences, self-care, and compassion satisfaction outcomes in mental health providers", *Journal of Clinical Psychology,* 75.6, 1066–1183.

Lee, J. and Miller, S. (2013) "A self-care framework for social workers: Building a strong foundation for practice", *Families in Society: The Journal of Contemporary Social Work,* 94.2, 96–103.

Lee, R. (2017) "The impact of engaging with clients' trauma stories: Personal and organizational strategies to manage probation practitioners' risk of developing vicarious traumatization", *Probation Journal,* 64.4, 372–387.

Lee, K., Pang, Y., Lee, J-A. and Melby, J, (2017) "A study of adverse childhood experiences, coping strategies, work stress and self-care in the child welfare profession", *Human Services Organisations: Management, Leadership and Governance,* 41.4, 389–402.

Lee, J., Miller, S. and Bride, B. (2020) "Development and initial validation of the self-care practices scale", *Social Work,* 65.1, 21–28.

132 Self-Care to Promote Self-Compassion

Lewis. M. and King, D. (2019) "Teaching self-care: The utilisation of self-care in social work practicum to prevent compassion fatigue, burnout and vicarious trauma", *Journal of Human Behaviour in the Social Environment*, 29.1, 96–106.

Lloyd, C., King, R. and Chenoweth, I. (2002) "Social work, stress and burnout: A review", *Journal of Mental Health*, 11.3, 255–265.

Local Government Association (2020) *The Standards for Employers of Social Workers in England*, London, Local Government Association.

Martin, E., Myers, K. and Brickman, K. (2020) "Self-preservation in the workplace: The importance of well-being for social work practitioners and supervisors", *Social Work*, 65.1, 74–81.

McGarrigle, T. and Walsh, C. (2011) "Mindfulness, self-care, and wellness in social work: Effects of contemplative training", *Journal of Religion and Spirituality in Social Work*, 30, 212–233.

Mette, J., Wirth, T., Nienhaus, A., Herth, V. and Mache, S. (2020) "'I need to take care of myself': A qualitative study on coping strategies, support and health promotion for social workers serving refugees and homeless people", *Journal of Occupational Medicine and Toxicology*, 15.1, 1–15.

Miller, J. (2020a) "Developing self-care competency among child welfare workers: A first step", *Children and Youth Services Review*, doi.org/10.1016/ j.child youth 2019.104528.

Miller, J. (2020b) "Building competency in self-care for social work students: A course-based case study", *Social Work Education*, doi.org/10.1080/02615479.2019.1620722.

Miller, J., Lianekhammy, J., Pope, N., Lee, J. and Grise -Owens, E. (2017) "Self-care among health care social workers: An exploratory study", *Social Work in Health Care*, 56, 865–883.

Miller, J., Donohoe-Dioh, J., Niu, C. and Shalash, N. (2018) "Exploring the self-care practices of child welfare workers; A research brief", *Children and Youth Services Review*, 84, 137–142.

Miller, J., Grise-Owens, E. and Shalash, N. (2018b) "Investigating the self-care practices of social work faculty: An exploratory study", *Social Work Education*, 37.8, 1044–1059.

Miller, J.,Donohoe-Dioh, J., Niu, C., Grise-Owens, E. and Poklembova, Z. (2019a) "Examining the self-care practices of child welfare workers: A national perspective", *Children and Youth Services Review*, 99, 240–245.

Miller, J., Lee, J., Niu, C., Grise-Owens, E. and Bode, M. (2019b) "Self-compassion as a predictor of self-care: A study of social work clinicians", *Clinical Social Work Journal*, DOI:10.100071/s 10615-019-00710-6.

Miller, J., Grise-Owens, E., Shalash, N. and Bode, M. (2020) "Self-care practices of self-identified social workers: Findings from a national study", *Social Work*, 65.1, 555–563.

Miller, J. and Cassar, J. (2021) "Self-care among health care social workers: The impact of COVID-19", *Social Work In Health Care*, 60.1, 1, 30–48.

Miller, J., Barnhart, S., Robinson, T., Pryor, M. and Arnott, K. (2021) "Assuaging COVID-19 peritraumatic distress among mental health clinicians: The potential of self-care", *Clinical Social Work Journal*, DOI:10.10007/s10615-021-00815.

Moore, S., Bledsoe, L., Perry, A. and Robinson, M. (2011) "Social work students and self-care: A model assignment for teaching", *Journal of Social Work Education*, 47.3, 544–553.

Mordue, S., Watson, L. and Hunter, S. (2020) *How to thrive in professional practice: A self-care handbook,* St. Albans, Critical Publishing.

Myers, K., Martin, E. and Brickman, K. (2020) "Protecting others from ourselves: Self-care in social work educators", *Social Work Education*, 37.8, 1044–1059.

National Association of Social Workers (2008) "Professional self-care and social work" in *Social Work Speaks, NASW Policy Statements, 2009–2012*, Washington DC, NASW. pp.268–272.

National Association of Social Workers (2021) *Code of Ethics*, Washington DC, NASW.

Newcomb, M., Burton, J. and Edwards, N. (2017) "Childhood adversity and self-care education for undergraduate social work and human service students", *Journal of Teaching in Social Work*, 4, 337–352.

Newcomb, M. (2021) "Self-care rhetoric in neoliberal organisations: social worker experiences", *Practice; Social Work in Action*, DOI:10.1080/09503153.2021.1998414.

Newell, J. and Nelson-Gardell, D. (2014) "A competency base approach to teaching self-care; An ethical consideration for social work educators", *Journal of Social Work Education*, 50.3, 427–439.

Nyak, S. (2020) "For women of colour in social work: Black feminist self-care practice based on Audre Lorde's radical pioneering principles", *Critical and Radical Social Work*, 1–17, DOI:10.1352/204986020x15945755847234.

O'Neill, M., Slater, G. and Batt, D. (2019) "Social work student self-care and academic stress", *Journal of Social Work Education*, 55.1, 141–152.

Owens-King, J. (2019)" Secondary traumatic stress and self-care are inextricably linked", *Journal of Human Behaviour in the Social Environment*, 29, 37–47.

Pack, M. (2012) "Two sides to every story: A phenomenological exploration of the meanings of clinical supervision from supervisee and supervisor", *Journal of Social Work Practice*, 26.2, 163–179.

Pack, M. (2014) "Vicarious resilience: A multi-layered model of stress and trauma", *Affilia: Journal of Women and Social Work*, 29.1, 18–29.

Parry, S. (ed.) (2017) *Effective self-care and resilience in clinical practice: Dealing with stress, compassion fatigue and burnout,* London, Jessica Kingsley.

Powers, M. and Engstrom, S. (2020) "Radical self-care for social workers in the global climate crisis", *Social Work*, 65.1, 29–37.

Pyles, L. (2020) "Healing justice, transformative justice and holistic self-care for social workers", *Social Work*, 65.2, 178–187.

Ravalier, J. (2017) *UK Social Workers: Working Conditions and Well Being*, London, BASW.

Rienks, S. (2020) "An exploration of child welfare caseworkers' experience of secondary trauma and strategies for coping", *Child Abuse and Neglect*, doi.org/10.1016/j.chiabu2020.104355.

Ruch, G. (2002) "From triangle to spiral: Reflective practice in social work education", *Social Work Education*, 21.2, 199–216

Salloum, A., Kondrat, D., Johnco, C. and Owen, K. (2015) "The role of self-care on compassion satisfaction, burnout and secondary trauma among child welfare workers", *Children and Youth Services Review*, 49, 54–61.

Salloum, A., Choi, M. and Stover, C. (2018) "Development of a trauma-informed self-care measure with child welfare workers", *Children and Youth Services Review*, 93, 108–116.

Schon, D. (1983) *The reflective practitioner: How professionals think in action*, London, Temple Smith.

Shannon, P., Simmelink-McCleary, J., Im, H., Becher, E. and Crook-Lyon, R. (2014) "Developing self-care practices in a trauma treatment course", *Journal of Social Work Education*, 50, 440–453.

Shepperd, M. and Newell, J. (2020) "Stress and health in social workers: Implications for self-care practice", *Best Practices in Mental Health*, 16.1, 46–65.

Smullens, S. (2015) *Burnout and Self-Care in Social Work*, Washington, NASW.

Stuart, H. (2021) "'Professional inefficacy is the exact opposite of the passionate social worker': Discourse analysis of neoliberalism within the writing on self-care in social work", *Journal of Progressive Human Services*, 32, 1, 1–16.

Van Hook, M. and Rothenberg (2009) "Quality of life and compassion satisfaction/fatigue and burnout in child welfare workers: A study of child welfare workers in community-based organizations in Central Florida", *Social Work and Christianity*, 36.1, 36–54.

Wang, Y., Zhang, H. and Yang, Y. (2020) "The moderating effect of professional self-care training on novice practitioners' organisational citizenship behaviour in China", *Social Work*, 65.1, 45–54.

Weinberg, M. (2014) "The ideological dilemma of subordination of self versus self-care: Identity construction of the 'ethical social worker'". *Discourse and Society*, 25.1, 84–99.

Willis, N. and Molina, V. (2019) "Self-care and the social worker: Taking our place in the code of ethics", *Social Work*, 64.1, 93–86.

Wyatt, J. and Ampadu, G. (2021) "Reclaiming self-care: Self-care as a social justice tool for black wellness", *Community Mental Health Journal*, DOI:10.1997/s10597-021-00884-9.

Xu, Y., Harmon-Darrow, C. and Frey, J. (2019) "Rethinking professional quality of life for social workers: Inclusion of ecological self-care barriers", *Journal of Human Behaviour in the Environment*, 29.1, 11–25.

6
SELF-COMPASSION

Introduction

As we saw in the previous chapter, more focus has been placed recently on social workers' self-care, with self-compassion forming an important part of self-care (Miller et al., 2019b). The events during the pandemic have also functioned as a stimulus for more focus on self-compassion, with Grant and Kinman (2020, p.6) pointing out that for practitioners "compassion towards the self as well as others is essential to sustain the wellbeing of helping professionals".

As self-compassion is a recently developed concept linked to the social work field, the purpose of this chapter is to consider definitions of self-compassion, to explore research about, and education and training for, self-compassion beyond the field of social work. Research linking the concept to social work students and to social workers will also be explored; its implications for social work education and practice will be discussed, along with criticisms and limitations of the concept, while clearly locating self-compassion in the wider context of social work.

Self-Compassion

Self-compassion plays a central part in the self-care process (Miller et al., 2019a). Self-compassion "can promote both personal and professional self-care behaviours as well as [being]a self-care practice in itself" (Miller et al., 2019a, p.11). In the latter's study of self-care, self-compassion was unique as the strongest predictor of personal and professional self-care for social workers.

Self-compassion has been researched in the past fifteen years, especially in the past five years. It has been particularly associated with the work of Kristin Neff and Christopher Germer in the USA and Paul Gilbert in the UK. However,

DOI: 10.4324/9781003112532-7

136 Self-Compassion

self-compassion also has a long history in some aspects of Buddhist philosophy (Iacono, 2017; Ying, 2009). It has been defined as allowing oneself to be affected by, and being open to, one's suffering while neither avoiding suffering nor becoming disconnected from it (Neff, 2003b). Self-compassion generates a desire to alleviate one's own suffering, while also healing oneself with warmth and loving kindness. It involves non-judgmentally accepting oneself, trying to understand one's pain, one's feelings of inadequacy and failure, without dwelling or ruminating on them, while also placing these experiences in the context of wider, broader human experience (Ying, 2009).

Self-compassion is perceived by Neff (2003b) as having three interacting components:

First, mindful awareness – the maintenance of moment-by-moment awareness in the presence of one's own experiences, accepting them and eventually letting them go, adapting a balanced approach and neither avoiding them nor becoming carried away, overwhelmed or over-identified with exaggerated negative thoughts and emotions.

Second, common humanity – a belief in connections between human beings, recognising that suffering, pain, mistakes, and imperfections are shared by all people, by everyone, thus protecting against feelings of isolation, loneliness, and withdrawing into one's own bad feelings or self-pity.

Third, self-kindness – which entails gentle, caring, nurturing, soothing, understanding of, and forgiving oneself for, one's failings and inadequacies, thus protecting oneself against critical self-judgement and self-blame.

Neff and colleagues have produced self-compassion scales that focus on the three elements noted above – mindful awareness, belief in common humanity, and self-kindness. The scales also focus on their negative counterparts, i.e. over-identification, isolation, and self-judgement. Overall, self-compassion acts as an emotion regulation strategy which neutralises negative emotions, while promoting positive feelings of connectedness, along with a better understanding of situations in more appropriate and effective ways (Neff et al., 2005). Self-compassion is also intended to bring healing, emotional well-being, increased contentment, self-understanding, and reduced guilt and self-criticism. Gilbert (2013) and Yarnell et al. (2015) suggest self-compassion helps people feel more cared for and calmer. People experience less threat and reduced defensiveness. Neff (2003b) and Miller et al., (2019a) argue self-compassion is a way of relating to the self as we would expect to relate to other people, i.e. by being non-judgmental, open, and curious, emphasising positives, accepting, tolerating flaws, and balancing strengths with challenges.

Overview of Research and Self-Compassion

In recent years, a considerable amount of research has been undertaken about self-compassion. By mid-2018, Bluth and Neff (2018) suggest more than 1,600 studies had been produced. The research is often linked to Neff's (2003a)

26-point scale or, its abbreviated version, Raes et al.'s (2011) 12-point scale. The scales measure individual beliefs and self-attitudes – the way people think about or relate to, themselves. Gilbert et al. (2017) have also created a scale that assesses aspects of compassion-engagement with suffering and action taken to alleviate it, as well as compassion for, and from, other people while Gu et al. (2020) have developed scales linked to compassion for others and for the self. Recently Neff and colleagues (2021) moved away from the emphasis on self-compassion as a rather static, dispositional trait by developing further long-, and short-form, state self-compassion scales that are more dynamic, process-oriented, and situationally influenced.

Self-compassion has been linked in a meta-analysis of 20 samples with over 4,000 participants with improved mental health outcomes such as increased life satisfaction, increased resilience to stress, decreased burnout, emotional exhaustion, anxiety, anger, depression, and shame while being negatively related to psychopathology (MacBeth and Gumley, 2012). It is significantly associated with a sense of adaptive strengths and with decreased self-criticism (Gilbert, 2013; Neff, 2009; Trompetter et al., 2017). In their research with over 3,000 subjects, Sirois et al. (2015) suggest self-compassion is connected to and can promote healthy behaviours. Along with others, Gerber et al.'s (2015) work suggests self-compassion improves coping skills, emotional functioning, autonomy, self-nourishing, relationship building, and compassion towards others. There is also considerable evidence in a meta-analysis involving nearly 16,500 people of the association of high levels of self-compassion with positive aspects of well-being (Zessin et al., 2015). Raes et al. (2011) in research with students and adults and Ferrari et al.'s (2019) meta-analysis of random controlled studies also suggest self-compassion can assist people in processing negative experiences more kindly, and in decreasing rumination, i.e. reducing dwelling on negative feelings and fear of failure. Of particular contemporary relevance is a study undertaken with over 400 people in Portugal during the first phase of COVID-19. More self-compassionate people were found to be less at risk of suffering from stress, anxiety, and depression. They also experienced less negative affect, and more positive affect, tending to engage in fewer dysfunctional coping strategies, and creatively adapting both emotion- and problem-focused coping styles (Beato et al., 2021).

Self-compassion is also positively associated with variables such as happiness, hope, optimism, empathy, wisdom, competence, conscientiousness, self-worth, self-determination, and social connectedness (Miller et al. 2019a, b; Neff, 2009). This is a long and impressive set of positive research findings.

Education and Training for Self-Compassion

Mindful Self-Compassion training (Neff and Germer, 2013) helps people to systematically develop self-compassion skills, especially through interpersonal exercises, mindfulness, and meditation linked to, for instance,

138 Self-Compassion

loving kindness, and breathing, as well as informal practices such as the self-compassion break, soothing touch, and written exercises. Baer (2010) emphasises self-compassion as "the key mechanism in these interventions' effectiveness" (Iacono, 2017, p.458). Neff and Germer (2013) discovered those who participated in eight-week long Mindful Self-Compassion training, compared with a control group, significantly increased their life satisfaction and self-compassion levels, along with a significant reduction in stress, anxiety, depression, and emotional avoidance. These gains were maintained at a one-year follow-up. In their meta-analysis of randomized controlled trials of self-compassion interventions, Ferrari et al. (2019) found increases in self-compassion and reductions in various aspects of psychopathology also evident in follow-up studies.

In a small-scale study of an eight-week Mindful Self-Compassion course for nurses in Ireland, Delaney (2018) discovered significant increases in self-compassion, mindfulness, resilience, and compassion satisfaction, accompanied by less secondary trauma and burnout. The nurses also reported feeling a higher degree of self- acceptance, with a more positive outlook, reduced self-criticism levels and better ability to cope with work demands.

Using a shorter, six-week adaptation of the Mindful Self-Compassion training, without formal meditation exercises, for health-care professionals, Neff et al. (2020) found significant gains in self-compassion, personal accomplishment, and well-being. Significant reductions were seen in depression, secondary traumatic stress, and burnout, which were maintained at follow-up for over three months. Participants originally lower in self-compassion before the training benefitted the most. This finding was encouraging in that health-care professionals who tended to be hard on themselves could find new ways of coping. Neff et al. (2020) emphasised one of the strengths of the course was its focus on tools and practices which could be used "on the job", not just within the context of the course. However, the programme did not significantly reduce participants' anxiety levels, with the researchers pointing out that fear of uncertainty, structural, and systemic issues in health-care organisations such as cuts in budgets and resources, staff departures, and illnesses exaggerated a sense of instability – experiences with which social workers are all too familiar. There have also been recent developments in producing shorter courses, for instance, one-day self-compassion training for nurses during the COVID-19 pandemic (Franco and Christie, 2021). The participants experienced significant increases in self-compassion, compassion satisfaction and resilience, with significant decreases in emotional exhaustion, stress, and anxiety, compared to a non-intervention group, after a three-month follow-up.

Online courses have also been produced in recent years, for example, for qualified psychologists, psychology trainees, women, and highly self-critical people. Internet-based interventions for self-compassion, it is argued, reduce possible feelings of stigma and/or shame which could be a barrier for some people in seeking face-to-face group-based programs (Krieger et al., 2016). Online programmes can be more accessible, flexible, and convenient. Four recent online programmes found significant increases in self-compassion. Krieger et al.'s (2016) study of a seven-week programme for "those suffering from harsh self-criticism" with very low self-compassion, found mindfulness, "reassuring self", and life satisfaction significantly increased, while perceived stress, fear of self-compassion, perceptions of "inadequate self", and "hated self" all decreased. A ten-week, online course for women by Nadeau et al. (2020) discovered decreases in self-judgement, shame, and perfectionism, although the study did not find any significant changes in anxiety and depression levels. However, in an online six-week course for trainee psychologists, participants experienced significant decreases in stress, depression, and emotion regulation difficulties (Finlay-Jones et al., 2017). Another six-week online course for qualified psychologists saw increases in self-compassion and mindfulness, also finding reductions in stress, burnout, and levels of self-judgement, isolation, and over-identification (Eriksson et al., 2018).

Recently, in a systematic review of the effects of self-compassion training on workers in various caring fields, Kotera and Van Gordon (2021) reported improvements in self-compassion and well-being related outcomes such as reduced stress, emotional exhaustion, and burnout and increased quality of life and resilience.

Two important, brief, self-compassion practices used when problematic circumstances occur include, firstly, the Self-Compassion Break and, secondly, Soften, Allow and Soothe (Germer, 2009). The Self-Compassion Break, in part, involves exercises reframing discomfort as a natural part of life, using phrases when problems occur such as "this is a moment of suffering" (mindfulness), "suffering is a part of life", " may I accept this as part of a life journey" (common humanity), and "may I be kind to myself" (self-kindness) (Germer and Neff, 2013; Iacono, 2017). These exercises can provide comfort, break patterns of rumination, and help people feel less isolated (Neff, 2011).

Soften (physical self-compassion), Allow (mental self-compassion), and Soothe (physical self-compassion) means locating problematic emotions which may occur during an experience, such as negative beliefs or feelings and thoughts of shame, within the body (Iacono, 2017). Taking deep breaths, one's hands can be placed on an area of the body which allows the discomfort to be there; that area is warmed, relaxed, softened, and soothed with kind intentions or words acting as "a balm to one's experiences of suffering and shame" (Iacono, 2017, p.465).

Self-compassion skills can include guided self-compassion meditations and Loving Kindness Meditation (Neff, 2011). Loving Kindness Meditation is a Buddhist practice that also develops compassionate thoughts, empathy, good will, and warm feelings for the self and others (Iacono, 2017). Self-compassionate meditations can involve repeating words such as "peace", "safe", "joy", "happiness", "ease", or cultivating compassionate images of a caring person or loved one. Iacono (2017) notes that compassion and self-compassionate meditation can involve encouraging positive self-talk, emotions, and intentions by repeating

140 Self-Compassion

sequences of phrases such as "may I/you be safe, may I/you be peaceful, may I/ you be good to myself/ yourself".

Another, different way of incorporating self-compassion is through undertaking written exercises, short letters to oneself, or diary keeping, to reflect on distressing or upsetting experiences that occur, without "judging" or "fixing" them, accompanied by comments about acceptance, strengths, hope, encouragement, and self-kindness (Coaston, 2019; Guan et al., 2021; Shapira and Mongrain, 2010). Bell et al. (2017) also draw attention to the idea of the self-compassionate "internal supervisor", whereby trainee therapists were given a short training course supplemented with video material, including guided practices and worksheets. Therapists were encouraged to use the voice and imagery of a valued, respected, kind, compassionate supervisor (or supervisors) that they had experienced, to help them feel more self-compassionate about work demands. Increases were found in levels of resilience and positive capabilities, as well as reductions in self-criticism, worries, and rumination.

A crucial point raised by the explorations of education and training above is that one needs to regularly practice and experience self-compassion in order to fully understand and use it (Germer, 2009). Also, as Neff (2003b) and others make clear, self-compassion is not a form of complacency, self-pity, or selfishness, but a matter of beliefs, a matter of commitment to developing one's thoughts more positively. However, clearly, only some of the procedures/practices noted above will appeal to social workers, but they offer possibilities, they provide opportunities; they raise the profile of, and consciousness about, self-compassion along with ways of expanding it.

Self-Compassion and Other Helping Professionals

Research findings have emerged about the role of self-compassion among helping professionals, such as counsellors, psychologists, and health-care workers, including nurses, where results demonstrate its benefits (Iacono, 2017). These encompass higher levels of worker resilience, service user satisfaction, enhancement of relationships with service users, and the maintenance and sustenance of caring for others. Health-care professionals who are more self-compassionate report greater inner resources, resilience, better mental health, less stress, and sleep disturbances (Neff et al., 2020). In a study in the NHS self-compassion was a strong predictor of compassion for others (Henshall et al., 2017). Physicians who are self-compassionate demonstrate greater work engagement and reduced physical and emotional exhaustion, along with increased satisfaction in their professional life (Babenko et al., 2019). Furthermore, Patsiopoulos and Buchanan (2011) and Gustin and Wagner (2013) found counsellors and nurses with a self-compassionate approach had a better ability to make relationships with, to meet the needs of, service users and patients, and to cope with stress and challenges. In many studies of nurses, self-compassion has been associated with higher levels of compassion satisfaction and lower levels of compassion fatigue and burnout (Dev et al., 2018; Durkin et al., 2016; Neff et al., 2020), but not all studies of nurses have found self-compassion strengthened positively the relationship between stress and burnout (for example, Dev et al., 2020). However, Iacono (2017) and Dodson and Heng (2021) point out that, among helping professionals generally, self-compassion has been usually, consistently associated with decreases in burnout and compassion fatigue, along with greater emotional regulation and compassion satisfaction – the positive feelings generated by work where one is offering help to others, as seen in Chapter 4.

In a study of nearly 200 psychologists and trainee psychologists in Australia by Finlay-Jones et al. (2015), self-compassion emerged as a significant predictor of stress symptoms with emotional regulation particularly prominent. The research suggested psychologists who were self-compassionate experienced more emotional clarity, were more accepting of problematic emotions, and were more able to access effective emotional regulation strategies. The findings also support the view that self-compassionate workers are more likely to cope with stressful work experiences, with demanding emotional states, to be kinder to themselves when they receive negative feedback or criticism and are more likely to use self-care strategies when encountering difficult situations. Finlay-Jones et al. (2015) also suggest the sense of common humanity, inherent as part of self-compassion, defuses reactions to challenging situations by encouraging feelings of interconnectedness, thus reducing a sense of isolation. They recognise that work in the helping professions inevitably means experiencing difficult demands and making mistakes, and although self-compassion encourages taking some individual responsibility for unpleasant events, it also encourages a reduction in the negative feelings which may surround these events, as does Leary et al. (2007). Findlay-Jones et al. (2015) conclude that self-compassion could be an important intervention target in stress programmes designed to promote stress resilience.

Nevertheless, Wilson and Joyce (2017) in an honest, open, refreshing, informative, incisive, and personal contribution point out that while clinical psychologists may well feel committed to self-compassion, it can be difficult to put this commitment into practice when encountering challenges and barriers to do so in stressful and pressurised workplace contexts, with heavy workloads and limited time. Self-compassion may be regarded as a vague, "fluffy" concept – a selfish luxury which might be frowned upon by colleagues, depending on their attitudes, workplace norms, and expectations. Wilson and Joyce (2017) argue that self-compassion involves ongoing work; effort on a moment-by-moment basis at personal, relational, institutional, and cultural levels; it is actually "easier said than done", which was the case as we saw in the previous chapter on self-care, and we shall see, is also the case with social work students and social workers and self-compassion. Andrews et al. (2020) came to similar conclusions in their qualitative study of nurses in the UK as Wilson and Joyce (2017), noting that

142 Self-Compassion

"internal" (personal) and "external" (organisational) permission was necessary to legitimise self-compassion efforts as a priority.

Social Workers, Social Work Students, and Self-Compassion Research

Research into self-compassion and social work is at an early stage. Indeed, in a recent article self-compassion was even described as being an "unusual word for social work" (Sicora, 2019, p.73). Research has been confined largely to the USA and parts of Europe, as seen particularly in the impressive, extensive work of Jay Miller and colleagues, again mainly based on Neff's scales. Little research has been undertaken on this topic in the UK, although one element of self-compassion – mindfulness – has clearly received attention and research has considered self-compassion as an outcome of mindfulness and resilience courses. In the UK, Kinman and Grant (2017) did consider self-compassion as part of research into a resilience course for newly qualified social workers. This included pre- and post-tests after two months. They found changes in self-compassion had increased "moderately", with participants tending to be more tolerant of their perceived shortcomings. This finding compared positively with members of a control group whose self-compassion had reduced. In a later research study, Kinman et al. (2019) examined self-compassion as part of a mindfulness course with social workers of varying lengths of experience. Qualitative analysis indicated some improvements in self-compassion. Harris (2017) researched an eight-week course for a small group of social workers in a local authority in Scotland. She discovered there was a small increase in total positive self-compassion scores and that self-kindness, common humanity, and mindfulness scores all increased, while self-judgment, isolation, and over-identification scores decreased. In the qualitative part of the study, "self-compassion and kindness were identified as key things many participants took from the course and were impacting on them most noticeably" (Harris, 2017, p.51).

Large-scale, extensive research studies in the USA found various types of social workers while believing in, and valuing, self-compassion only "moderately" and "sometimes" engaged in self-compassion; they were "fairly" self-compassionate (Lianekhammy et al., 2018; Miller et al., 2018, 2019a, b). A significant, positive relationship was found between age and experience, i.e. older and more experienced workers were more self-compassionate. Also, respondents perceiving themselves to enjoy good health noted less self-criticism, with less "over-identification" – defined as ruminating on negative feelings (Lianekhammy et al., 2018; Miller et al., 2018, 2019a, b). As was the case with self-care, satisfaction with one's own financial resources was also predictive of overall self-compassion suggesting, perhaps not surprisingly, that those workers who perceived their financial resources to be in a secure, strong position, could feel more self-compassion. Workers who perceived themselves to have more limited financial resources and who did not

Self-Compassion **143**

have partners were more likely to experience isolation and over-identification. Miller et al. (2018; 2019a, b) also discovered higher level educational qualifications were predictive of self-compassion, as was membership of a professional association and experience as a supervisor. In addition, social workers with high overall self-compassion scores experienced greater mindfulness, accompanied by stronger feelings of self-kindness rather than self-judgement and over-identification with negative thoughts and feelings (Miller et al., 2019a). More recently, a long-term study of social service workers in the USA found self-compassion significantly reduced feelings of exhaustion, along with increased feelings of self-worth, self-control, and organisational belonging (Schabram and Heng, 2021).

Research about self-compassion and social work students is also at its earliest stages – again mainly focused upon the USA (Gottleib and Shibusawa, 2019; Ying, 2009; Ying and Han, 2009). Such studies have also shown self-compassion to be linked to, and associated with, positive mental health outcomes, less stress, and better ability to cope with challenges. Ying (2009) found that among social work students the six key elements of self-compassion were associated with overall competence, although the common humanity element was not related to mental health. Ying (2008) also found the mindfulness element of self-compassion reduced the depressive and anxiety symptoms of students, while Ying (2009) found that over-identification and isolation elements were associated with such symptoms. Ying and Han (2009), again in a study of social work students, found self-compassion positively influenced the stress and coping process; it was associated with less stress, with greater satisfaction when compared to reliance on religious and spiritual beliefs. In one of the few studies to consider cultural competence, Gottleib and Shibusawa's (2019) study of nearly 260 social work students, including over a third "who identified as people of colour", discovered higher rates of self-compassion predicted higher levels of "cultural competence". These findings suggested self-compassion could encourage, could ease, movement towards "cultural competence", with less avoidance of culturally unfamiliar situations, promotion of exploration of personal and professional identities and their possible association with privilege and oppression. However, this research did not comment specifically on those students described as "people of colour", making no comments about explorations either of racism or anti-racism and self-compassion.

In a study with undergraduate students in Ireland, Kotera et al. (2021) discovered self-compassion was positively associated with resilience, engagement in course work, and intrinsic rather than extrinsic motivation for the work. In the UK, in a rare study of social work students that has considered self-compassion, Kotera et al. (2019b) also found it was a significant, independent, negative predictor of mental health symptoms in a sample of nearly 90 students. Self-compassion made greater impact than resilience upon mental health, which led Kotera et al. (2019a, b) to argue for much more attention to be given to self-compassion in social work and social work education.

144 Self-Compassion

Implications for Social Work, Social Work Education, and On-Going Professional Development

As is the case with self-care, self-compassion encourages social workers to give more attention to their emotional needs, to be more sensitive, more responsive to their attitudes and beliefs about themselves. Exploration of the self-compassion concept reveals there are clear parallels to traditional social work values and work with service users. Social workers and practitioners in training are helped to feel greater acceptance of service users, to be more respectful, less judgmental towards them and less critical; they are better able to recognise positives and strengths in service users' situations (Kotera et al., 2019a, b). Self-compassion encourages workers to be more self-accepting, more respectful, and less judgmental in their attitudes to themselves, along with greater recognition of one's own positives and strengths. Recent research about perfectionism among social workers in the UK by Kinman and Grant (2022) highlighted the dangers of practitioners setting, and fixating on, excessively exacting standards, strong self-criticisms, and ruminative, obsessive concern with failing to meet those standards. Added to this can be workers' perceptions of the high expectations of other people both within, and external to, the social work profession, that they will always excel. This, in turn, significantly relates to feelings of stress, inadequacy, inefficacy, social isolation, and cynicism (Kinman and Grant, 2022).

The point is reinforced by the earlier work of Mathew Gibson (for instance, 2013, 2016, 2019) who has drawn attention to the shame and guilt that social workers can feel, while the work of Alessandro Sicora (2019) has explored reflection, with a focus on the mistakes and the errors, made by social work practitioners and students. Indeed, Germer and Neff (2013) have emphasised that self-compassion directly targets shame. As we have seen, self-compassion encourages practitioners to regulate their emotions, to self-soothe, feel less shame, and less guilt, and to be less critical about themselves, placing perceptions of mistakes, errors, and failures into a much broader, wider context of human experience (Wakelin et al., 2021).

Neff (2011) and Miller et al. (2018) have argued the "common human experience" element in self-compassion helps in assisting workers to develop more positive, supportive relationships with colleagues. It is suggested that as workers feel kinder towards themselves and colleagues, they may be better able to be more empathically engaged and be more compassionate in working with service users. While not being discouraged from feeling a sense of responsibility, practitioners can be helped to feel less responsible for situations that are perhaps linked more to the responsibilities of service users, the policies, procedures, and practices of social work agencies, legislative requirements, and national government policies (Gibson, 2019; Miller et al., 2019b). As Miller et al. (2018) point out, the value, and the importance, of self-compassion, as is the case with self-care, should be recognised at institutional levels, as an important part of the identity of the professional social worker – not just as an "adjunct" or "add-on".

Kinman et al. (2019) noted that practitioners in their study felt guilty about prioritising self-compassion, partly seeing it as an "indulgence", while finding it difficult to set aside time for such work. Hence there are extremely important implications here for social work education and social work organisations to give higher priority to the promotion and the facilitation of self-compassion. During the recent coronavirus epidemic, some social work educators have been making more active use of self-compassion. For example, Gates et al. (2020, p.8) who are members of a group of international social work lecturing colleagues, describe their use of self-compassion to inform their teaching and learning practices, and their efforts to model such behaviours when interacting with students online and to "practice... self-compassion [to] counter the emotional and relational impacts of unexpected, rapid and disruptive change".

As we have noted previously, while the social work qualifying curriculum is already crowded with theories, models, and topics competing for limited time and space, developing knowledge and skills surrounding self-compassion is an important, vital task. Equally, opportunities could be made available to qualified social workers to either learn about the concept during on-going professional development or to consolidate existing awareness of self-compassion. Ferrari et al.'s (2019) meta-analysis of self-compassion interventions discovered that group-based work had a significant, large effect on self-compassion, whereas individual "delivery" produced a significant, yet smaller effect. These authors (2019, p.1470) suggest that group-based approaches facilitate an "experiential, lived experience of connection which aligns to the core theoretical framework for self-compassion... to encourage sharing and discussing the personal relevance of [self-compassion], reinforcing common humanity and acceptance of flaws". However, in view of time and priority pressures, Kinman et al., (2019) make an important point by advocating mixed method approaches to learning about the topic, which could involve face-to-face group interactions, blended with online, distance learning opportunities. Social work tutors, practice teachers, line managers, and social work leaders all have a role to play in making a commitment to tasks to assist such developments, while Coaston (2019) provides an excellent, detailed, informative account of the important role of self-compassion in supervision situations.

Therefore, continuing professional development opportunities are needed to maintain, to develop the required knowledge about, and awareness of, self-compassion, which links to the role of agency policies, procedures, and practices in facilitating the use, regular review, and evaluation of self-compassion approaches. This is a task that could well prove daunting, in view of the generally limited opportunities for education and training opportunities for practitioners and line managers in the UK (Turner-Daly and Jack, 2017). Hence opportunities for the development, the growth of learning about self-compassionate approaches, are partly dependent on organisational, managerial, leadership, and supervisory modelling and backing, which goes beyond the individual social worker and social work student, as is the case with the nursing profession

146 Self-Compassion

(Andrews et al., 2020). The aspiration is to establish, to encourage a culture of caring self-kindness and sharing, based upon common human experiences in working together in a mutual community, to reduce feelings of isolation and self-criticism. The ideal would be for a balanced approach to be taken, involving both social work agency, and individual responsibilities, to initiate, develop, and maintain a focus on self-compassion. As we saw in an earlier chapter, a clear danger is too much responsibility might fall on individual practitioners' initiatives, while organisational responsibilities about self-compassion to help workers cope within a context of excessive workloads, competing demands, and limited resources can be neglected (Jennings et al., 2022; Schabram and Heng, 2021).

Some Further Strengths and Limitations of Self-Compassion

Self-compassion is a developing area that, as we have seen, is only just starting to make in-roads into social work education and practice. It is a concept that requires further refinement; many areas require further exploration. For instance, as with self-care, some attention has been given to the impact of Adverse Childhood Experiences on self-compassion, such as disparaging criticisms and rejection by parental figures, "disturbed" family functioning, and insecure attachments (Miller et al., 2019a; Reizer, 2019). This could make it harder for some workers to be self-compassionate. However, developing knowledge and skills about self-compassion could well provide a good opportunity to explore and to reduce the impact of such experiences (Reizer, 2019; Robinson et al., 2016). It might be that self-compassion also has more meaning for those practitioners who experience particularly self-critical, negative beliefs, and attitudes about themselves, set unrealistically high standards, doubt themselves, attribute successes to luck, to other people, to external sources, feel unworthy, fear failure, discount praise, are particularly self-punishing and "hard on themselves" – the imposter phenomena which seems to occur more frequently among social workers than might be expected (Unwin, 2018). Self-compassion offers an opportunity to help such workers feel less isolated, more appreciative of the flaws, the imperfections amongst people generally as "common humanity", in working towards developing kinder attitudes towards themselves (Patzak et al., 2017).

This leads on to the point that workers may have very different feelings about perfectionism, guilt, shame, inadequacy, self-pity, and about a sense of failure, capacity for rumination, sensitivity to suffering, and self-kindness, depending on their personal and professional experiences, their current work location, the cultural and structural context for their work at any particular time (Robinson et al., 2016). Such factors will clearly impact significantly upon workers' capacity for self-compassion. Also, much of the research about self-compassion relies on quantitative approaches. In the UK, more qualitative approaches to such research might be helpful. This would allow individual social workers more freedom to express their perceptions, views, definitions, and interpretations of self-compassion.

From a different perspective, another critical point can be made about self-compassion. It could have the potential to encourage complacency, indifference to making mistakes, excusing faults, errors, and negative experiences, involving a reduced commitment to professional standards in social work (Leary et al., 2007; Wilson and Joyce, 2017). Nevertheless, research on self-compassion with students would suggest this might not be the case; it has been found that self-compassion is not related to a lack of stringency about students' own standards related to academic work and other situations (Leary et al., 2007; Neff et al., 2005). Indeed, these researchers found that those people with elevated levels of self-compassion were *more* likely to be open to perceiving, viewing, and reviewing bad experiences, mistakes, and failures as challenges, as providing motivation and opportunities for learning, for positive re-interpretation and growth.

However, social workers are qualified professionals, responsible and accountable not only to themselves and their own learning, but also to their profession, their agencies, and service users. Social workers can encounter, may have to respond to, serious "uncontrollable", unexpected disappointments, accidents, traumas, tragedies, and losses in their work with service users, where it may well be appropriate to be self-compassionate, to see oneself as "less responsible". Yet, on the other hand, excessive acceptance of complacency, repeated mistakes, and/or errors could lead to restrictions on service users' access to resources, limitations of their rights, flawed judgements, incomplete evaluations, misleading assessments, and poorly informed decision making by practitioners, which could have serious consequences in service users' lives. Hence the suggestion would be that professional practitioners' self-compassion should be exercised with care, especially amongst the small number of social workers who may be lacking in accountability, motivation, or commitment to their professional tasks (Collins, 2016).

One possible, practical starting point might be for practitioners, supervisors, managers, and leaders to assess, to evaluate or re-evaluate their own levels of self-compassion, using one or more of the relevant scales (for example, Gilbert et al., 2017; Gu et al., 2020; Miller et al., 2019a; Neff, 2003a) and, if needed, to consider possible strategies to work on developing more (or less) self-compassion. At the same time, we should acknowledge that Neff's earlier scales have received criticisms. For example, Muris and Petrocchi (2017) criticise the negative indicators that comprise one half of the self-compassion scales, i.e. self-judgement, over-identification, and isolation. They claim these indicators are already known to be related to psychopathology, inflate it, and argue they should be seen as different, distinct, and separate constructs to self-compassion. In turn, Neff refutes these claims in debates with Muris and colleagues in various articles, with Neff et al. (2018) citing supporting research, which validates their approach, while arguing for the vital importance of self-compassion as a holistic construct, requiring a balance between both the positive and negative elements. These disputes have continued to the present time.

148 Self-Compassion

Furthermore, as is the case with resilience and self-care, the self-compassion concept could be criticised for its lack of attention not only to the organisational context of social work, but also to wider, broader, structural matters, including, as previously noted, the severe impact of neoliberalism, austerity, extensive poverty, and unequal opportunities upon social workers (Garrett, 2018). Another important, associated point is that little research seems to have been undertaken to consider the implications of culture for self-compassion and social work (an exception, already noted, is Gottleib and Shibusawa, 2019).

A significant link was found between self-compassion and positive mental health across three different cultures, amongst Thai, Taiwanese, and Americans (Neff et al., 2008). But different, alternative, complex views are presented about culture and self-compassion. Wakelin et al. (2021) argue that most research about self-compassion has focused on white people in Western cultures, despite the discrimination, stress, and adversity faced by ethnic minority groups who therefore may perceive it in diverse ways and may respond differently to self-compassion interventions. These authors and Guan et al. (2021) also note the majority of self-compassion research is not representative, for instance, of Eastern cultures. Yet, others present self-compassion research that has taken place among such cultures (for example, Arimitsu, 2014, 2016; Chio et al., 2021a; Finlay-Jones et al., 2018; Huang et al., 2021; Wong and Mak, 2013, 2016; Wong and Yeung, 2017) and with more diverse populations such as Iranian Muslims, older Chinese women, and LGBTQ adults (Bluth and Neff, 2018). Ferrari et al. (2019) in their meta-analysis also comment on the recent growth in the number of studies demonstrating the efficacy of the self-compassion construct in several cultural contexts. They note the support these studies offer to "the universality of self-compassion [and] whether individuals respond to pain and distress with self-compassion and kindness seems to be important across different cultural contexts" (Ferrari et al., 2019, p.1469).

Nevertheless, other researchers have drawn attention to the point that there are contradictory, conflicting, and contrasting cultural perspectives on self-compassion within countries at national, regional, and local levels (Chio et al., 2021a; Huang et al., 2021). Therefore, culture intersecting with other social divisions, could have an important impact on people's attitudes and commitment to self-compassion. Also, little self-compassion research seems to have been undertaken with Black or Asian people in the USA and especially in the UK, although a recent study of American students found self-compassion resources buffered the impact of depressive feelings associated with racial discrimination (Liu et al., 2020). These points also have relevance to, and important implications for, social workers, in view of their varied cultural, ethnic backgrounds, and the possible impact upon their self-compassion.

Early explorations about gender issues also seem to have been limited, but a meta-analysis and research suggests males are likely to be slightly more self-compassionate than females, but with larger differences between males and females among ethnic minority groups (MacBeth and Gumley, 2012; Yarnell et al.,

2015, 2019). In fact, in most self-compassion research studies the participants are predominantly females. Interestingly, just recently, research on self-compassion and gender has started to move away from looking at differences between males and females to gender role orientation that considers the identification of males and females with "masculine" and "feminine" traits (Patzak et al., 2017; Yarnell et al., 2019). It is argued that most variance in self-compassion occurs not *between* but *within* gender groups, where men and women can associate themselves with, for instance, "masculine", "feminine", "undifferentiated", and "androgynous" characteristics. Yarnell et al. (2019) in their work on gender role orientation found that men and women high in masculinity, femininity, and androgyny tend to have the highest levels of self-compassion. Although self-compassion researchers and theorists seem to come to different conclusions about males, females and self-compassion education and training, the overall conclusion seems to be that both would benefit, for different reasons, for example, to help overcome male reluctance to undertake such training and the greater need for females to develop more self-compassion (Neff et al., 2020; Patzak et al., 2017). However, the implications of sexuality and disability for self-compassion still do not seem clear. Therefore, if research about self-compassion generally is at a quite early stage, then this is even more the case when considering self-compassion and social work, where research is only just beginning about the impact of the structural context and social divisions.

A further criticism of self-compassion is that it may encourage a tendency towards excessive acceptance of suffering in situations that are perceived as outside social workers' control – the idea of accepting "the real world as it is" and "this is the way things are", with little that can be done to change circumstances; a passivity, a neglect, an under-valuing of "righteous anger" and active resistance (Ying, 2009, p.11). This can lead to a danger of passive, acquiescent attitudes towards injustice, wider social discrimination, and underlying oppression (Garrett, 2018; IFSW, 2014). However, clinical psychologists such as Wilson and Joyce (2017) and social work writers such as Iacono (2017) suggest self-compassion approaches are compatible with social justice, anti-discriminatory, and anti-oppressive approaches. Furthermore, recently, Neff (2021) discusses "fierce" self-compassion, particularly related to women, including the importance of "acting on the world" to alleviate suffering and to fight injustice. Nevertheless, it seems likely that debates will continue about the role of self-compassion and its potential, or otherwise, for linkage to social justice, radical, and structural approaches to social work.

Self-compassion can therefore be criticised for an excessive "inward", intrapersonal, and individualistic focus (Dev et al., 2018; Reizer, 2019). There seems to be uncertainty, doubt, and debate surrounding the extent to which self-compassion might involve an excessive "internal" focus, even amongst self-compassion researchers and theorists. Miller et al. (2018; 2019b) argue self-compassion is an intrapersonal rather than an interpersonal concept in contrast to compassion which focuses on others, while Neff's (2003a) original scales also seem to

150 Self-Compassion

measure intrapersonal rather than interpersonal elements (MacBeth and Gumley, 2012). Furthermore, Neff et al. (2005, p.283) state self-compassion "is an internal process that does not necessarily involve interpersonal discussion"; it can be seen as being concerned mainly with one's own feelings; it is significantly associated with processing them internally and emphasising self-reflection, but less so with the expression of feelings in reflective discussions with other professional colleagues and in interactions in on-going professional development opportunities. In fact, Sinclair et al., (2017) and Quaglia et al. (2021) in meta-analyses have criticised self-compassion for its allegedly inward focus, at the expense of considering a multi-faceted model of compassion and expressing compassion for other people. Sinclair et al. (2017, p.177) argue that "the quintessential features of compassion, such as action, altruism, a virtuous response and the use of self in alleviating the suffering of another is lacking". They argue for the need, not to turn inward towards the self, but to turn outward, beyond the self, towards compassion for other people and the suffering of other people. Recently, Dodson and Heng (2021), while noting many strengths in self-compassion approaches, have also argued for a more process-oriented model of self-compassion, more closely linked to wider actions. Also, in recent research, Chio et al. (2021b) and Quaglia et al. (2021), for example, have emphasised the value of combining *both* self-compassion *and* compassion training, an approach also suggested by the implications of Paul Gilbert's work.

On the other hand, Neff, at the same time, also consistently emphasises relatedness, connectedness, and common human experiences as one of the three key elements of self-compassion. She and others (for instance, Gerber et al., 2015; Miller et al., 2018, 2019b; Neff, 2021; Neff, 2003b; Neff and Pommier, 2013) do consider links between self-compassion and compassion, empathic concern for others, altruism, demonstrating understanding of, and acting upon, the suffering and stress of others. Recently, Neff and Germer (2018) and Yarnell et al. (2019) point out self-compassion has both "yin" and "yang" qualities. They argue self-compassion has "yin" qualities such as soothing, comforting, and validating, but also "yang" qualities such as protecting, providing, and motivating action to change, to eradicate suffering. Several other researchers also clearly link self-compassion to recognition of the importance of collective, mutual support, and concern for other people (Gerber et al., 2015; Jennings et al., 2022; Liu et al., 2020; Miller et al., 2019a; Ying, 2009). As we noted previously when discussing self-care, the implication seems to be that, although perhaps initially focused on the self, knowing about, using, and practising self-compassion can also lead to increased empathy, better concern for, and understanding of other people – both service users and colleagues – although Sinclair et al. (2017) suggest there is little empirical evidence of this from service user/client perspectives.

Another aspect that may require further consideration in the future is the relationship of self-compassion to other psychological theories and concepts. As we have already noted, self-compassion is also a key element of self-care, while mindfulness is one of the three key elements of self-compassion. Mindfulness has clearly received and should receive, considerable attention in and of itself, as we shall see in the next chapter. Like self-care, self-compassion is also considered to be part of coping, especially emotional coping (Ewert et al., 2021; Gerber et al., 2015; Lianekhammy et al., 2018; Neff, 2003b; Ying, 2009;). There is a case that coping should receive more attention from social workers (Collins, 2020; Neff, 2003b; Ying and Han, 2009). Self-compassion is also linked to resilience (Kinman and Grant, 2017; Kotera et al., 2019a, b; Miller et al., 2018; Neff, 2009) and support (Miller et al., 2019a, b) – both of which have received considerable attention in the social work literature (Collins, 2020). Therefore, it seems important to see self-compassion not only as a part of self-care, but also, as is the case with other concepts discussed in this book, as having significant links with a range of psychological concepts such as those noted above, as well as other concepts such as self-efficacy (confidence) and control/agency – all of which have important implications for social workers (Collins, 2020; Liao et al., 2021; Yarnell et al., 2019). The message for social workers, social work students, supervisors, and line managers is that it is helpful to see self-compassion as a valuable concept clearly linked to other psychological concepts. There may be dangers in over-emphasising it – in and of itself – at the expense of these other concepts, as well as the need for more recognition of the impact of the institutional and structural context of social work.

Conclusion

We have considered the recent development of the self-compassion concept. We have explored key aspects of self-compassion-mindful awareness, a belief in common humanity involving the connectedness between people's suffering and pain, self-kindness, and their "negative" counterparts. We have discussed recent research undertaken by Neff and others about self-compassion which has produced a wide range of positive findings, including improved life satisfaction, better well-being, improved physical and mental health, reduction in stress, fewer negative feelings, and reduced fears of failure and self-criticism. Research indicates that a wide range of participants have benefitted from education and training in self-compassion, leading to greater acceptance of their thoughts and feelings, stronger motivation for learning, and development of more confidence, as well as better ability to cope with the challenge. Research with a range of helping professionals has also demonstrated many positive gains associated with self-compassion.

As regards social work, as we have seen, research is at an early stage; it has mainly taken place in the USA; it is largely based upon use of Neff's scales. Nevertheless, the benefits of self-compassion are considerable. As is the case with self-care, social workers and social work students are encouraged to give more attention to their wishes, wants, needs, attitudes, feelings, and beliefs

152 Self-Compassion

about themselves. Research with social work students indicates higher levels of self-compassion were associated with positive mental health, less stress, and better coping ability. Research with qualified social workers has found that self-compassion helps practitioners to be more accepting of painful experiences and suffering, it helps them to be less preoccupied with negative thoughts and negative feelings, to feel less isolated, guilty, self-critical, and judgemental, and kinder to themselves, more accepting of making mistakes and errors. In the USA, older, more experienced workers with higher educational qualifications, who were healthier, perceived themselves to be wealthier, and had partners, who were members of a professional association and occupied supervisory roles, were likely to have higher levels of self-compassion. However, studies have indicated that, like self-care, while social workers may "believe" in self-compassion, they only engaged "moderately" in self-compassion activities. There are also indications that expectations of professional standards and behaviour, responsibilities to the profession, social work agencies, and service users impose some important limits on operationalising the concept.

The maintenance and development of learning experiences that are part of self-compassion are seen as a joint venture, a partnership between individuals and their organisations. Without provision and support from the policies, procedures, and practices of educational institutions and social work agencies, along with appropriately knowledgeable, well-motivated supervisory staff, the development of self-compassion could be problematic for both social workers and social work students.

We have also seen that the development of self-compassion in social work in the UK is at a very early stage; more evidence-based and evidence-informed knowledge is required. Furthermore, both generally and in relation to social work, more attention needs to be given, for example, to the impact of discrimination and oppression, culture, ethnicity, gender, sexuality, disability, and religion upon self-compassion. There are also debates about the extent to which the acceptance elements of self-compassion allow opportunity to give sufficient recognition to social justice, to the need for practitioners to make efforts to work to change the political, structural, and institutional context of social work – all of which create a negative climate for the development of self-compassion. Alternatively, one could argue that this discouraging background actually reinforces even further the need for social workers to be self-compassionate.

What is clear is that self-compassion potentially has much to offer social workers, although it is surrounded by critical issues. In the coming years, it will be interesting to see how self-compassion develops in social work, the extent to which, and ways in which, individual social workers practice it, and the extent to which social work education and social work agencies accept their responsibilities to enable, empower, and facilitate self-compassion within a structural context.

References

Andrews, H., Tierney, S. and Sears, K. (2020) "Needing permission: The experiences of self-care and self-compassion in nursing; a constructivist grounded theory study", *International Journal of Nursing Studies*, 101, 1–10.

Arimitsu, K. (2014) "Development and validation of the Japanese version of the self-compassion scale", *The Japanese Journal of Psychology*, 85, 50–59.

Arimitsu, K. (2016) "The effects of a programme to enhance self-compassion in Japanese individuals: A randomised controlled pilot study", *Journal of Positive Psychology*, 11, 559–571.

Babenko, O., Mosewich, A., Lee, A. and Koppula, S. (2019) "Association of physicians' self-compassion with work engagement, exhaustion and professional life satisfaction", *Medical Science*, 7.2, 29.

Baer, R. (2010) "Self-compassion as a mechanism of change in mindfulness-and acceptance-based treatment" in Baer, R. (ed.) *Assessing Mindfulness and Acceptance Processes in Clients: Illuminating the Theory and Practice of Change*, Oakland CA, New Harbinger, pp.135–154.

Beato, A., da Costa, L. and Nogueira, R. (2021) "'Everything is gonna be alright with me': The role of self-compassion, affect, and coping in negative emotional symptoms during coronavirus quarantine", *International Journal of Environmental Research and Public Health*, DOI:10.3390/ ijerph 18042017.

Bell, T., Dixon, A. and Kolts, R. (2017) "Developing a compassionate internal supervisor: Compassion-focussed therapy for trainee therapists", *Clinical Psychology and Psychotherapy*, 24, 632–648.

Bluth, K. and Neff, K. (2018) "New frontiers in understanding the benefits of self-compassion", *Self and Identity*, 17.6, 605–608.

Chio, F., Mak, W. and Yu, B. (2021a) "Meta-analytic review on the differential effects of self-compassion components on well-being and psychological distress: The moderating role of dialecticism on self-compassion", *Clinical Psychology Review*, DOI:10.1016/j. cpr.101986.

Chio, F., Mak, W., Cheung, R., Hsu, A. and Kwan, H. (2021b) "Can compassion to the self be extended to others: the association of self-compassion and other-focused concern", *The Journal of Positive Psychology*, DOI:10.1080/17439760.2021.191638.

Coaston, S. (2019) "Cultivating self-compassion within the supervision relationship", *The Clinical Supervisor*, 38.1, 79–96.

Collins, S. (2016) "The commitment of social workers in the UK: Commitment to the profession, the organisation and service users?", *Practice: Social Work in Action*, 28.3, 139–179.

Collins, S. (2020) *The Positive Social Worker*, London, Routledge.

Delaney, M. (2018) "Caring for the care givers: Evaluation of the effects of an eight-week pilot mindful self-compassion (MSC) training program on nurses' compassion fatigue and resilience", *PLoS One*, 13.11, 1207261.

Dev, V., Fernando, A, Lim, A. and Consedine, N. (2018) "Does self-compassion mitigate the relationship between burnout and barriers to compassion? A cross-sectional quantitative study of 799 nurses", *International Journal of Nursing Studies*, 81, 81–88.

Dev, V., Nagao, A. and Consedine, N. (2020) "Self-compassion as a stress moderator: A cross-sectional study of 1700 doctors, nurses and medical students", *Mindfulness*, 11.5, 1170–1181.

154 Self-Compassion

Dodson, S. and Heng, Y. (2021) "Self-compassion in organizations: A review and future research agenda", *Journal of Organizational Behaviour*, DOI:10.1002/job.2556.

Durkin, M., Beaumont, E., Hollins Martin, C. and Carson, J. (2016) "A pilot study exploring the relationship between self-compassion, self-judgement, self-kindness, compassion, professional quality of life and wellbeing among UK community nurses", *Nurse Education Today*, 46, 109–114.

Eriksson, T., Germundsjo, L., Astrom, E. and Ronnlund, M. (2018) "Mindful self-compassion training reduces stress and burnout symptoms among practicing psychologists: A randomized controlled trial of a brief web-based intervention", *Frontiers in Psychology*, 9, Article 2340.

Ewert, C., Vater, A. and Schroder-Abe, M. (2021) "Self-compassion and coping: A meta-analysis", *Mindfulness*, DOI:https:// doi.org/10.1007/s12671-020-01563-8.

Ferrari, M., Hunt, C., Harrysunker, A., Abbott, M., Beath, A. and Einstein, D. (2019) "Self-compassion interventions and psychosocial outcomes: A meta-analysis of RCTs", *Mindfulness*, DOI:10.1, 1455–1473.

Finlay-Jones, A. Rees, C. and Kane, R. (2015) "Self-compassion, emotion regulation and stress among Australian psychologists: Testing an emotion-regulation model of self-compassion using structural equation modeling", *PLoS ONE*, DOI:10.7, e0133491.doi.10.1371/journal. pone 0133481.

Finlay-Jones, A., Kane, R. and Rees, C. (2017) "Self-compassion online: A pilot study of an internet based self-compassion cultivation program for psychology trainees", *Journal of Clinical Psychology*, 73.7, 797–816.

Finlay-Jones, A., Xie, Q., Huang, X., Ma, X. and Guo, X. (2018) "A pilot study of the 8-week mindful self-compassion training program in a Chinese community sample", *Mindfulness*, DOI:10.1007/s12671-017-0838-3.

Franco, P. and Christie, L. (2021) "Effectiveness of a one-day self-compassion training for pediatric nurses' resilience", *Journal of Pediatric Nursing*, 61, 109–114.

Garrett, P.M. (2018) *Welfare Words*, London, Sage.

Gates, T., Ross, D., Bennett, B. and Jonathan, K. (2020) "Teaching mental health and well-being online in a crisis: Fostering love and self-compassion in clinical social work education", *Clinical Social Work Journal*, DOI:https;//doi.org/10.1007/s10615-021-00786-z

Gerber, Z., Tolmacz, R. and Doron, Y. (2015) "Self-compassion and forms of concern for others", *Personality and Individual Differences*, 86, 394–400.

Germer, C. (2009) *The Mindful Path to Self-Compassion: Freeing Yourself from Destructive Thoughts and Emotions,* New York, Guilford Press.

Germer, C. and Neff, K. (2013) "Self-compassion in clinical practice", *Journal of Clinical Psychology*, 69.8, 856–867.

Gibson, M. (2013) "Social worker shame in child and family social work; inadequacy, failure, and the struggle to practice humanely", *Journal of Social Work Practice*, 28.4, 417–431.

Gibson, M. (2016) "Shame in child and family social work: A scoping review", *British Journal of Social Work*, 46, 549–565.

Gibson, M. (2019) "The role of pride, shame, guilt and humiliation in social service organizations: A conceptual framework from a qualitative case study", *Journal of Social Service Research*, 45.1, 12–128.

Gilbert, P. (2013) *The Compassionate Mind*, London, Robinson.

Gilbert, P., Catarino, F., Duarte, C., Matos, M., Kolts, R., Stubbs, J., Cerasatto, L., Duarte, J., Pinto-Gouveia, J. and Bascan, J. (2017) "The development of compassionate engagement and action scales for self and others", *Journal of Compassionate Health Care*, 4.4, 1–24.

Gottleib, M. and Shibusawa, T. (2019) "The impact of self-compassion on cultural competence: Results from a quantitative study of MSW students", *Journal of Social Work Education*, DOI:10.1080/1043777.2019.1633976.

Grant, L. and Kinman, G. (2020*) Developing Emotional Resilience and Wellbeing: A Practical Guide for Social Workers,* London, Community Care.

Gu, J., Baer, R., Cavanagh, K., Kuyken, W. and Strauss, C. (2020) "Development and psychometric properties of the Sussex-Oxford compassion scales (SOCS)", *Assessment,* 27.1, 3–20.

Guan, F., Wu, Y., Ren, W, Zhang, P., Jing, J., Zhuo, X., Wu, S-T., Peng, K-P. and He, J-B. (2021) "Self-compassion and the mitigation of negative affect in the era of social distancing", *Mindfulness,* DOI:10.1007s12671-021-01674-w.

Gustin, L. and Wagner, L. (2013) "The butterfly effect of caring-clinical nursing teachers understanding of self-compassion as a source of compassionate care", *Scandinavian Journal of Caring Services,* 27, 175–183.

Harris, M. (2017) "'We forget that we are human too': An exploration of the impact of a MBLC (compassion focused mindfulness) on social work staff", *Unpublished M. Sc. Dissertation,* Aberdeen University, Aberdeen.

Henshall, L., Alexander, T, Molyneaux, P., Gardiner, E. and McLellan, A. (2017) "The relationship between perceived organisational threat and compassion for others: Implications for the NHS", *Journal of Clinical Psychology and Psychotherapy*, 25.2, 231–249.

Huang, J., Lin, K., Qiao, S. and Wang, Y. (2021) "The effects of a self-compassion intervention on future-oriented coping and psychological well-being: A randomized controlled trial in Chinese college students", *Mindfulness*, 12, 1451–1458.

Iacono, G. (2017) "A call for self-compassion in social work education", *Journal of Teaching in Social Work,* 5, 454–576.

International Federation of Social Workers (2014) *Global Definition of the Social Work Profession,* Rheinfelden, International Federation of Social Workers.

Jennings, R., Lanaj, K. and Kim, Y. (2022) "Self-compassion at work: A self-regulation perspective on its beneficial effects for work performance and wellbeing", *Personnel Psychology,* 2, 1–31.

Kinman, G. and Grant, L. (2017) "Building resilience in early -career social workers: Evaluating a multi-modal intervention", *British Journal of Social Work*, 47, 1979–1998.

Kinman, G. and Grant, L. (2022) "Being 'good enough': Perfectionism and well-being in social workers", *British Journal of Social Work*, DOI:19.1093/bjsw/bcac010.

Kinman, G. Grant, L and Kelly, S. (2019) "'It's my secret space': The benefits of mindfulness for social workers", *British Journal of Social Work,* 1–20, DOI:10.1093/bjsw/bcz73.

Kotera, Y., Green, P. and Sheffield, D. (2019a) "Mental health attitudes, self-criticism, compassion and role identity among UK social work students", *British Journal of Social Work*, 49, 351–370.

Kotera, Y., Green, P. and Sheffield, D. (2019b) "The role of positive psychology for mental health in UK social work students: Self-compassion as a predictor of better mental health", *British Journal of Social Work,*bcz149, DOI:https://doi.org/doi 10.1093/bjsw149.

Kotera, Y., Tsuda-McCaie, F., Edwards, A-M., Bhandari, D. and Maughan, G. (2021) "Self-compassion and Irish social work students: Relationships between resilience, engagement and motivation", *International Journal of Environmental Research and Public Health,* DOI:10.3390/ijerph 18158187.

Kotera, Y. and Van Gordon, W. (2021) "Effects of self-compassion training on work-related well-being: A systematic review", *Frontiers in Psychology,* DOI:10.3389/fpsyg2021 630798.

156 Self-Compassion

Krieger, T., Martig, D., van den Brink, E. and Berger, T. (2016) "Working on self-compassion online: A proof of concept and feasibility study", *Internet Interventions*, 6, 64–70.

Leary. M., Tate, E., Adams, C., Batts Allen, A. and Hancock, J. (2007) "Self-compassion and reactions to unpleasant self-relevant events: The implications of treating oneself kindly", *Journal of Personality and Social Psychology*, 92.5, 887–904.

Liao, K., Stead, G. and Liao, C. (2021) "A meta-analysis of the relation between self-compassion and self-efficacy", *Mindfulness,* 12, 1878–1891.

Lianekhammy, J., Miller, J., Lee, J., Pope, N., Barhart, S. and Grise-Owens, E. (2018) "Exploring the self-compassion of health care social workers; How do they fare?", *Social Work In Health Care*, 57.7, 563–580.

Liu, S., Li, C-L., Wang, C., Wei, M. and Ko, S. (2020) "Self-compassion and social connectedness buffering racial discrimination on depression among Asian Americans", *Mindfulness*, 11, 762682.

MacBeth, A. and Gumley, A. (2012) "Exploring compassion-a meta-analysis of the association between self-compassion and psychopathology", *Clinical Psychology Review*, 32, 545–552.

Miller, J., Lee, J., Benner, K., Shalash, N., Barhart, S. and Grise-Owens, E. (2018) "Self-compassion among child welfare workers: An exploratory study", *Children and Youth Services Review*, 89, 205–211.

Miller, J., Lee, J., Shalash, N. and Poklembova, Z. (2019a) "Self-compassion among social workers", *Journal of Social Work*, DOI:10.1177/1468017319829404.

Miller, J., Lee, J., Niu, C., Grise-Owens, E. and Bode, M. (2019b) "Self-compassion as a predictor of self-care: A study of social work clinicians", *Clinical Social Work Journal*, DOI:10.10007/s1065-019-00710-6.

Muris, P. and Petrocchi, N. (2017) "Protection or vulnerability? A meta-analysis of the relations between the positive and negative components of self-compassion and psychopathology", *Clinical Psychology and Psychotherapy*, 24, 373–383.

Nadeau, M., Caporale-Berkowitz, N. and Rochlen, A. (2020) "Improving women's self-compassion through an online program: A randomized controlled trial", *Journal of Counselling and Development,* 99.4, 47–59.

Neff, K. (2003a) "The development and validation of a scale to measure self-compassion", *Self and Identity*, 2.3, 223–250.

Neff, K. (2003b) "Self-compassion: An alternative conceptualization of a healthy attitude towards oneself", *Self and Identity*, 2.2, 85–101.

Neff, K. (2009) "The role of self-compassion in development: A healthier way to relate to oneself", *Human Development*, 52.4, 211–214.

Neff, K. (2011) *Self-Compassion: The Proven Power of Being Kind to Yourself*, New York, Harper Collins.

Neff, K. (2021) *Fierce Self-Compassion*, New York, Harper Collins.

Neff, K., Hsieh, Y-P. and Dejitterat, K. (2005) "Self-compassion, achievement goals, coping and academic failure", *Self and Identity*, 4, 263–287.

Neff, K., Pisitungkagarn, K. and Hsieh, Y-P. (2008) "Self-compassion and self-construal In the United States, Thailand and Taiwan", *Journal of Cross-Cultural Psychology*, 39.3, 267–285.

Neff, K. and Germer, C. (2013) "A pilot study and randomized controlled trial of the mindfulness self-compassion programme", *Journal of Clinical Psychology*, 69.1, 28–44.

Neff, K. and Pommier, E. (2013) "The relationship between self-compassion and other-focused concern among college undergraduates, community adults and practicing meditators", *Self and Identity*, 12, 160–173.

Neff, K. and Germer, C. (2018) *The Mindful Self-Compassion Workbook*, New York, Guilford Press.

Neff, K., Long, P., Knox, M., Davidson, O., Kuchar, A. and Breines, J. (2018) "The forest and the trees: Examining the association of self-compassion and its positive and negative components with psychological functioning", *Self and Identity*, 17.6, 627–645.

Neff, K., Knox, M., Long, P. and Gregory, C. (2020) "Caring for others without losing yourself: An adaptation of the mindful self-compassion program for healthcare communities", *Journal of Clinical Psychology*, 76, 1543–1562.

Neff, K., Toth-Kiraly, I., Knox, M., Kuchar, A. and Davidson, O. (2021) "The development and validation of the state self-compassion scale (long-and short form)", *Mindfulness,* DOI:https://doi.org/10.1007/s12671-020-01505-4.

Patsiopoulos, A. and Buchanan, M. (2011) "The practice of self-compassion in counselling: A narrative inquiry", *Professional Psychology: Research and Practice,* 42.4, 301–307.

Patzak, A., Kolllmayer, M. and Schober, B. (2017) "Buffering imposter feelings with kindness: The mediating role of self-compassion between gender-role orientation and the imposter phenomenon", *Frontiers in Psychology*, 8, 1–12.

Quaglia, J., Soisson, A. and Simmer -Brown, S. (2021) "Compassion for self versus other: A critical review of compassion training research", *Journal of Positive Psychology*, 16.5, 675–690.

Raes, F., Pommier, E., Neff, K. and Van Gucht, D. (2011) "Construction and factorial validation of a short form of the self-compassion scale", *Clinical Psychology and Psychotherapy*, 18.3, 250–255.

Reizer, A. (2019) "Bringing self-kindness into the workplace: Exploring the mediating role of self-compassion in the associations between attachment and organizational outcomes", *Frontiers in Psychology*, DOI:10.3389/fpsyg.2019.01148.

Robinson, K., Mayer, S., Allen, A., Terry, M., Chilton, A. and Leary, M. (2016) "Resisting self-compassion: Why are some people opposed to being kind to themselves?", *Self and Identity*, 15.5, 505–524.

Schabram, K. and Heng, Y. (2021) "How other-and self-compassion reduce burnout through resource replenishment", *Academy of Management Journal*, DOI:10.5465 amj2019.0493.

Shapira, L. and Mongrain, M. (2010) "The benefits of self-compassion and optimism exercises for individuals vulnerable to depression", *Journal of Positive Psychology*, 5.5, 377–389.

Sicora, A. (2019) "Reflective practice and learning from mistakes in social work student placement", *Social Work Education*, 38.1, 63–74.

Sinclair, S., Kondejewski, J., Raffin-Bouchel, S., King-Shier, K. and Singh, P. (2017) "Can self-compassion promote health care provider well-being and compassionate care to others? Results of a systematic review", *Applied Psychology: Health and Well Being*, 9.2, 168–206.

Sirois, F., Kitner, R. and Hirch, J. (2015) "Self-compassion, affect and health promoting behaviours", *Health Psychology*, 34.6, 661–669.

Trompetter, H., de Kleine, E. and Bohlmeijer, E. (2017) "Why does positive mental health buffer against psychopathology? An exploratory study on self-compassion as a resilience mechanism and adaptive regulatory strategy", *Cognitive Therapy and Research*, 41.3, 459–468.

Turner-Daly, B. and Jack, G. (2017) "Rhetoric versus reality in social work supervision: The experiences of a group of childcare social workers in England", *Child and Family Social Work*, 22.1, 36–46.

Unwin, J. (2018) "Imposter phenomena and experience levels in social work: An initial investigation", *British Journal of Social Work*, 48.5, 1432–1446.

158 Self-Compassion

Wakelin, K., Perman, G. and Simonds, L. (2021) "Effectiveness of self-compassion-related interventions for reducing self-criticism: A systematic review and meta-analysis", *Clinical Psychology and Psychotherapy*, DOI:10.1002/cpp2586.

Wilson, H. and Joyce, C. (2017) "Modelling imperfection and developing the imperfect self: Reflections on the process of applying self-compassion" in Parry, S. (ed.) *Effective Self-Care and Resilience in Clinical Practice,* London, Jessica Kingsley, pp.33–43.

Wong, C. and Mak, W. (2013) "Differentiating the role of self-compassion components in buffering cognitive personality vulnerability to depression among Chinese in Hong Kong", *Journal of Counselling Psychology,* 60, 162–169.

Wong, C. and Mak, W. (2016) "Writing can heal: Effects of self-compassion writing among Hong Kong Chinese college students", *Asian American Journal of Psychology*, 7, 74–82.

Wong, C. and Yeung, N. (2017) "Self-compassion and posttraumatic growth: Cognitive processes as mediators", *Mindfulness*, 8, 1078–1087.

Yarnell, L., Stafford, R., Neff, K., Reilly, E., Knox, M. and Mullarkey, M. (2015) "Meta-analysis of gender differences in self-compassion", *Self and Identity*, 14.5, 499–520.

Yarnell, L., Neff, K., Davidson, O. and Mullarkey, M. (2019) "Gender differences in self-compassion: Examining the role of gender role orientation", *Mindfulness*, 10.6, 1136–1152.

Ying, Y-W. (2008) "The buffering effect of self-detachment against emotional exhaustion among social work students", *Journal of Religion and Spirituality in Social Work: Social Thought*, 27, 1.2, 131–150.

Ying, Y-W. (2009) Contribution of self-compassion to competence and mental health in social work students", *Journal of Social Work Education*, 45.2, 309–323.

Ying, Y-W. and Han, M. (2009) "Stress and coping with professional challenge in entering masters of social work students: The role of self-compassion", *Journal of Religion and Spirituality in Social Work: Social Thought*, 29, 263–283.

Zessin, U., Dickhauser, O. and Garbade, S. (2015) "The relationship between self-compassion and well-being: A meta-analysis", *Applied Psychology: Health and Well-Being*, 7.3, 340–364.

7
MINDFULNESS

Introduction

In the previous chapter focused on self-compassion we noted that, according to Kirsten Neff (2003, 2011) and others, mindfulness was one of the three core components of self-compassion. In this chapter, we will concentrate our attention on mindfulness. There are countless texts, articles and research works published about mindfulness, with a journal specifically focused on the topic. Nevertheless, there are few books that explore mindfulness and social work, examples being the works of Steven Hick (2009), Matt Boone (2014), and Terry Northcut (2017), published in the USA. In the UK, Mark Hamer's (2006) book touches on some aspects of mindfulness. There are also relatively few articles and pieces of research about mindfulness and social work.

In this chapter, we will consider definitions of mindfulness, critical perspectives that surround it, and its role in the workplace in the UK. We will examine general research findings on the topic as well as research specifically linked to mindfulness training, social work students, and social workers in the USA and the UK. We shall consider different perceptions of the role of mindfulness in social work, debates about it, and criticisms of it, set within educational, organisational, and structural contexts. We will explore ways in which mindfulness might be developed further in social work education at qualifying and post-qualifying levels and in social work agencies. However, first of all, we shall examine definitions of mindfulness.

Mindfulness

Nairn defines mindfulness as "knowing what is happening, while it is happening" (Mindfulness Association, 2013, p.4). This resonates with Salzburg's (2013, p.177)

DOI: 10.4324/9781003112532-8

160 Mindfulness

definition: "being aware of our present moment's experience" without diverting into ruminative, worrying thoughts about either the past or the future, and that of Kabat-Zinn (2004, p.4) who describes mindfulness as "paying attention in a particular way...in the present moment, and nonjudgmentally". Bishop et al. (2004, p.232) consider mindfulness to be "a two-component model consisting of (a) self-regulation...and (b) adopting a particular orientation towards one's experience...characterized by curiosity, openness, and acceptance". One of the important features of mindfulness is that, like a camera zoom lens, it can move between a larger awareness of what is happening such as open monitoring of wide sensory and affective/cognitive fields in the environment and/or a focus of attention on narrower, particular details, such as a given object, sensation, or image (Chiesa, 2013). Mindfulness encourages not only observation and awareness of experiences, but engagement, participation, and involvement in them, without becoming swamped or overwhelmed by them.

Mindfulness can be defined as a state, a practice, and a trait. The *state* of mindfulness is characterised as "an attentive and non-judgemental...monitoring of moment-by-moment cognition, emotion, perception, and sensation" (Garland, 2013, p.440). However, mindfulness is also a *practice* designed to facilitate this state, and a *trait* or disposition that is within a personality and also can be developed over time. Garland (2013, p.440) argues that the interaction of these aspects is integral to mindfulness in that the "recurrent activation of the mindful state via mindfulness practices leaves lasting traces that may accrue into durable changes in trait mindfulness".

While there may be differences in definitions, intention, and motivation, mindfulness can be understood, therefore, as a purposeful practice of training one's mind, consisting of three main core themes: being aware, attending to, and focusing on being in the present, immediate moment, and accepting, not judging, or evaluating the experience (Harris, 2017).

As Harris (2017) also points out, mindfulness has evolved from over 2,500 years of Buddhist teaching, but it has given birth to an industry estimated to be worth over £1 billion in the Unites States. Extensive criticisms have been made of "corporate mindfulness" training programmes as expounded by several American organisations – an approach trenchantly and vigorously criticised by Zack Walsh (2018). The latter vibrantly highlights the dangers of mindfulness being accommodated, annexed, and rebranded to promote neoliberal practices in support of adaptation, and of adjustment, to the status quo rather than changing it, minimising political, social, cultural, and economic dimensions while maximising individual responsibility in an uncritical manner. This, in turn, undermines the role of social welfare and state agencies, turning attention away from social justice.

In Buddhist teaching, mindfulness is the means by which the practitioner develops "awareness and clear comprehension...to recognise the nature of reality" (Salzburg, 2013, p.177), but that reality can be perceived to be dominated by neoliberalism – with no alternative (Walsh, 2018). Secular mindfulness has been criticised for reducing mindfulness to self-help techniques, more concerned with relieving individual stress than developing insights into the true nature of the mind (Bodhi, 2013; Gethin, 2013; Harris, 2017; Nilsson and Kazemi, 2016). It has also been criticised as cultural appropriation, misrepresenting Buddhism and "sterilising it to fit Western agendas" (Dzonsgar Khyentse Rinpoche, 1997, p.3). Nilsson and Kazemi (2016, p.8) suggest mindfulness has become "A self-regulatory practice that enables individuals to adapt to society – enhancing their sense of health and well-being[while]improving the quality of their work and relationships within a western capitalist framework". Boone (2014, p3) cautions that mindfulness risks becoming "yet another superficial salve residing in our self-care medicine cabinets, something to be taken out when times are tough, but not something that fundamentally influences the way we live". As Harris (2017) highlights, this point focuses upon the heart of the commodification and commercialisation of mindfulness, as also seen in the term "McMindfulness", "conveniently side-stepping any serious soul searching into the causes of widespread social suffering" (Purser and Cooper, 2014, para. 3).

However, despite concerns about the appropriation or misinterpretation of sacred teachings, secular mindfulness can be seen as an effective, skilful way of presenting Buddhist ideas, while making them accessible to the secular world (Bodhi, 2013; Gethin, 2013). Harris (2017) notes that Purser and Cooper (2014, para.18) argue secular mindfulness has "extracted the juice from Buddhism", enabling access to the essence of the teachings. Bodhi (2013) argues that Buddhism will inevitably develop new expression in the Western world and, although he warns that secular mindfulness should respect sacred traditions, he concludes that in acting with prudence and compassion, it is important and valid in the task of helping other people. This is seen in the use of mindfulness in the context of the workplace in the UK.

Mindfulness in the Workplace

As interest in mindfulness has grown, more and more organisations have sought to introduce it to their workforce to support staff and/or improve performance (Harris, 2017; Mental Health Foundation, 2010). In the UK, a Mindfulness All-Party Parliamentary Group recommended the use of mindfulness in health, education, and the criminal justice system to support employee well-being, to address absenteeism, occupational stress, and mental ill health (MAPPG, 2015). Interestingly enough in view of earlier comments in this chapter about the possible restrictions, the limitations of mindfulness, its alleged conservatism, its reproduction and perpetuation of neoliberalism and neglect of the structural context, the MAPPG (2015, p.8) also called for the development of mindfulness programmes for public sector staff to "improve organisational effectiveness".

In their integrative review, Good et al. (2016) found that mindfulness was associated with improved functioning in the workplace, attentional stability, improved cognitive capacity and cognitive flexibility. They found mindfulness

162 Mindfulness

linked to reduced reactivity to stress, emotional stimuli, and better relational functioning, including "greater attention to others, better communication, reduced conflict...and greater expression of other-directed emotions, such as compassion and empathy" (Good et al., 2016. p.126). Recent systematic reviews of the empirical literature on mindfulness in the workplace found it to be associated with reduced mental health issues, less stress, improved well-being, resilience, work engagement, and job satisfaction (Bartlett et al., 2019; Lomas et al. 2017, 2018, 2019; Vonderlin et al., 2020). There is, therefore, a developing evidence base suggesting mindfulness is associated with a range of features which can improve employee workplace functioning. Despite the growing research base, MAPPG (2015) cautions that, while the existing research on mindfulness in the workplace is promising, more research is required. For a recent, thought-provoking, extensive consideration of the pros and cons of mindfulness in work contexts, see Choi et al. (2021) and for an example of criticisms of mindfulness and mindfulness research, see Van Dam et al. (2018).

Education and Training for Mindfulness

Neff (2003, 2011) and Stickle (2016) maintain that mindfulness training can foster resilience, enabling practitioners to engage more effectively with the emotional world of the people they work with, without losing perspective. This, they argue, requires self-awareness, a focus on strengths, resources, the ability to regulate one's thoughts and emotions, and being curious and open to experiences. Education for mindfulness involves observing, exploring our thoughts and feelings, to some extent accepting and decentring, detaching from them, being neither engulfed nor over-identified with them, and letting them come, go, and pass by (Bartlett et al., 2019). Mindfulness training can also develop sensitivity to, and awareness of, our repeated habitual reactions when we are in danger of acting automatically, "acting on autopilot", without thinking through, reflecting on, or reappraising these actions.

Mindfulness-Based Interventions (MBIs) are intended to increase compassion and kindness for the self and other people. MBIs are perceived, interpreted, and practiced in a variety of ways. However, many MBIs derive from Mindfulness-Based Stress Reduction courses (MBSR) (Kabat-Zinn, 1991; Rosch, 2015). This is one prominent approach to mindfulness training; it is the best known; it is used more often than other approaches in the education of social workers, sometimes in a shorter form, with different means of delivery, for instance, taught partly online, and/or with additional exercises (Beer et al., 2019). For example, in Kinman et al.'s (2019) research study in the UK, the eight-week-long mindfulness course for qualified social workers was an adapted form of MBSR and Mindfulness-Based Cognitive Therapy (MBCT). This included practices and reflective exercises linked to body scans and breathing to help reduce the impact of anxiety, worry, and rumination; it was designed to improve well-being.

The "standard", or more "traditional" MBSR course entails eight weekly sessions of about two and a half hours each, often accompanied by about forty-five minutes of personal "homework" practice for most days in the week. Such courses often incorporate meditation practices involving awareness of the present moment and the surrounding environment, giving attention to breathing, to body sensitivity linked to sound, sight, smell, and taste, along with a blend of didactic approaches, experiential learning, and shared group discussion, with physical exercises drawn from yoga (McCusker, 2020). Attention to breathing entails becoming aware of the sensations of breathing, for example, deep, shallow, long, and short breaths. Body scanning focuses attention on sensations in each part of the body. This involves thoughts and feelings about the body parts, which may be associated with pain, tension, or relaxation. Body stretching entails scanning each part of the body while stretching and becoming more aware of thoughts, feelings, movement, and non-movement.

MBSR courses aim to instil hope, to foster mutual aid, and individual and collective empowerment (Gockel et al., 2019). They are founded on the belief that the capacity for mindfulness exists in every person. The strengths-based perspectives associated with MBSR fit well with strengths-based approaches to social work, for instance, with the emphasis on "there is more right with[you] than is wrong with [you]", along with the idea that challenges and difficulties can be worked on, and worked through (Santorelli and Kabat-Zinn, 2009, p.2).

Similar to MBSR is the Mindfulness-Based Living Course (MBLC), as used in Harris' (2017) course for social workers, which also takes place over eight weeks in sessions of about two hours, with an introduction session and a follow-up session one month after the ending of the course (Mindfulness Association, 2016b). A day of silent practice can also be included between weeks six and seven. The course is based on the Mindfulness Association's Level 1 Mindfulness Training (Mindfulness Association, 2016a). Participants are introduced gradually to a range of mindfulness practices including sitting meditation, body scan, mindful movement, and mindful walking. While the course is largely similar to other MBIs, the MBLC has a more explicit focus on compassion, self-compassion, kindness, and acceptance (Mindfulness Association, 2011). A 'three circles' model also focuses on emotional regulation, responding to over-stimulation, and providing active soothing and contentment systems that help maintain a balanced approach (Gilbert, 2013; Gilbert and Choden, 2013; Harris, 2017).

In previous chapters, we have drawn attention to various scales which might be of interest to readers and can be used to "measure" the concepts we have discussed, as part of education and training experiences. Two of the most popular mindfulness scales are Brown and Ryan's (2003) Mindfulness Awareness and Attention Scale which is focused on one characteristic – awareness – and Baer et al.'s (2006) Five Facets of Mindfulness Scale which considers the dimensions: observing, describing, acting with self-awareness, non-judgement of, and non-reactivity to, inner experience. However, while several mindfulness scales

164 Mindfulness

exist, they have been criticised by researchers on account of the varied factors and mechanisms associated with mindfulness. For instance, Grossman and Van Dam (2011, p.226) argue because "there is ...no gold standard that can be used to evaluate questionnaires purporting to measure mindfulness...we cannot know whether a questionnaire reliably measures some aspects of mindfulness". The suggestion is that alternative approaches might be used, for example, in-depth interviews, a focus on outcome measures, and specification of the effects of mindfulness and the longer-term changes which can occur as a result of the practice and process of mindfulness (Grossman and van Dam, 2011; Purser and Milillo, 2015; Vonderlin et al., 2020).

Mindfulness Education and Training for Health-Care Workers and Others

Health care and education are areas that have received particular attention in workplace research about mindfulness, while less attention has been given to the impact of mindfulness on performance in other work settings. In considering rare studies which have examined service user experiences of working with health-care workers following mindfulness-based programmes, Dobkin et al. (2016) pointed out that clinicians who scored high on mindfulness were more likely to engage in service user-centred communication. They demonstrated more interest in, and gave more attention to, the service user as a person, made more effort to understand their feelings and stories, showing a better understanding of their illnesses, while also giving more attention to their social contexts. The workers reported giving more attention to service users' concerns, particularly listening more carefully, offering more empathy, reduced judgmental attitudes, increased positive regard, more self-control, less need to control other people, reduced emotional reactions, and improvements in handling conflict. McCorquodale's (2015) review of the literature also suggests mindfulness can enhance professional practice in health care, contributing to reflective and relational work, emotional attunement, and intuitive knowledge. In an interesting study of health-care professionals, Moll et al. (2015) found that health-care workers participating in a mindfulness programme were initially primarily concerned with reducing *intrapersonal* stress, with less than one in ten interested in its impact on *interpersonal* interactions. However, after completing the programme, more than half of the participants referred to its social impact and interpersonal interactions with service users, colleagues, and family. Wasylkiw et al. (2015) discovered health-care managers also benefitted from mindfulness training, with participants reporting reduced stress, as well as improved work–life balance, and leadership effectiveness.

Mindfulness courses have also been effective in reducing stress, anxiety, burnout, and emotional exhaustion in nursing staff, and in increasing job control, emotional regulation, and use of emotional support (Baer et al., 2012; Cohen-Katz et al., 2005; MacKenzie et al., 2006).

In comprehensive and detailed meta-analyses of research with health-care professionals and students, Wasson et al. (2020) and Conversano et al. (2020) discovered mindfulness-based interventions improved compassion and self-compassion. They also found important support for the idea of flexibility, of differences, in the format and implementation of mindfulness programmes, i.e., the validity of a range of sessions, hours and location, including home-based practices in a variety of formats, with the most significant changes occurring in organisational-based experiences. The value of the experiences of both very brief, so-called "lower doses" as well as "higher doses" of more in-depth mindfulness training was emphasised. These meta-analyses suggested mindfulness interventions with health-care staff could be implemented with an expectation that improvements would be seen in levels of stress, depression, and anxiety, with the effects being maintained and strengthened over time.

Flook et al. (2013) also found teachers who had received mindfulness training showed significant reductions in stress and burnout, improved work performance, and increased self-compassion. A systematic review of teaching mindfulness to teachers reported mindfulness-based interventions showed the strongest promise in their positive effects on emotional regulation, while increased emotional awareness, emotion recognition, and understanding were also helpful (Emerson et al., 2017).

Psychotherapists in training following mindfulness programmes received higher ratings from service users related to their ability to communicate clearly, to establish and maintain therapeutic relationships, and solve problems (Irving et al., 2009). Amongst therapists and counsellors, including some social workers, Martin-Cuellar et al.'s (2018) research findings indicated mindfulness was significant in supporting participants' compassion satisfaction and in acting as a protective factor for practitioners who worked with traumatised service users. They pointed out that the evidence of many studies indicated mindfulness was significant in decreasing clinicians' negative emotions, anxiety, and rumination, emphasising a worker's ability to concentrate better, and to give closer attention to service users' concerns in counselling. Martin-Cuellar et al. (2018) went on to cite evidence that mindfulness experiences also enabled counsellors to practice more effectively their skills, such as non-verbally attending, using open-ended questions, reflecting on feelings and other skills, which clearly have relevance for the day-to-day work of social workers.

However, not all research about mindfulness training in the workplace has had positive outcomes. One example is the work of Brooker et al. (2013) with staff employed in the disability sector. They discovered participants positively evaluated the training programme, and reported growing awareness of the signs, the sources of stress, accompanied by positive changes in self-care, attitudes, behaviours, and interactions with colleagues and service users. They also found significant increases in positive affect. However, job satisfaction declined, perceived stress, anxiety, and negative emotional symptoms increased significantly, while other aspects did not change significantly, such as rates of depression,

166 Mindfulness

burnout, compassion satisfaction, compassion fatigue, and four out of five mindfulness facets – describing, awareness, non-judgment, and non-reactivity. The authors claimed some of the "negative" results following the mindfulness training involved participants developing increasing awareness of the adverse impact of workplace settings, circumstances, negative emotions, and feelings they experienced which, while not changing setting and circumstances, were seen as "the first step towards positive change" (Brooker et al., 2013, p.133). Hence, mindfulness training can sensitise employees more extensively and deeply, raising their consciousness, and their awareness of organisational cultures and climates which may support negativity and undesirable behaviours.

Mindfulness and Social Work Education

The previous examples indicate the different, varied approaches to mindfulness training which can make it difficult to compare research findings (Beer et al., 2019). Consequently, there are also a variety of approaches to learning about mindfulness in qualifying and post-qualifying social work education and training. Gockel and Deng (2016, p.234) point out the breadth, the range of such possibilities, observing "there is no one monolithic model for integrating mindfulness training into social work education". They suggest

> each approach will have its own particular benefits and limitations…the best fit for any one situation will depend on the instructor's goals, the course goals, the instructor's training and experience with mindfulness, the nature of the student population, the particular format of the course and the unique context of the programme
>
> *(Gockel and Deng, 2016, p.234).*

In addition, while there are clearly "special", specific, particular aspects of knowledge and skills surrounding mindfulness such as developing awareness through meditation and giving attention to breathing and body, it seems helpful to consider existing learning already familiar to social workers that might transfer to learning about mindfulness (McCusker, 2021). Some of the core elements of mindfulness such as accepting, and not judging one's experiences and situations, link in closely with some of the basic, traditional values of social work, albeit with slightly altered meanings, where acceptance and non-judgmental approaches are more closely linked to working with the behaviours of service users rather than one's own attitudes and behaviours. The idea is that the social work student or social worker is not a "tabula rasa", a blank screen, but has existing experiences that may help (or hinder) learning about mindfulness (Kessen and Turner, 2016). Another example is learning about interview skills in social work courses, which usually includes an emphasis on being highly attentive, on very carefully listening to service users, on making sensitive, empathic responses and, possibly, on the counselling skill of immediacy – the focus on the here-and-now feelings of the worker in response to interactions with service users. In mindfulness the focus initially is more about concentration upon, being more attentive to oneself, listening carefully to oneself, and being empathic in response to one's own feelings and thoughts.

Furthermore, social work courses also place considerable emphasis on reflection and reflective approaches, the development of self-awareness throughout the course in behaviours in both academic and fieldwork contexts, in supervision, in written assignments, and in fieldwork placement reports. Reflection and self-awareness are also key components of mindfulness, as well as social work (Fieze and Faver, 2019; Richards et al., 2010). Thus, social work students and social workers are likely to approach mindfulness with foundations for understanding some of the concepts that they will encounter. Indeed, some practitioners may also already have undertaken or experienced formal or informal learning opportunities specifically about mindfulness before undertaking such experiences as part of a qualifying social work course, or post-qualifying learning experience, although little information is available about this point.

Also, as we have seen consistently and persistently throughout the previous chapters, single theoretical concepts clearly cannot exist alone. Mindfulness education and training is one approach that is said to comprise part of a "tool box" or "tool kit" among several inter-related concepts, such as knowledge and understanding of anti-discriminatory, anti-oppressive approaches, stress, resilience, coping, support, and self-confidence (Kinman et al., 2019; Maddock et al., 2021) These topics have been, and are being, explored by several writers and researchers (for example, Collins, 2007, 2017, 2020; Grant and Kinman, 2014).

Mindfulness in Social Work: The Research Evidence

While mindfulness for health professionals has received considerable attention in the research literature, the same cannot be said for social work (Beer et al., 2019; Harris, 2017). Trowbridge and Lawson's (2016, p.118) systematic review of the literature found limited evidence about the use of mindfulness by social workers, then identifying only ten papers which, offered a "meagre glimpse" into such practices; they concluded the existing evidence was "statistically limited, and low level", highlighting the need for more robust, systematic research. More recently, the overall conclusion is that the empirical literature on mindfulness for social workers is still limited (Beer et al., 2019). What follows in this section is an examination of some of the research literature.

Mindfulness and Social Work Students

For many, the focus has been on how mindfulness can benefit social work students, better preparing them for practice (Grant and Kinman, 2012; McCusker, 2021). Birnbaum's (2005) study of Israeli social work students who attended up to four mindfulness meditation sessions, found the outcomes included improved

168 Mindfulness

emotional regulation, self-awareness, self-reflection, and self-acceptance. In later research following an eight-week course, Birnbaum (2008) again found participants experienced improvements in their capacity to regulate emotions, to cope with intense emotions, and to gain respite from excessive demands. Mindfulness, she argued, created an inner reflective space in which students could safely explore feelings, conflicts, and dilemmas. Napoli and Bonifas's (2011) research produced similar findings while noting the increased quality of life, but no decrease in perceived stress. On the other hand, Ying (2009) also explored the impact of mindfulness upon social work students, discovering mindfulness to be associated with reductions in perceived stress, negative emotional contagion, and emotional exhaustion.

Goh (2012) found students' listening, communication and engagement skills improved following mindfulness training, with a reduction of mind wandering, multi-tasking thoughts and excessive thinking ahead. Students in Gockel et al.'s (2013) research about very brief interventions indicated mindfulness was beneficial in developing self-awareness, non-judgmental attitudes, confidence in remaining attentive and making emotional connections with service users. Bonifas and Napoli's (2014) study of the impact of a 13-week mindfulness course on students found improved quality of life, and improved coping and stress management skills, although, again, there were no significant reductions in perceived stress itself. Also, following a mindfulness-based course, Lee and Himmelheber (2016) discovered significant increases in students' mindful practices such as observational skills, acceptance, and reduction of excessive emotional reactions. At a Scottish university, Howie et al. (2016) offered a four-week long mindfulness course to final-year social work students. Participants noted personal and professional benefits, including decreased anxiety, better sleep, increased awareness, growing recognition of the importance of self-acceptance and self-compassion. Constantine Brown et al. (2017) discovered students with lower levels of mindfulness had higher levels of compassion fatigue, concluding that mindfulness protected against compassion fatigue.

In a study in Northern Ireland, Roulston et al. (2018) found significant, positive changes in stress levels, well-being, and resilience following mindfulness training, but such training did not appeal to a number of students, although the reasons for this were not explained. Furthermore, not all studies of social work students and mindfulness have been "positive". For instance, in the USA, both Ying (2008) and Kessen and Turner (2016) noted MSW students' mindfulness levels *decreased* during their final year of study, although in the latter study it seemed students did not actually receive mindfulness-based training. In their research, Trowbridge and Lawson (2016) expressed doubts about social work students' carry over of the use of mindfulness into full-time work after qualification.

Nevertheless, earlier, Gockel et al. (2013) found students had been willing and able to follow-up course-based learning experiences with important, regular, home-based practices four months afterwards. Impressively, nearly one half practised mindfulness either every day or every other day; over a third pursued weekly practice, with only one quarter practising less than weekly. Griffiths et al. (2019) went on to note several studies have indicated that students continued to use mindfulness techniques after making the transition to full-time employment. In the UK, McCusker (2021) conducted small-scale qualitative research with students, and followed up six months later into their initial transition to newly qualified social workers. Critical framing of mindfulness encouraged reflective forms of working in three ways. Firstly, validating the importance of self-care and developing awareness of internalised oppression in an organisational, social, and cultural context related to gender, mental health, and disability. Secondly, better mitigation of stress and role conflict. Thirdly, supporting engagement with service users. Regarding the latter point, participants reported enhanced awareness of their emotional states and their potential negative impact on interactions with service users. Students were helped to become more reflective about emotionally demanding situations, including dealing with service users' anger and minimising blame, with encouragement to identify broader social factors impacting service users, such as trauma and negative labelling. As with other studies, mindful practices provided participants with an opportunity to set boundaries, to contain, to not become overwhelmed by negative emotional experiences.

Also in the UK, Maddock et al.'s (2021) small-scale study of a six-week online programme, undertaken during the COVID-19 pandemic with students from two universities, produced positive findings similar to previous research. These included significant reductions in stress, burnout, anxiety, and rumination, along with increases in mental health, well-being, self-compassion, and various aspects of related core mindfulness skills, linked to, for instance, attention giving, emotion regulation, acceptance, and non-judgement. The programme was felt to be particularly successful because of the way it combined didactic input, application of mindfulness theory, experiential learning about mindful practice, and integration with social work practice through case studies and role-plays.

Mindfulness and Social Workers

As Trowbridge and Lawson (2016) and Beer et al. (2019) highlight, there is less empirical literature available relating mindfulness to more experienced, qualified social work professionals. For instance, Thomas (2012) and Thomas and Otis (2010) in their research with over 170 social workers in the USA discovered elevated levels of mindfulness played a significant role in reducing personal distress, compassion fatigue, burnout and in increasing compassion satisfaction. McGarrigle and Walsh's (2011) smaller scale, mixed-methods study on the impact of an eight-week course, also found significant reductions in perceived stress, accompanied by increases in dispositional, trait mindfulness among the participants, who also spoke of increased awareness of stress and coping strategies, the necessity for self-care, accompanied by the need for the workplace to allow space and time to practice mindfulness.

170 Mindfulness

In Canada, Crowder and Sears (2017) explored the impact of an eight-week mindfulness programme on social workers using a control group, along with a follow-up group after six months. They found the mindfulness group showed significant reductions in perceived stress and risk of burnout, alongside increases in self-compassion, job satisfaction, and ability to manage emotions, while identifying less with negative thoughts and emotions. Participants also spoke of being more "present", more attentive, "in the moment", with service users, along with more positive relationships with colleagues and supervisors. They experienced improved sleep, energy levels, and well-being. In a shorter, two-day workplace-based course with paediatric social workers in the USA, Trowbridge et al. (2017) discovered significant pre- and post-differences in outcomes related to decreases in secondary traumatic stress, increases in mindful attention, awareness, and practitioners' belief in their ability to care.

In Scotland, Harris (2017) researched an eight-week course for social workers employed by one local authority. Findings again included increased awareness of stress and significant decreases in perceived stress. Participants had more realistic, balanced expectations and perceptions of work; they could focus, they could concentrate better in the workplace on particular, specific tasks without becoming distracted by other, competing thoughts and tasks. They were sensitive to, and contained their emotions more readily, while also managing their workloads more effectively. They perceived improved listening and relationship skills in interactions with service users. They also experienced improved sleep patterns, higher levels of self-compassion, self-acceptance, and enhanced self-awareness.

Kinman et al. (2019) in research with social workers in the UK, also incorporated both pre- and post-tests linked to a mindfulness training programme of eight weeks, while considering its impact on resiliency resources. The researchers observed increases in emotional self-efficacy, psychological flexibility, self-compassion, and compassion satisfaction, with reductions in compassion fatigue and perceived stress. They also suggested participants were calmer, could concentrate more on the present moment, manage emotions better, were better able to recognise the value, the importance, and make use of, breaks in the working day.

Finally, during the recent COVID-19 pandemic, a study of practitioners in Turkey who followed a four-week mindfulness-based programme reported statistically significant increases in psychological flexibility and self-compassion, accompanied by lower rates of depression, compared to a control group at post-test and one month follow-up. However, differences in stress and anxiety were not statistically significant (Hosseinzadeh Asl, 2021)

One key focus of mindfulness on self-awareness, emotional containment and "holding" is of particular interest, given the extent to which self-awareness and emotional regulation is highlighted in the social work literature as a key component of resilience (Adamson et al., 2014; Grant and Kinman, 2014). Adamson et al. (2014) state that self-awareness is fundamental for resilient social workers, while Grant and Kinman (2014) describe it as one of the most

Mindfulness **171**

accurate predictors of resilience. Thus, as participation in mindfulness courses contributes to increased self-awareness; this is one way in which social workers can build and can sustain resilience in practice. Furthermore, Bogo et al. (2017) have also identified the importance, the role and utility of mindfulness in initial and post-qualifying social work education, through research which again indicates it increases self-awareness and emotional regulation. Therefore, mindfulness can address emotional factors, which may interfere with self-efficacy or confidence in performing social work roles and tasks, thus helping practitioners with both high and low levels of confidence to improve the overall quality of their work, with a particular focus on their interactions with service users. Hence mindfulness would seem to have an important role in developing students' and workers' self-confidence, as well as their resilience.

In addition, in their personal and professional lives, many social workers have also spoken about taking on too much individual responsibility (for example, see Harris, 2017; Kinman et al., 2019). In contrast, mindful, resilient, and self-confident, social workers seem better able to manage expectations, to be clearer and more realistic about what they can achieve (Beddoe et al., 2013). Participation in mindfulness courses appears to help facilitate these resilient capabilities, helping staff regain a better, more balanced perspective on their role, to step back from an over-involvement in work that risks excessive focus on the responsibility of the individual social worker and emotional exhaustion.

Organisational Perspectives

As we have already noted in previous chapters, most social workers often work within social work agencies where there is usually considerable pressure. Although mindfulness courses clearly have a preventative, reactive role to play in facilitating social workers' endeavours to cope, to develop resilience and self-confidence, this does not alter the organisational context of social work, unless significant numbers of practitioners have participated in such courses and try to influence the culture and practices of their social work agency. Leaders of social work agencies, line managers, and team colleagues need to have a commitment to initiate, to support, and to develop an organisational culture and climate in which knowledge, understanding of, and skills in mindfulness approaches can thrive (Choi et al., 2021; Liu et al., 2020). It is essential that appropriate opportunities be provided for this (Beer et al., 2019; Grant and Kinman, 2014; McGarrigle and Walsh, 2011; Trowbridge et al., 2017). The intention is that, like self-care, while mindfulness practices are, in part, an individual's responsibility, they are also a responsibility of the social work agency – one that assists workers to undertake mindfulness experiences not only in their own time but also in work time, with the sanction and the approval of the organisation. Interesting points have been raised by Shier and Graham (2011) and Lynn and Mensinga (2015) about social workers approaching mindfulness as a "personal" interest and how this "fits" with work as a practitioner and a professional knowledge base. Encouragement

172 Mindfulness

to work on further blending a "personal" interest with professional practice is endorsed by support from the social work agency.

There is also an educational task to be undertaken in providing more opportunities to learn about mindfulness as part of on-going post-qualifying education, opportunities for practice teachers, workers, and their managers to either start to learn, to experience more about mindfulness, and/or to consolidate their existing learning about it. One way of doing this is that leaders of social work organisations might sanction, provide, promote, and encourage attendance at mindfulness-based courses as part of professional development. Providing opportunity and permission to attend, while facilitating motivation and engagement with mindfulness could be seen as important as a sign of appreciation of, and care for, staff. In turn, development of mindfulness skills could be encouraged such as attention giving and awareness, accompanied by other skills linked to coping and control. A mindfulness course can provide a safe space, a time to reflect, to share common issues both as people and as professional practitioners, moving towards more self-acceptance and confidence in dealing with demanding work situations.

Furthermore, as we have noted, it can clearly be difficult for individual, isolated practitioners who either have experienced or who do experience mindfulness training, to share this and make an impact upon their workplace, to change the functioning of organisations and teams. While they can work on themselves, they may well have problems in changing workplace perceptions of mindfulness, without the support of colleagues and line managers. Rupprecht et al. (2019) emphasise the interactions of individuals, teams, and organisations to use mindfulness to help reduce conflict, improve inter-personal relationships, to develop an awareness of problems in the workplace while endeavouring to resolve them. Rupprecht et al. (2019, p.33) provide a definition of *team* mindfulness "as collectively paying attention to… team experiences and their underlying objectives, tasks, roles, and structures in a …consistent and non-judgmental way". Drawing parallels with individual mindfulness through reflection and attention to the present moment, collective awareness of organisational culture, climate and purpose, performance and problems, teams can work to develop more effective functioning (Liu et al., 2020). This would also involve mindful line managers, along with mindful workplace leaders whose leadership would encourage mindfulness, humility, altruism, open and honest discussion, and in creating improved cohesion, optimism, hope and feelings of confidence in teams. Hence the ideal is to develop a multi-level model of mindfulness in social work organisations which engages individual social workers, teams, line managers and leaders, rather than just self-selected individuals with a somewhat restricted interest in practising mindfulness (Choi et al., 2021).

Possible Educational Developments

In the USA and the UK, it is understood that a high percentage of medical schools include explorations of mindfulness within their curricula. So, questions

Mindfulness **173**

could be asked about the teaching of, learning about, mindfulness in qualifying social work educational programmes. As is the case with other concepts discussed in this book, should these learning opportunities take place in stand-alone workshops or be integrated into other existing core modules such as social work theory, or in "new" modules, based around stress and its alternatives? Issues also exist also, as with the other concepts previously discussed, about the extent to which such opportunities should be of a mandatory or voluntary nature, with some literature and research suggesting the former (for example, Maddock et al., 2021) and others, the latter (for instance, Gockel and Deng, 2016; Roulston et al., 2018). A further issue surrounds whether there is a need for formal assessment through particular learning assignments about mindfulness, although Gockel and Deng (2016) argue against this. Although these various issues are clearly important, a practical point is that mindfulness will undoubtedly compete for attention in the already overcrowded social work education curriculum in the UK, along with other topics that have strong claims for attention. It remains to be seen if mindfulness either can, or will, start to occupy a more prominent position in social work curricula.

Those who teach, those who help people to learn about mindfulness "are expected to embody mindful attention, curiosity [and]acceptance…creating a warm and responsive environment" (Santorelli and Kabat-Zinn, 2009 in Gockel et al., 2019, p.284). At the same time, Rupprecht et al. (2019) importantly point out that mindfulness educators should not just be "experts" in, and just focus on, mindfulness, but also be knowledgeable and skilled in making links between mindfulness practices, organisational functioning, and group dynamics – the important contexts within which such learning is located and takes place.

Educational tasks surrounding mindfulness could take place either through face-to-face contact in "traditional" MBSR eight-week courses taking place once per week, or in modified versions of MBSR courses, or via shorter, or much shorter courses, "blended" learning, telephone apps or online experiences (see, for instance, Beer et al., 2019; Kinman et al., 2019; Maddock et al., 2021; Trowbridge et al., 2017). A great deal depends on the motivation, commitment to, and belief in, mindfulness learning experiences on the part of practitioners and on the quality of institutional provision. Also, as Bartlett et al. (2019) point out, the demands of mindfulness training should not involve substantial additions to existing workload demands – a difficult balance to achieve.

Furthermore, there is clearly a need to undertake more research about mindfulness and social work. This could, for example, involve larger samples of students and workers in a wider range of settings, including more males, more ethnic minorities, more (dis)abled people, and more LBGTQ representation. Following participants' attendance at courses, there is a need to make more use of particularly qualitative, and quantitative research, pre-tests, post-tests, and control groups with those who have not undertaken mindfulness training, with more consistent, specific measures of mindfulness levels, more focus on the impact of mindfulness on practitioners' stress levels, longer-term follow-up interviews

174 Mindfulness

beyond a few months to assess the maintenance of changes, or otherwise. In particular, it is important to explore further the complexities of the direct effects of mindfulness education on practitioners' interaction with wider structural perspectives, relationships within the workplace, with team members, colleagues, supervisors and, most importantly, practices with families and service users. Indeed, there is an especial need to consider the impact of mindfulness training experiences upon social workers' interactions with service users, from the service user perspective.

Some Ethical and Critical Questions, Individuality and Wider Perspectives

Chiesa (2013) reminds us that mindfulness is associated with ethical developments which involve not only "guarding" oneself to act in the service of others, but also "guarding" people more generally by actively practising patience, loving kindness, and mindfulness. Such ethical development is seen as a vital component in Buddhist mindfulness, which is in danger of getting either neglected or lost (Choi et al., 2021). It involves the eightfold path to enlightenment, moving towards the alleviation of the causes of people's suffering and, ideally, the end of suffering. The eightfold path embraces several "right" elements, one of which is right mindfulness (Ovrelid, 2008). Right mindfulness provides an overall framework for re-calling and for remembering one's motivation, experiences, and skilled and unskilled behaviours. Other elements include morality linked to ethical behaviour, i.e., right livelihood, intention, speech and action, right commitment to understanding, to working on suffering, right effort involving maintaining and developing skills such as concentration and, finally, wisdom associated with right view, thoughts, and intentions surrounding mindfulness. For a more detailed examination of these aspects see Purser and Milillo (2015). Walsh (2017) emphasises the need to give much more attention to mindfulness as right livelihood, which has positive implications for the social work profession, with its concern for benevolence, doing no harm and for the good and well-being of people generally. Hence, mindfulness practice is not necessarily seen as ethically neutral.

Therefore, mindfulness can involve, contrary to some beliefs, judgements of what is considered ethical, "good" and "skilful" (Bodhi, 2013; Chiesa, 2013; Gethin, 2013; Ovrelid, 2008; Purser and Milillo, 2015). Inevitably these terms are open to differing perceptions, to varying interpretations, according to culture and context. They reveal tensions, paradoxes, and contradictions in view of earlier comments about core aspects of mindfulness related to acceptance and to suspension of judgment, but social work practice also reveals tensions, paradoxes, and contradictions. At times, social workers will suspend judgment, will observe, be open to experiences, and communicate acceptance in their behaviours in interview situations in counselling or helping roles. But on other occasions, in other roles and settings, practitioners will be more likely to make formal

Mindfulness **175**

judgments, be required to compile evaluations and assessments, and provide recommendations and decisions in reviews and formal reports for panels and courts. The point here is again that mindfulness may be labelled, may be stereotyped for passivity, "neutrality", detachment, and inaction, when this is not always the case.

Furthermore, as we saw earlier in the chapter, there are different perceptions of the mindfulness concept in the approaches taken to its alleged focus on individuality and consideration of its potential for developing a more critical, radical perspective, linking it further to social justice and anti-oppressive approaches. This is a disputed area with varying interpretations of the focus and potential of mindfulness. Mindfulness has been criticised for so-called extensive "navel gazing", for focusing on an "observer" role, for being non-political and being primarily concerned with self-help (for instance, Rosencrantz et al., 2019; Walsh, 2018). When exploring mindfulness and social work recently, Malcom Payne (2020, p.74) reached rather limited, and limiting, conclusions about the practice implications of mindfulness for social work "shifting you from 'acting'[and] 'doing'...towards 'being' and 'feeling', while cautioning "Restrain your desire to take action... Mindfulness does not seek to... develop critical analyses of action...or thoughts". Malcolm Payne (2020, p.74) continues "Do not move on... to getting clients to plan actions or carry out changes... it is not part of mindfulness. If you need to act or clients want to make changes, make that explicitly a non-mindfulness part of the social work process". Choi et al. (2021) endorse this comment, relating it to mindfulness generally, suggesting that mindfulness does not really examine decision making and action elements. In their book chapter on mindfulness and social work, Parkes and Kelly (2014, p.114) also warn workers to "resist the temptation to change how things are", while Malcolm Payne (2020, p.70) goes on to argue "proposing mindfulness as a response to... problems of oppression or poverty...can seem insubstantial...it does not help people solve broader social or relationship issues".

Taking this further, as we have seen, mindfulness can be criticised, like some of the other concepts discussed in this book, not only for its "psychologised", inward, interior, individualistic focus, but also for apparently encouraging an acceptance of, and adjustment to, the wider status quo, institutional domination, and endorsement of a neoliberal hegemony "in which external stressors do not necessarily change, but the person's ability to manage it does" (McCusker, 2020, p.9). However, Kabat-Zinn (1991, p.28) a founder of MBSR argues acceptance "has nothing to do with passive resignation [but with] an attitude that sets the stage for acting" and decision making in difficult circumstances. Also, writers such as Cook (2016, p.151) have cautioned against over-emphasising mindfulness as part of a neoliberal hegemony. She argues there are limits to neoliberalism's influence and its "totalising" effects. She suggests neoliberalism's diverse, multiple meanings include interacting with other political, economic, and cultural forms, such as mindfulness, and different "forms of identity, collectivist and interpersonal connections which may ...contest neoliberal frames".

176 Mindfulness

McCusker (2020, p.14) cautiously suggests while mindfulness, in and of itself,

> cannot address the structural origins of problems facing social workers...
> it does represent one of a number of strategies that can engender a more
> aware...caring and compassionate sense of what the role actually involves
> [while] future opportunities lie in extending understanding of mindfulness
> as an enabler.

An enabler, that is, as we shall see, of environmental, critical, radical, social justice oriented, and anti-oppressive approaches to social work.

Mindfulness theorists, along with various social work writers, remind us that the traditional aims underlying mindfulness include the alleviation of collective suffering of all people, which is compatible with the intentions of social workers to work for social justice (Crowder, 2016; Dylan and Coates, 2016; Scherer and Waistell, 2018; Walsh, 2017, 2018). Walsh (2018, pp.118119) highlights that it is important for mindfulness "to probe the systemic conditions of suffering... to re-orientate oneself in solidarity...in a communion of subjects". Despite criticisms of mindfulness for its apparent political passivity, Walsh (2018, p.118) argues that all human activity is political, including the practice of mindfulness, hence the need to "retranslate mindfulness for social and political activism". This has important implications for social workers, while Walsh (2017, 2018) also concentrates on the opportunities for re-thinking, re-orientating, and developing more critically questioning mindfulness alternatives.

This involves a heightened awareness of power and privilege, oppression, marginalisation, democratisation, and social transformation. The importance of a relentless critical questioning of mindfulness is emphasised in order to deconstruct and reconstruct it, using wide-ranging critical perspectives (Walsh, 2017). He considers the value of such critique in seeking to develop socially and ecologically engaged mindfulness practices. He quotes examples of mindfulness programmes supporting social, environmental, and economic justice, combining personal well-being with political struggle such as the Mindfulness for Social Change programme developed by Paula Haddock in the UK. He also discusses The East Bay Meditation Centre in Oakland, California that works with socially engaged mindfulness to support social justice. A focus is on provision for, and use by, "people of colour", gay, lesbian, and transgender people, away from a focus on white, male, middle-class European perspectives in order to decolonise mindfulness. The danger of replicating and perpetuating existing oppressions such as those of capitalism, patriarchy, racism, sexism, and homophobia is highlighted. Walsh (2017) then goes further to point out the importance of mindfulness movements interlinking and making alliances with other campaigns and justice movements such as Black Lives Matter, which also emphasise connections to, and criticisms of, colonialism, racism, and control.

Indeed, only a small number of social work writers have considered the potential of mindfulness for raising practitioners' sensitivity, awareness, and

Mindfulness **177**

responsiveness to, for example, issues surrounding age, gender, sexuality, (dis) ability, and cultural and ethnic differences. Napoli and Bonifas (2013) described the links between social work, mindfulness and the cultures and practices of Native North Americans; they found similarities in connections made between mind, body, and spirit. They suggested mindfulness helped practitioners interact in more culturally sensitive ways as seen, for instance, in their increased awareness about, and use of, silences, in respecting silences and becoming more able to tolerate them after having undertaken mindfulness experiences (Napoli and Bonifas, 2013). In research with female service users who experienced intimate partner violence, Crowder (2016) compared a mindfulness-based group experience with feminist-based groupwork, while considering a fusion of the two approaches. Iacono (2019) has written about the implications of mindfulness for working with LBGTQ youth and adults. Several scholars recognise that mindfulness can also assist social work students and workers in tolerating discomfort when reflecting on, when challenging, privilege, stereotyping, discrimination, and oppression, and in developing less avoidant and judgemental attitudes towards religious and ethnic groups (Langer and Moldoveanu, 2000; McCusker, 2021; Maddock et al., 2021; Wong, 2004). Mishna and Bogo (2007) have also argued that mindfulness helps social work educators and practitioners to meet, encounter, and face up to tensions, challenges and conflicts about anti-discriminatory and anti-oppressive practices, rather than avoiding them.

At an early stage in an edited book on mindfulness and social work, Steven Hick (2009, p.4) notes social workers' rather passive "acceptance of that which is uncontrollable or lack of resistance to that which is already happening". However, later in the book, then in another article, he approaches mindfulness from a different perspective, seeing that it has much wider potential as an enabler of radical, critical, structural, environmental, and eco-social work approaches (see also, for example, Berila, 2016; Hick and Furlotte, 2009; McCusker, 2020, 2021; Ng, 2016; Wong, 2004, 2013;). Therefore, social work writers have responded to this challenge by examining, by advocating for, the contribution of mindfulness to promoting eco-social work, which involves engagement with the natural world, including issues surrounding environmental crises such as global warming (see, for instance, Crews and Besthorn, 2016; Lysack, 2009).

In their inspiring, stimulating, thought-provoking article, Hick and Furlotte (2009) express commitment to combining mindfulness in social work with social justice approaches. They suggest these concepts converge around ideas linked to social relations, dialectics, consciousness-raising, developing awareness of thoughts, emotions and feelings, self-reflection, and critical reflection. They argue for a linkage between definitions of mindfulness based on health and wellness (Bishop et al., 2004) and society-oriented definitions, with some roots in social psychology and education (Langer, 1989). For instance, Langer and Moldoveanu (2000, p.2) see mindfulness as being grounded in "greater sensitivity to one's environment, increased openness to new information...new categories

178 Mindfulness

for structuring perception and enhanced awareness of multiple perspectives in problem solving".

Hick and Furlotte (2009) go on to consider how the introspective awareness encouraged by mindfulness simultaneously fuels the development of uncovering, discovering, and understanding a critical consciousness, raising an increased awareness of the surrounding world, its systems, and institutions, while critical reflection sensitises us to how knowledge and power are perpetuated; how power operates through systems. These authors, Crowder (2016) and Donald et al. (2019), argue the interconnectedness element in mindfulness discussed earlier, encourages identification with people, and being with people in broader society and the environment. Donald et al.'s (2019) review also emphasises the manner in which mindfulness is particularly related to pro-social behaviours, the well-being of other people, and enhancing the quality of their lives. This involves a developing realisation that new forms of interaction, of organising and working towards transformative social change are possible. It recognises and acknowledges, the internal world, lived experiences, and external social structures as related, reciprocal, co-existing constructs mutually reinforcing each other. As Cheung (2016, p.70) puts it, in social work: "mindfulness…results in an inner strength and practice which brings empowerment for a person to confront social justice and human rights issues".

Other social work writers have taken up this theme of mindfulness emphasising the duality of "inner" work on the self, with "outer" social responsibility, social engagement, and social action (for example, Dylan and Coates, 2016; Ovrelid, 2008; Todd, 2009). Social action is intended to involve empowerment, the promotion of human welfare, social justice, and social change (London, 2009; Nilsson and Kazemi, 2016). It entails solidarity, sharing, and working in collectives: it is a more social justice-oriented, socially "engaged" form of Buddhist mindfulness that can have a broader, wider impact on communities and society generally (Purser and Milillo, 2015; Walsh, 2017; 2018). Therefore, mindfulness is seen as a socio-political tool that can contribute to human rights and to social justice approaches which are lie at the heart of social work (Nilsson and Kazemi, 2016). Cheung (2016, p.70), linking social work and mindfulness, concludes that mindfulness "is based on a synthesis of critical consciousness with mindful awareness of the structural causes of injustice and the dynamics surrounding oppression".

Conclusion

Mindfulness is seen to be an important contributor to self-compassion and self-care, which we have explored in earlier chapters of this book. In particular, mindfulness in, and for, social work usually takes place within a variety, a range of social work organisations which will impact on when and how it is used and applied. In turn, it will also be located within an environmental and structural context that includes class, "race", gender, age, sexuality, (dis)ability language and religion. Mindfulness will be operating in an ecological framework, a context of interacting, interlocking, interconnected systems which are also in state of constant change and flux. Mindfulness will be subject to different perceptions and different interpretations; it will be used in diverse ways by individuals, teams, groups, and organisations. Hence learning about mindfulness should be always located within a wider, broader, theoretical, conceptual, critical, organisational, and structural framework, which highlights collective and service user perspectives, as is the case with all the central concepts we have discussed throughout this book.

References

Adamson, C., Beddoe, L. and Davys, A. (2014) "Building resilient practitioners: Definitions and practitioner understandings", *The British Journal of Social Work*, 44.3, 522–541.

Baer, R., Smith, G., Hopkins, J., Kreitmeyer, J. and Toney, L. (2006) "Five facet mindfulness questionnaire", *Assessment*, 13, 27–45.

Baer, R., Carmody, J. and Hunsinger, M. (2012) "Weekly change in mindfulness and perceived stress in a mindfulness-based stress reduction program", *Journal of Clinical Psychology*, 68.7, 755–765.

Bartlett, L., Martin, A., Neil, A., Memish, K., Otahal, P., Kirkpatrick, M. and Sanderson, K. (2019) "A systematic review and meta-analysis of workplace mindfulness training randomized controlled trials", *Journal of Occupational Health Psychology*, 24, 108–126.

Beddoe, L., Davys, A. and Adamson, C. (2013) "Educating resilient practitioners", *Social Work Education*, 32.1, 100–117.

Beer, W., Phillips, R., Stepney, L. and Quinn, C. (2019) "The feasibility of mindfulness training to reduce stress among social workers: A conceptual paper", *British Journal of Social Work*, DOI:10.1093/bjsw/bcz104.

Berila, B. (2016) *Integrating Mindfulness into Anti-Oppression Pedagogy*, New York, Routledge.

Birnbaum, L. (2005) "Connecting to inner guidance: mindfulness meditation and transformation of professional self-concept in social work students", *Critical Social Work*, 6.2.

Birnbaum, L. (2008) "The use of mindfulness training to create an 'accompanying place' for social work students", *Social Work Education*, 27.8, 837–852.

Bishop, S., Lau, M., Shapiro, S., Carlson, L., Anderson, N., Carmody, J., Segal, Z., Abbey, S., Speca, M., Velting, D. and Devins, G. (2004) "Mindfulness: A proposed operational definition", *Clinical Psychology*, 11.3, 230–241.

Bodhi, B. (2013) "What does mindfulness really mean? A canonical perspective", in Williams, J. and Kabat-Zinn, J. (eds.) *Mindfulness: Diverse Perspectives on its Meaning, Origins and Applications*, Abingdon, Routledge, pp.19–41.

Bogo, M., Regehr, C., Baird, S., Paterson, J. and LeBlanc, V. (2017) "Cognitive and affective elements of practice confidence in social work students and practitioners", *British Journal of Social Work*, 47, 701–718.

Bonifas, R. and Napoli, M. (2014) "Mindfully increasing quality of life: A promising curriculum for MSW students", *Social Work Education*, 33.4, 469–484.

Boone, M. (ed.) (2014) *Mindfulness and Acceptance in Social Work: Evidence-Based Interventions*, Oakland, New Harbinger.

180 Mindfulness

Brooker, J., Julian, J., Webber, L., Chan, J., Shawyer, F. and Meadows, G. (2013) "Evaluation of an occupational mindfulness program for staff employed in the disability sector in Australia", *Mindfulness*, 4, 122–136.

Brown, K. and Ryan, R. (2003) "The benefits of being present: Mindfulness and its role in psychological well-being", *Journal of Personality and Social Psychology*, 84.4, 822–848.

Cheung, M. (2016) "The intersection between mindfulness and human rights: The case of Falun Gong and its implications for social work", *Journal of Religion and Spirituality in Social Work: Social Thought*, 35, 12, 57–75.

Chiesa, A. (2013) "The difficulty of defining mindfulness: Current thought and critical issues", *Mindfulness*, 4, 255–268.

Choi, F., Gruman, J. and Leonard, C. (2021) "A balanced view of mindfulness at work", *Organizational Psychology Review,* DOI:10.1177120413866211036930.

Cohen-Katz, J., Wiley, S., Capuano, T., Baker, D., Kimmel, S. and Shapiro, S. (2005) "The effects of mindfulness-based stress reduction on nurse stress and burnout, Part II: A quantitative and qualitative study", *Holistic Nurse Practice,* 19.1, 2635.

Collins, S. (2007) "Social workers, resilience, positive emotions and optimism", *Practice: Social Work in Action,* 19.4, 255–269.

Collins, S. (2017) "Social workers and resilience revisited", *Practice: Social Work in Action,* 29.2, 85–105.

Collins, S. (2020) *The Positive Social Worker,* London, Routledge.

Constantine Brown, J., Ong, J. and Mathers, J. (2017) "Compassion fatigue and mindfulness: Comparing mental health professionals and MSW student interns", *Journal of Evidence Informed Social Work,* 14.3, 119130.

Conversano, C, Ciacchini, R., Orru, G., Giuseppe, M., Gemignani, A. and Poli, A. (2020) "Mindfulness, compassion, and self-compassion among health care professionals: What's new? A systematic review", *Frontiers in Psychology*, DOI:10.3389/fpsyg.2020.016833.

Cook, J. (2016) "Mindful in Westminster: The politics of meditation and the limited neoliberal critique", *HAU: Journal of Ethnographic Theory*, 6.1, 141–161.

Crews, D. and Besthorn, F. (2016) "Eco-social work and transformed consciousness; Reflections on eco-mindfulness engagement with the silence of the world", *Journal of Religion and Spirituality: Social Thought,* 35, 12, 91–107.

Crowder, R. (2016) "Mindfulness based feminist theory: The intermingling edges of self-compassion and social justice", *Journal of Religion and Spirituality in Social Work: Social Thought,* 35, 12, 24–40.

Crowder, R. and Sears, A. (2017) "Building resilience in social workers: An exploratory study on the impacts of a mindfulness-based intervention", *Australian Social Work,* 70.1, 17–29.

Dobkin, P., Bernardi, N. and Bagnis, C. (2016) "Enhancing clinicians' well-being and patient-centred care through mindfulness", *Journal of Continuing Education in the Health Professions,* 36, 11–16.

Donald, J., Belinda S., Van Zanden, B., Duinveld, J., Atkins, P., Marshall, S. and Ciarrochi, J. (2019) "A systematic review and meta-analysis of the links between mindfulness and pro-social behaviour", *British Journal of Psychology,* 110, 101–125.

Dylan, A. and Coates, J. (2016) "Introduction to special issue: Mindfulness and social work", *Journal of Religion and Spirituality in Social Work: Social Thought*, 35, 1–2, 1–6.

Dzonsgar Khyenste Rinpoche (1997) *The Distortions We Bring to the Study of Buddhism.* www.lions roar: buddhist wisdom for our time.com [accessed 8 Mar. 2020].

Emerson, L-M., Leyland, A., Hudson, K., Rowse, G., Hanley, P. and Hugh-Jones, P. (2017) "Teaching mindfulness to teachers: A systematic review and narrative synthesis", *Mindfulness*, 8, 1136–1149.

Fieze, L. and Faver, C. (2019) "Teaching self-awareness: Social work educators' endeavours and struggles", *Social Work Education*, 38.2, 159–176.

Flook, L., Goldberg, S., Pinger, L., Bonus, K. and Davidson, R. (2013) "Mindfulness for teachers: A pilot study to assess effects on stress, burnout and teaching efficacy", *Mind, Brain, and Education*, 7.3, 182–195.

Garland, E. (2013) "Mindfulness research in social work: Conceptual and methodological recommendations.", *Social Work Research*, 4, 439–448.

Gethin, R. (2013) "On some definitions of mindfulness" in Williams, J. and Kabat-Zinn, J. (eds.) *Mindfulness: Diverse Perspectives on its Meaning, Origins and Applications*, Abingdon, Routledge, pp.263–281.

Gilbert, P. (2013) *The Compassionate Mind: A New Approach to Life's Challenges*, London, Robinson.

Gilbert, P. and Choden (2013) *Mindful Compassion*, London, Constable and Robinson.

Gockel, A., Burton, D., James, S. and Bryer, E. (2013) "Introducing mindfulness as a self-care and clinical training strategy for beginning social work students", *Mindfulness*, 4.343353.

Gockel, A. and Deng, X. (2016) "Mindfulness training as social work pedagogy: Exploring benefits, challenges, and issues for consideration in integrating mindfulness into social work education", *Journal of Religion and Spiritualty in Social Work: Social Thought*, 35.3, 222–234.

Gockel, A., Deng, X., Gleeson, S. and Leamon, A. (2019) "The serene student: Evaluating a group -based mindfulness training program for social work students", *Social Work with Groups*, 42.4, 275–290.

Goh, E. (2012) "Integrating mindfulness and reflection in the teaching and learning of listening skills for undergraduate students in Singapore", *Social Work Education*, 31.5, 587–604.

Good, D., Lyddy, C., Glomb, T., Bono, J., Brown, K., Duffy, M., Baer, R., Brewer, J. and Lazar, S. (2016) "Contemplating mindfulness at work: An integrative review", *Journal of Management*, 42.1, 114–142.

Grant, L. and Kinman, G. (2012) "Enhancing wellbeing in social work students: Building resilience in the next generation", *Social Work Education*, 31.5, 605–621.

Grant, L. and Kinman, G. (2014) "What is resilience?" in Grant, L. and Kinman, G. (eds.), *Developing Resilience for Social Work Practice*, London, Palgrave, pp.1630.

Griffiths, A., Royse, D., Murphy, A. and Starks, S. (2019) "Self-care practice in social work education: A systematic review of interventions", *Journal of Social Work Education*, 55.1, 102–114.

Grossman, P. and Van Dam, N. (2011) "Mindfulness, by any other name …Trials and tribulations of sati in Western psychology and science", *Contemporary Buddhism*, 12, 219239.

Hamer, M. (2006) *The Barefoot Helper: Mindfulness and Creativity in Social Work and the Helping Professions*, Lyme Regis, Jessica Kingsley.

Harris, M. (2017) "'We Forget We Are Human Too'. An exploration of the impact of a M B L C (compassion focussed mindfulness) on social work staff", *Unpublished M. Sc. dissertation*, Aberdeen University, Aberdeen.

Hick, S. (ed.) (2009) *Mindfulness and Social Work*, Chicago, Lyceum.

Hick, S. and Furlotte, C. (2009) "Mindfulness and social justice approaches: Bridging the mind and society in social work practice", *Canadian Social Work Review*, 26.1, 5–24.

182 Mindfulness

Hosseinzadeh Asl (2021) "A randomized controlled trial of a mindfulness-based intervention in social workers working during the COVID-19 crisis", *Current Psychology*, DOI:10.1007/s12144-02102150-3.

Howie, J., Innes, D. and Harvey, P. (2016) "Promoting conscious competence by introducing mindfulness to social work students", *Journal of Practice Teaching and Learning*, 14.1, 88–104.

Iacono, G. (2019) "An affirmative mindfulness approach for lesbian, gay, bisexual, transgender and queer youth mental health", *Clinical Social Work Journal*, 47, 156–166.

Irving, J., Dobkin, P. and Park, J. (2009) "Cultivating mindfulness in health care professionals: A review of empirical studies of mindfulness-based stress reduction (MBSR)", *Contemporary Therapies in Clinical Practice*, 15, 61–66.

Kabat-Zinn, J. (1991) *Full Catastrophe Living: Using the Wisdom of Your Body and Mind to Face Stress, Pain and Illness*, New York, Delta Trade Paperbacks.

Kabat-Zinn, J. (2004) *Wherever You Go, There You Are: Mindfulness Meditation for Everyday Life*, London, Piatkus.

Kessen, C. and Turner, K. (2016) "Are graduate social work students mindful?" *Journal of Religion and Spirituality in Social Work: Social Thought*, 35, 12, 76–90.

Kinman, G., Grant, L. and Kelly, S. (2019) "'It's my secret space': The benefits of mindfulness for social workers" *British Journal of Social Work*, DOI:10.1093/bjsw/bcz073.

Langer, E. (1989) *Mindfulness*, Boston, Addison Wesley Longman.

Langer, E. and Moldoveanu, M. (2000) "Mindfulness research and the future", *Journal of Social Issues*, 56.1, 129–139.

Lee, J. and Himmelheber, S. (2016) "Field education in the present moment: Evaluating a 14-week pedagogical model to increase mindful practice", *Journal of Social Work Education*, 52, 473–483.

Liu, S., Xia, H., He, J. and Liu, J. (2020) "The influence of individual and team mindfulness on work engagement", *Frontiers in Psychology*, 10, 2928.

Lomas, T., Medina, J., Ivtzan, I., Rupprecht, S., Hart, R. and Eiroa-Orosa, J. (2017) "The impact of mindfulness on well-being and performance in the workplace: An inclusive systematic review of the empirical literature", *European Journal of Work and Organizational Psychology*, 26.4, 492–513.

Lomas, T., Medina, J., Ivtzan, I., Rupprecht, S. and Eiroa-Orosa, F. (2018) "A systematic review of the impact of mindfulness on the well-being of healthcare professionals", *Journal of Clinical Psychology*, 74., 319–355.

Lomas, T., Ivtzan, I., Rupprecht, S. and Eiroa-Orosa, F. (2019) "Mindfulness based interventions in the workplace: An inclusive systematic review and meta-analysis", *The Journal of Positive Psychology*, 14, 625–640.

London, T. (2009) "Mindfulness in activism: Fighting for justice as a self-reflective emancipatory practice" in S. Hick (ed.) *Mindfulness and Social Work*, Chicago, IL, Lyceum, pp.188–201.

Lynn, R. and Mensinga, J. (2015) "Social workers' narratives of integrating mindfulness into practice", *Journal of Social Work Practice*, 29.3, 255–270.

Lysack, M. (2009) "From environmental despair to the ecological self: Mindfulness and community action" in Hick, S. (ed.) *Mindfulness and Social Work*, Chicago, IL, Lyceum, pp.202–218.

Mackenzie, C., Poulin, P. and Seidman-Carlson, R. (2006) "A brief mindfulness-based stress reduction intervention for nurses and nurse aides", *Applied Nursing Research*, 19, 2, 105–109.

Maddock, A., McCusker, P., Blair, C., and Roulston, A. (2021) "The mindfulness‑based social work and self‑care programme: A mixed methods evaluation study", *British Journal of Social Work*, DOI:10.1093/ bjsw/ bcab 203.

MAPPG (2015) *Mindful Nation UK*, London, Mindfulness All Party Parliamentary Group.

Martin‑Cuellar, A., Atencio, D., Kelly, R. and Lardier, D. (2018) "Mindfulness as a moderator of clinical history of trauma on compassion satisfaction", *The Family Journal: Counselling and Therapy for Couples and Families*, 26.3, 358–368.

McCorquodale, L. (2015) "Mindfulness and professional practice: A generative dialogue", *Reflective Practice: International and Multidisciplinary Perspectives*, 16.2, 230–241.

McCusker, P. (2020) *Mindfulness in Social Work Education and Practice*, Dundee/Glasgow. Iriss.

McCusker, P. (2021) "Critical mindfulness in social work: Exploring the potential of reflexive self‑care in the journey from student to social worker", *British Journal of Social Work*, DOI:10.1093/bjsw/bcaa246.

McGarrigle, T. and Walsh, C. (2011) "Mindfulness, self‑care, and wellness in social work: Effects of contemplative training", *Journal of Religion and Spirituality in Social Work: Social Thought*, 30.3, 212–233.

Mental Health Foundation (2010) *Mindfulness Report*, London, Mental Health Foundation.

Mindfulness Association (2011) *Mindfulness Based Living Course Manual*, Edinburgh, Mindfulness Association.

Mindfulness Association (2013) *Mindfulness Module Weekend 1 Manual*, Edinburgh, Mindfulness Association

Mindfulness Association (2016a) *Level1: Being Present* [Online] www.mindfulness assocation.net/ Courses.aspx [accessed 15 Aug. 2020].

Mindfulness Association (2016b) *Mindfulness Based Living Eight Week Course* [Online] www. mindfulness association.net/ M B L C.aspx [accessed 15 Aug. 2020].

Mishna, F. and Bogo, M. (2007) "Reflective practice in contemporary social work classrooms", *Journal of Social Work Education*, 43.3, 529–544.

Moll, S., Frolic, A. and Key, B. (2015) "Investing in compassion: Exploring mindfulness as a strategy to enhance interpersonal relationships in healthcare practice", *Journal of Hospital Administration*, 4.6, 36–45.

Napoli, M. and Bonifas, R. (2011) "From theory towards empathic self‑care: Creating a mindfulness classroom for social work students", *Social Work Education*, 30.6, 635–649.

Napoli, M. and Bonifas, R. (2013) "Becoming culturally competent: Mindful engagement with American Indian Clients", *Journal of Ethnic and Cultural Diversity in Social Work*, 22.34, 198–212.

Neff, K. (2003) "The development and validation of a scale to measure self‑compassion", *Self and Identity*, 2.3, 223–250.

Neff, K. (2011) *Self‑Compassion: Stop Beating Yourself Up and Leave Insecurity Behind*, New York, William Morrow.

Ng, E. (2016) "The critique of mindfulness and the mindfulness of critique: paying attention to the politics of ourselves with Foucault's analytic of governmentality" in Purser, R. Forbes, D. and Burke, A. (eds.) *Handbook of Mindfulness, Culture, Context and Social Engagement*, Switzerland, Springer Link, pp.135–153.

Ovrelid, B. (2008) "The cultivation of moral character: A Buddhist challenge to social workers", *Ethics and Social Welfare*, 7.7, 243–261.

184 Mindfulness

Nilsson, H. and Kazemi, A. (2016) "From Buddhist sati to western mindfulness practice: A contextual analysis", *Journal of Religion and Spirituality in Social Work: Social Thought,* 36, 12, 223–250.

Northcut, T. (ed.) (2017) *Cultivating Mindfulness in Clinical Social Work: Narratives from Practice,* Cham, Springer.

Parkes, R. and Kelly, S. (2014) "Mindfulness for resilience in social work" in Grant, L. and Kinman, G., (eds.) *Developing Resilience for Social Work Practice,* London, Palgrave, pp.110–127.

Payne, M. (2020) *How to Use Theory in Social Work Practice: An Essential Guide,* Bristol, Policy Press.

Purser, R. and Cooper, A. (2014) *"Mindfulness' 'Truthiness' Problem: Sam Harris, Science, and the Truth about Buddhist Tradition"* www.salon.com/2014/12/06mindfulness truthiness problem sam harris science, and the truth about budhist tradition [accessed 10 Dec. 2020].

Purser, R. and Milillo, J. (2015) "Mindfulness revisited: A Buddhist-based conceptualization", *Journal of Management Inquiry,* 4.1, 3–24.

Richards, K., Campenni, E. and Muse-Burke, J. (2010) "Self-care and well-being in mental health professionals: The mediating effects of self-awareness and mindfulness", *Journal of Mental Health Counselling,* 323, 247–264.

Rosch, E. (2015) "The Emperor's clothes: A look behind the western mindfulness mystique" in Ostafin, B., Robinson, M. and Meier, B. (eds.) *Handbook of Mindfulness and Self-Regulation,* New York, Springer, pp.271–292.

Rosencrantz, M., Dunne, J. and Davidson, R. (2019) "The next generation of mindfulness-based intervention research: What have we learned and where are we headed?", *Current Opinion in Psychology,* 28, 179–183.

Roulston, A., Montgomery, L., Campbell, A. and Davidson, G. (2018) "Exploring the impact of mindfulness on mental wellbeing, stress, and resilience of undergraduate social work students", *Social Work Education,* 37.2, 157–172.

Rupprecht, S., Koole, W., Chaskalson, M., Tamdjidi, C. and West, M. (2019) "Running too far ahead? Towards a broader understanding of mindfulness in organisations", *Current Opinion in Psychology,* 28, 32–36.

Salzburg, S. (2013) "Mindfulness and loving kindness" in Williams, J. and Kabat-Zinn, J. (eds.), *Mindfulness: Diverse Perspectives on its Meaning, Origins and Perspectives,* Abingdon, Routledge, pp.177–182.

Santorelli, S. and Kabat-Zinn, J. (eds.) (2009) *Mindfulness-Based Stress Reduction (MBSR) Professional Education and Training: MBSR Curriculum and Supporting Materials,* Worcester, MA, U. Mass Medical School, Centre for Mindfulness in Medicine, Health, Care and Society.

Scherer, B. and Waistell, J. (2018) "Incorporating mindfulness: questioning capitalism", *Journal of Management, Spirituality and Religion",* 15, 2, 123–140.

Shier, M. and Graham, J. (2011) "Mindfulness, subjective well-being, and social work: Insight into their interconnection from social work practitioners", *Social Work Education,* 30.1, 29–44.

Stickle, M. (2016) "The expression of compassion in social work practice", *Journal of Religion and Spirituality in Social Work: Social Thought,* 36.12, 120–131.

Thomas, J. (2012) "Does personal distress mediate the effect of mindfulness on professional quality of life", *Advances in Social Work,* 13, 561–585.

Thomas, J. and Otis, M. (2010) "Intrapsychic correlates of professional quality of life: mindfulness, empathy and emotional separation", *Journal of the Society for Social Work and Research,* 1.2, 83–98.

Todd, S. (2009) "Mobilising communities for social change: Integrating mindfulness and passionate politics" in Hick, S. (ed.) *Mindfulness and Social Work,* Chicago, Lyceum, pp.177–187.

Trowbridge, K. and Lawson, L. (2016) "Mindfulness-based interventions with social workers and the potential for enhanced patient-centered care: A systematic review of the literature", *Social Work in Health Care,* 55.2, 101–124.

Trowbridge, K., Lawson, L., Andrews, S., Pecora, J. and Boyd, S. (2017) "Preliminary investigation of workplace-provided compressed mindfulness-based stress reduction with paediatric social workers", *Health and Social Work,* 42.4, 207–214.

Van Dam, N., van Vogt, M., Vago, D., Schwaltz, L., Saron, C., Oledski, A., Meissner, T., Lazar, S., Kerr, C., Gorchov, J., Fox, C., Field, B., Britton, W., Brefczynski, J. and Meyer, D. (2018) "Mind the hype: A critical evaluation and prescriptive agenda for research on mindfulness and meditation", *Perspectives in Psychological Science,* 13, 36–61.

Vonderlin, J., Biermann, M., Bohus, M. and Lyssenko, L. (2020) "Mindfulness based programs in the workplace: A meta-analysis of random controlled trials", *Mindfulness,* 11, 1579–1698.

Walsh, Z. (2017) "Contemplative praxis for social ecological transformation", *The Arrow: A Journal of Wakeful Society, Culture and Politics,* 4, 1, 1–19.

Walsh, Z. (2018) "Mindfulness under neoliberal governmentality: Critiquing the operation of biopower in corporate mindfulness and constructing queer alternatives", *Journal of Management, Spirituality and Religion,* 15.2, 109–122.

Wasylkiw, L., Holton, J., Azar, R. and Cook, W. (2015) "The impact of mindfulness on leadership effectiveness in a health care setting: A pilot study", *Journal of Health Organization and Management,* 29.7, 893–911.

Wasson, R., Barratt, C. and O'Brien, W. (2020) "Effects of mindfulness-based interventions on self-compassion in health care professionals: A meta-analysis", *Mindfulness,* DOI:https:// doi.org/10.1007/s12671-020-01342-5.

Wong, Y-L. R. (2004) "Knowing through discomfort: A mindfulness based critical social work pedagogy", *Critical Social Work,* 5.1.

Wong, Y-L. R (2013) "Returning to silence, connecting to wholeness: Contemplative pedagogy for critical social work education", *Journal of Religion and Spirituality in Social Work: Social Thought,* 32, 269–285.

Ying, Y. W. (2008) "Variation in personal competence and mental health between entering and graduating MSW students: The contribution of mindfulness", *Journal of Religion and Spirituality: Social Thought,* 32, 3, 402–422.

Ying, Y. W. (2009) "Contribution of self-compassion to competence and mental health in social work students", *Journal of Social Work Education,* 45.2, 309–323.

NAME INDEX

Acker, G. 14, 25, 115, 129
Adams, R. 20, 25, 67–68, 70, 75, 78, 81–82, 156
Adamson, C. 75, 81, 85, 122, 129, 170, 179
Alkema, K. 115, 117, 129
Allen, R. 7, 24, 30
Ampadu, G. 120–121
Andrew, T. 22, 29
Andrews, H. 141, 146, 163
Antonopoulu, P. 18, 20, 24
Arimitsu, K. 148, 153
Armes, S. 66–67, 82, 124, 129
Armstrong, K. 34, 56
Arnold, D. 39, 105
Ashley – Binge, S. 80, 82, 112, 127, 129
Astvik, W. 25, 101, 105
Atkins, P. 13, 25, 180
Audin, K. 95–96, 105

Babenko, O. 149, 153
Badger, K. 71, 82
Bae, J. 24–25, 92, 94–95, 97, 99–101, 104, 138
Baer, R. 58, 61, 138, 153, 155, 163–164, 178, 181
Baginski, M. 17, 26, 91, 165
Baines, D. 18, 26
Baldschun, A. 76, 82, 95, 105
Barnes, V. 49, 53, 56
Bartlett, L. 162, 173, 179
Batson, C. 36–56
Baugerud, G. 24, 26, 64, 78, 82, 92, 94–95, 97, 99, 105

Baum, N. 75, 78, 82, 89, 105
Beato, A. 137, 153
Beddoe, L. 24, 26, 51, 53, 56, 65, 67, 75, 82, 90, 92, 105, 113, 122, 129, 171, 179
Beehr, T. 12, 26
Beer, O. 22–23, 26, 162, 166–167, 169, 171, 173, 179
Bell, T. 140–153
Bellinger, A. 103, 105
Ben Porat, A. 65, 83, 87, 89, 105
Ben Zur, H. 13, 26
Beresford, P. 53, 56
Berila, B. 177–179
Berlant, L. 39–40, 56
Besthorn, S. 177, 180
Billingham, J. 20, 31
Bilson, A. 45, 56
Birnbaum, L. 167–168, 179
Bishop, K. 160, 177, 179
Bloomquist, K. 113–114, 116, 118, 120, 122, 125–126, 129
Bluth, K. 136, 148, 153
Bober, T. 116, 129
Bodhi, B. 161, 174, 179
Bogo, M. 171, 177, 179, 183
Bonifas, R. 168, 177, 179, 183
Boone, M. 160–161, 179
Boscarino, J. 25, 79, 81–82
Bourassa, D. 20, 26, 73, 75, 77–78, 82
Bourdieu, P. 48, 56, 61
Bradshaw, A. 43, 56
Bramley, L. 37, 46, 56
Brent- Godley, T. 65, 82

188 Name Index

Bressi, S. 113, 120–121, 126, 129
Bride, S. 65, 67, 75–76, 82, 84, 126, 129, 131
Brill, M. 45, 56
Briskman, L. 55, 62
Brooker, J. 165–166, 180
Brown, B. 53, 56–57
Brown, K. 163, 180
Brown, M-E. 124, 129
Brown, P. 41, 58
Brown, W. 10, 26
Buchanan, M. 140, 157
Burns, C. 91, 100, 105
Burns, K. 12, 18, 24, 26
Butler, J. 9, 26
Butler, L. 65, 78, 80, 82
Butler, P. 8, 26

Calhoun, S. 89, 110
Calnan, M. 12, 32
Campos-Vidal, J. 24, 27, 75, 77, 83, 94, 97, 106, 116, 118–119, 127, 130
Canda, E. 19, 45, 56
Caringi, J. 77, 82
Carpenter, J. 20, 26, 103, 107
Carter, B. 103, 106
Chablah, R. 91, 107
Charlesworth, S. 9, 26
Cheung, M. 178, 180
Chiesa, A. 160, 174, 180
Chio, F. 148, 150, 153
Choden 39, 58, 163, 181
Choi, F. 162, 171–172, 174–175, 180
Choi, G. 66, 83
Christie, L. 138, 154
Cieslak, R. 74, 83
Clark, S. 44, 57
Clossley, L. 89, 110
Coaston, S. 140, 145, 153
Coates, J. 176, 178, 180
Cocker, P. 76, 83
Coffey, M. 14, 20, 26, 63, 83, 90, 106, 112, 129
Cohen- Katz, J. 164, 180
Cohen, P. 10, 26
Collins, M. 45, 47, 57
Collins, S. 2, 5, 11–13, 21–26, 34, 39, 49, 51, 55, 57, 66, 73–74, 83, 90–93, 100–104, 106, 112–113, 117, 119–120, 125, 127–130, 147, 151, 153, 167, 180
Collins, W. 118, 129
Conrad, D. 66, 69, 77, 83, 93–95, 106
Consedine, N. 30, 4–42, 55, 57, 73, 76, 83
Constantine- Brown, J. 168, 180
Conversano, C. 165, 180
Cook, J. 175, 180
Cook, L. 17, 27

Cooper, A. 161, 184
Cooper, C. 11–13, 26–27, 30, 90, 106, 109
Cooper, J. 19, 24, 27, 91, 106
Cooperrider, D. 102, 106, 110
Corcoran, T. 73, 75, 80
Cornwell, J. 43, 59
Cousins, C. 80, 82, 112, 127, 129
Cox, K. 111, 130
Craig, C. 77, 80, 82–83, 94, 96, 106
Crawford, P. 40, 44, 56–57
Crews, D. 177, 180
Crowder, R. 170, 176–180, 180
Cuartero, M. 24, 27, 75, 77, 83, 94, 97, 106, 116, 118–119, 127, 130
Curry, A. 123, 130

Dalai Lama 34–35, 37, 57
Dalphon, H. 114, 120
Davidson, R. 34, 57
De Zulueta, P. 2, 5, 40, 57
Decker, J. 97, 106
Dekel, R. 67, 83
Delaney, M. 138, 153
Deng, X. 166, 173, 181
Denne, E. 77, 83
Dev, V. 141, 153
Dewar, B. 50, 57
Dewe, P. 77, 83
Diaconescu, M. 64, 83
Diebold, J. 116, 122, 130
Diener, E. 92, 106
Dobkin, P. 164, 180
Dodson, S. 141, 150, 154
Dombo, A. 66, 83
Dombo, E. 113–115, 130
Donald, J. 178, 180
Donovan, T. 15, 27
Doris, J. 34, 57
Dorociak, K. 114, 126, 120
Downing, K. 125, 130
Durkin, M. 141, 154
Duschinski, R. 9, 11, 23, 25, 27
Dutton, J. 39–40, 46, 50, 57
Dylan, A. 176, 178, 180

Ebbinghaus, A. 39, 57
Edwards, K. 100, 106
Egan, G. 38, 47, 57, 69, 83
Ekman, P. 37, 57
Elliott, T. 103, 105
Emerson, L-M. 165, 181
Eng, I. 73, 83
Engstrom, S. 121, 127, 133
Epley, P. 123, 130
Epstein, M. 36, 57
Eriksson, T. 139, 154

Name Index

Evans, S. 20, 27, 63, 83, 91, 99, 106–107, 127, 130–131

Farnfield, S. 53, 57
Faver, C. 167, 181
Ferguson, H. 17, 27, 30, 52, 54, 57
Fernando, A. 30, 41–42, 55, 57, 73, 76, 83
Ferrari, M. 137–138, 145, 148
Fieze, L. 167, 181
Figley, C. 45, 60, 66, 68–71, 75–76, 81–85, 93, 106
Finlay- Jones, A. 139, 141, 154
Finzi- Dottan, R. 99, 106
Firth- Cozens, J. 43, 59
Fitzpatrick, S. 8, 27
Flook, L. 165–181
Flores, R. 41, 58
Folkman, S. 12, 27
Fox, M. 79, 83, 117–118, 126–127, 130
Franco, P. 138, 154
Frey, L. 98, 100, 106
Frost, L. 48, 51, 58, 121, 127, 130
Furlotte, C. 177–178, 181

Garland, E. 160, 181
Garrett, P.M. 10, 15, 24, 27, 148–149, 154
Gates, T. 145, 154
Geoffrion, S. 76, 84
Gerber, Z. 137, 150–151, 154
Germer, C. 135, 137–140, 144, 150, 154, 156–157
Gethin, R. 161, 174, 181
Ghesquiere, A. 77, 84, 95, 107
Gibbs, P. 36, 46, 58
Gibson, M. 144, 154
Gilbert, P. 34–40, 42, 44, 47, 58, 135–137, 147, 150, 154, 163, 181
Giordano, A. 74, 84
Glassburn, S. 123, 130
Gockel, A. 166, 173, 181
Godfrey, M. 2
Goetz, J. 37, 58
Goh, E. 168, 181
Goldberg, D. 14, 27
Good, E. 161–162, 181
Gottleib, M. 143, 148, 155
Goussios, A. 101, 106
Grabner, S. 12, 26
Graham, J. 12, 27, 92, 107, 171, 184
Grant, L. 23–24, 27–28, 39, 59, 69, 77, 84, 88, 95, 102, 107–108, 114, 120, 122, 125–127, 130–131, 135, 142, 144, 151, 155, 167, 170–171, 181–182, 184
Grant, S. 12, 15, 24, 37, 103, 107
Gray, R. 113–115, 130
Gregory J. 36, 58

Griffiths, A. 112–115, 122, 130, 169, 181
Grise- Owens, E. 113, 116, 122, 124, 131–132, 156
Grossman, P. 164, 181
Gu, J. 38, 137
Guan, F. 140, 148, 155
Gumley, A. 37, 59, 137, 148, 150, 156
Gustin, L. 140, 155

Hamer, M. 159, 181
Han, M. 143, 151
Harr, C. 64, 68–69, 77, 81, 84, 91, 93–94, 96, 99, 102, 104, 107, 128, 131
Harrington, A. 34, 87
Harris J. 10, 27
Harris, D. 36, 40–41, 47, 78, 80, 85, 102, 107
Harris, M. 142, 155, 161, 163, 167, 170–171, 181
Harrop, A. 8, 28
Hay, J. 39, 54, 58
Hendrix, E. 120, 126, 131
Heng, Y. 141, 143, 146, 150, 154, 157
Henshall, L. 40, 43, 58, 140, 155
Hermon, S. 91, 107
Hernandez- Wolfe, P. 89, 99, 107
Hick, S. 159, 177–178, 181
Hillock, S. 72–73, 87
Himmelheber, J. 168, 182
Hoggett, P. 39, 48, 51, 55, 58
Holmes, M. 92, 95, 107
Hombrados- Mendieta, I. 65, 84
Horsell, C. 44–45, 51, 55, 58
Hosseinzadeh Asl 178, 182
Howard, A. 20, 28, 96, 98, 107
Howie, J. 168, 182
Huang, J. 148, 155
Hudson, J. 20, 28
Hughes, M. 103, 107
Hugman, B. 45, 58
Humphries, M. 103, 107
Hunter, S. 90, 107, 132
Hurley, D. 90. 107, 121, 131
Huxley, P. 63, 83, 91, 99, 106, 127, 130

Iacono, G. 136, 139, 141, 149, 155, 177, 182
Ingram, R. 14, 28
Irving, J. 165, 182
Ivtzan, J. 36–37, 58, 105

Jack, G. 145, 157
Jazaieri, H. 42, 58
Jeffrey, L. 113, 131
Jen, J. 44, 57
Jennings, R. 146, 150, 155
Jinpa, J. 37, 39, 42, 58

190 Name Index

Johnson, C. 15–18, 21–24, 28, 91, 99, 108
Joinson, C. 63, 84
Jones, C. 14, 28
Joss, N. 76, 83
Joyce, C. 141, 147, 149, 158

Kabat-Zinn, J. 160, 162–163, 173, 175, 182, 184
Kalliath, P. 22–23, 88, 127
Kalliath, T. 22–23, 28, 127
Kanov, J. 38, 40, 58
Kapoulitsas, M. 73, 75, 84
Karptetis, G. 24, 28, 91, 108
Kaszap, P. 53, 57
Kazemi, A. 141, 178, 184
Kearns, S. 13, 28
Keller- Guenther, Y. 64, 69, 77, 83, 93–95, 106
Kelly, S. 175, 184
Kessen, C. 166, 168, 182
Killian, K. 20, 28, 98, 108, 116, 131
Kim, M. 73, 76–76, 84
King, D. 122, 124, 132
Kingstone, T. 16, 28
Kinman, G. 22–24, 27–28, 39, 59, 69, 77, 84, 88, 95, 102, 107–108, 114, 120, 122, 125–127, 130–131, 135, 142, 144–145, 151, 155, 162, 167, 170–171, 181–182, 184
Kirby, J. 36, 41–42, 59
Kleinman, A. 51, 59
Klimecki, C. 42, 59
Klimecki, O. 42, 61
Knight, C. 80, 84
Kong, S-T. 25, 28, 54, 59
Kormosh, M. 99, 106
Kotera, Y. 139, 143–144, 151, 155
Kreitzer, L. 72–73, 80, 84
Krieger, T. 138–139, 156

La Mott, J. 113, 115, 131
Langer, E. 177, 182
Larkin, P. 38, 59
Lavalette, M. 8, 10, 29
Lawson, L. 167–169, 185
Leary, M. 141, 147, 156
Ledoux, K. 34, 42–43, 59, 68, 72, 79, 84
Lee, F. 65–66, 74, 76, 84
Lee, J. 66, 76, 84, 112–114, 124, 126–127, 131, 168, 182
Lee, K. 127, 131
Lee, R. 65, 84, 112–113, 120, 127, 131
Lefevre, M. 13, 29
Letson, M. 102, 108

Lev-Weisel, R. 67, 84, 89, 108
Lewis, M. 122, 124, 138
Lianekhammy, J. 142, 151, 156
Liao, K. 151, 156
Ling, D. 35–36, 41–42, 59
Littlechild, B. 18–19, 29
Liu, S. 148, 150, 171–172, 182
Lizano, E. 65, 84
Lloyd, C. 14, 20, 29, 112, 132
Lomas, T. 162, 182
London, T. 178, 182
Ludick, M. 75, 84
Lutz, A. 42, 59
Lynn, R. 171, 182
Lysack, M. 177, 182

Macbeth, A. 37, 59, 137, 148, 150, 156
Mackenzie, G. 164, 182
MacNeil, G. 64–65, 72, 85
Maddock, A. 167, 169, 173, 177, 183
Maddox, L. 65, 67, 70, 72, 75, 87
Madigan, J. 39, 46, 62
Mak, W. 148, 158
Manthorpe, G. 17, 26
Marlowe, J. 75, 81, 85
Marmot, M. 8, 29
Martin- Cuellar, A. 20, 29, 65, 78, 85, 97–98, 108, 165, 183
Martin, L. 113, 115, 131
Maslach, C. 14, 29, 64, 72, 85
Masson, F. 74, 85
Masters, K. 39, 61
Matiti, M. 37, 46, 56
Matos, M. 42, 59
McArdle, K. 13, 28
McCann, I. 65, 85
McCorquodale, L. 164, 183
McCusker, P. 163, 166–167, 169, 175–177, 183
McElvaney, R. 90, 99, 110
McFadden, P. 11, 15–16, 20–22, 24, 29, 63, 73, 85, 91–92, 108
McGarrigle, T. 113, 126–127, 132, 169, 171
McLean, J. 22, 29
McNay, L. 49, 54, 59
Mee, S. 39–41, 43–44, 61, 101, 109
Mendez- Fernandez, A. 65–66, 72, 75, 85
Mensinga, J. 171, 182
Mette, J. 113, 132
Michael, K. 13, 26
Mickel, A. 15, 29, 73, 85, 90, 108
Middleton, J. 65, 85, 96, 109
Milillo, J. 164, 174, 178, 181
Miller, B. 69–70, 75, 85

Name Index **191**

Miller, J. 112–117, 119, 121–122, 125–126,
    131–132, 135–137, 142–144, 146–147,
    149–151, 156
Mishna, F. 177, 183
Moldoveanu, M. 177, 182
Molina, V. 112, 134
Moll, S. 164, 183
Molnar, B. 89, 108
Mongrain, M. 140, 157
Moore, B 64, 81, 84, 94, 96, 107
Moore, S. 118, 124, 132
Moorhouse, A. 90, 99, 108
Mor-Barak, M. 65, 84
Mordue, S. 11, 132
Morgan, G. 51, 53, 59
Moriarty, J. 12, 14, 86
Morris, L. 20, 29–30
Moskowitz, J. 12, 27
Mueller-Hirth, N. 49, 52, 62
Munro, E. 49, 52, 59
Muris, P. 147, 156
Myers, D. 90, 108
Myers, K. 122–123, 132

Nadeau, M. 139, 156
Nahmani, M. 45, 56
Napoli, M. 45, 56
Neff, K. 135–142, 144, 147–151, 154,
    156–157, 159, 162, 183
Nelson, D. 12–13, 30–31
Nelson-Gardell, D. 78, 85, 122
Newcomb, M. 112, 120–123, 125–127, 133
Newell, J. 64–65, 69–70, 72, 75, 85,
    116–117, 133
Newsome, S. 22, 30
Ng, E. 177, 183
Nillson, P. 45, 59
Nilsson, H. 161, 178, 184
Noone, C. 25, 28, 54, 59
Northcut, T. 159, 184
Nouwen, H. 35, 59
Nussbaum, M. 34–36, 39, 46, 55–56, 59
Nuttman- Schwartz, O. 75, 85
Nyak, S. 119–120, 128, 133

O' Connell, M. 35, 59
O' Leary, P. 53, 60
O' Neill, S. 116–133
O'Byrne, P. 104, 108
Orb, A. 34–36, 39, 43, 46, 51
Ortego- Galan, A. 33, 60
Otis, M. 20, 31, 78, 87, 98, 110, 119, 169,
    184
Ovrelid, B. 35–36, 39, 49, 60, 174, 178, 183

Owens- King, J. 113, 115
Ozawa De Silva, B. 34–35, 42, 60

Pack, M. 89, 121, 123, 133
Papadopoulos, I. 44, 60
Parker, S. 13, 25
Parkes, R. 175, 184
Parry, S. 111, 133
Parton, N. 104, 108
Patsiopoulos, A. 140, 157
Patzak, A. 147, 157
Payne, M. 175, 184
Pearlman, L. 65–66, 72, 85
Pearson, A. 53, 60
Peeters, M. 12, 31
Pelon, S. 64, 69, 77, 94–95
Pentaraki, M. 10, 30
Petrocchi, N. 147, 156
Phillips, J. 23, 30
Pink, S. 17, 30
Pithouse, A. 12, 18, 24, 30, 96, 109
Podsakoff, N. 11, 30
Pommier, E. 38, 60, 150, 156
Pooler, D. 91–92, 109
Potter, C. 65, 85
Powers, M. 121, 127, 133
Price, J. 34, 60
Prost, S. 96, 109
Purser, R. 161, 164, 174, 178, 184
Pyles, L. 112, 120–121, 128, 133

Quaglia, J. 150, 157
Quinn, A. 55, 85

Radey, M. 45, 60, 68–69, 75, 85
Raes, F. 137, 157
Rajan-Rankin, S. 22, 30
Ramon, S. 20, 30
Ravalier, J. 7, 9, 11, 14–15, 19–21, 24, 30,
    63, 86, 91, 101, 112, 133
Rayner, S. 67, 69, 86
Regehr, C. 89, 109, 116, 129
Reid, H. 8, 28
Reizer, A. 146, 149, 157
Rhodes, M. 44, 46, 60, 62
Richards, K. 167, 184
Rienks, S. 65, 67, 113, 124, 133
Roberts, L. 52, 60
Robertson, I. 11–12, 30, 90, 109
Robinson, G. 103, 109
Robinson, K. 146, 157
Rogers, C. 38, 47, 60, 69, 86
Ron, P. 67, 86, 89, 109
Rose, M. 24, 30, 70, 109

192 Name Index

Rosencrantz, M. 175, 184
Rothenberg, M. 79, 87, 94, 110, 118, 134
Roulston, A. 168, 173, 184
Royse, D. 113, 115, 130
Ruch, G. 14, 30, 61, 71–72, 86, 98, 109, 123, 133
Rupprecht, S. 172–173, 184
Ryan, R. 163, 180

Saakvitne, K. 66, 72, 86
Sabo, B. 74, 86
Saleebey, D. 7, 30
Salloum, A. 96, 109, 113–116, 118, 126, 133
Salzburg, S. 159–160, 184
Samios, C. 89, 97, 109
Santorelli, S. 163, 173, 184
Savaya, R. 24, 30. 92, 109
Schabram, K. 143, 146, 157
Schaub, J. 41, 49, 60
Scherer, B. 176, 184
Schon, D. 123, 133
Schopenhauer, A. 34, 60
Schrag, R. 66, 72–74, 77–80, 86
Sears, A. 170, 180
Selye, H. 12, 31
Senreich, E. 24, 31, 64, 66, 73, 86, 88, 92, 94, 96–97, 99–100, 109
Shamai, M. 67, 86, 91, 109
Shannon, P. 118, 122, 124, 133
Shapira, L. 140, 157
Shaufeli, W. 12, 31
Shell, E. 74, 86
Sheppard, M. 46, 60
Shepperd, M. 116–117, 133
Shibusawa, T. 143, 148, 155
Shier, M. 12, 27, 92, 107, 171, 184
Shraer, R. 15, 31
Sicora, A. 142, 144, 157
Silman, J. 17–18, 23, 31
Simmons, B. 12–13, 30–31
Simpson, A. 40–41, 60
Sinclair, S. 35–36, 38, 41–43, 52–54, 60–61
Singer, T. 42, 57, 61
Singh, J. 72, 86
Singh, P. 41, 61
Singleton, V. 39–41, 43–44, 61, 101, 109
Sirois, F. 137, 157
Smith, M. 48, 61
Smullens, S. 111, 135
Sodeke- Gregson, E. 94, 109
Spandler, H. 45, 61
Sprang, G. 69–70, 75, 77–78, 80, 83, 85–86, 94, 96, 106
Stalker, C. 12, 24, 31, 76, 86, 91–92, 99, 109

Stamm, B. 64, 68–70, 73, 75–76, 83, 86, 93, 99–100, 106, 110
Stanford, S. 63, 86
Stanley, S. 22, 31
Steffen, P. 39, 61
Steiner, S. 111, 130
Stickle, M. 39, 42, 44–45, 61, 62, 184
Stickley, T. 45, 61
Storey, J. 20, 31
Strauss, C. 38, 41, 44, 46, 58, 61
Stuart, H. 120–121, 127–128, 134

Tanner, D. 35, 39, 42, 44–45, 49, 53–54, 61, 64, 68, 86
Tavormina, M. 89, 110
Teater, B. 103, 110
Tedam, P. 21, 31
Tedeshci, R. 89, 110
Tham, P. 18, 31
Thomas, J. 20–21, 31, 69–71, 77–78, 87, 96–98, 110, 169, 184
Ting, I. 14, 31
Todd, S. 178, 185
Tosone, C. 20, 31, 78, 87
Trompetter, H. 137, 157
Trosten-Bloom, A. 102, 110
Trowbridge, K. 167–171, 173, 185
Tsang, N. 39, 44, 49, 61
Turgoose, D. 65, 67, 70, 72, 75, 87
Turner- Daly, P. 145, 157
Turner, D. 7, 32
Turner, K. 166, 168, 182

Unwin, J. 146, 157

Vaden, E. 113, 120–121, 126, 129
Van Dam, N.J. 161, 162, 164, 181, 185
Van de Cingel, M. 34, 61
Van Gordon, W. 139, 155
van Heugten, K. 11, 18, 32, 66, 81, 87
Van Hook, M. 79, 87, 94, 110, 118, 134
Vittelone, N. 40, 61
Voltaire 1, 5
Von Dietze, E. 34–36, 39, 43, 46, 51
Vonderlin, J. 162, 164, 185

Wachter, K. 77, 10–101, 110
Wagaman, M. 23, 32, 65, 69, 87, 93–97, 102, 110
Wagner, L. 140–155
Wainwright, D. 12, 32
Waistell, J. 176, 184
Wakelin, K. 148, 158
Walsh, C. 113, 126–127, 132, 169, 171, 183

Name Index

Walsh, J. 53, 61, 144, 148, 158
Walsh, Z. 160, 174–176, 178, 185
Wang, Y. 122, 134
Ward, A. 53, 61
Warner, J. 51, 54–55, 61
Wasson, R. 165, 185
Wasylkiw, L. 164, 185
Watson, J. 43, 61
Webber, M. 20, 28
Weinberg, M. 117, 134
Weiss-Dagan, S. 67, 77, 87, 69, 110
Wendt, S. 101, 110
Weng, H. 42, 61
Wheeler, A. 90, 99, 110
Whitebrooke, M. 40, 47, 55, 61
Whiting- Blome, W. 66, 83
Whiting, P. 46, 62
Whitney, D. 102, 106, 110
Wilberforce, N. 21, 32
Wilkin, L. 72–73, 87
Williams, C. 54–55, 62

Williams, P. 14, 27
Willis, N. 112, 134
Wilson, H. 141, 147, 149, 158
Wong, C. 148, 158
Wong, Y-L. 177, 185
Worline, M. 46, 62
Wulfekuhler, H. 44, 46, 62

Xu, Y. 96, 100, 110, 115–116, 119, 122, 126, 134

Yarnell, L. 136, 148–151, 158
Yeung, N. 148, 158
Yi, J. 23, 32, 69–71, 77–79, 97–98, 110
Ying, Y-W. 136, 143, 149–151, 158, 168, 185
Younas, A. 19, 46, 62
Yuill, C. 12, 24, 32, 45, 49, 52, 62

Zembylas, M. 46, 62
Zessin, U. 137, 158
Zschomler, D. 17, 27

SUBJECT INDEX

abuse: of children 20, 89; domestic 9; of service users 8, 79; sexual 65, 78; of social workers 18–20, 78; and social work students 78; *see also* child; children; domestic violence
accomplishment *see* personal accomplishment
ADASS 9, 25
adoption and fostering 79
adult: poverty 8; protection 73, 77, 95; services 9, 16; social care 8; trauma 78–79; workers 73, 77, 95
adverse childhood experiences 20, 79; and social workers 20; and social work students 78–79, 125; *see also* self-care; self-compassion
affect 1, 42, 66, 97–98, 137, 165; *see also* emotions
affective 37–38, 42, 46, 97, 137, 140
ageism 5; *see also* older people
agency 36, 49, 51, 75, 104, 113, 151; *see also* control; social work agency
aggression 8, 19, 74
altruism 36, 42, 150, 177
anti-discriminatory approaches 4, 47, 55, 149, 167, 177
anti-oppressive approaches 4, 47, 55, 149, 167, 175–177
anti-racism 143; *see also* racism
appraisals 12–14
appreciative inquiry 102–104
Asian people 7, 74, 96, 113
assessment 10, 18, 48, 77, 173–175; and compassion fatigue 72; and compassion

satisfaction 101; and COVID-19 8, 17; and self-care 124; and self-compassion 147
assets *see* strengths
austerity 6, 9–10, 40, 101, 148
authority 49–50, 53; *see also* power; surveillance
autonomy 10, 18, 50, 100, 131

BAME 7, 21–22; *see also* Asian; COVID-19
BASW 8–9, 17, 19, 23, 26, 44, 111, 113–114, 120, 129
Black Lives Matter 176
black people 7, 21, 74, 96, 119–120, 148, 176
BMA 43, 56
Buddhism 34, 161
burnout 2, 5, 13–14, 22, 64–65, 67–68, 74, 88; and compassion fatigue 68–69, 72–73, 76, 81, 94, 98; and compassion satisfaction 91, 94; and helping professionals 64, 141; and measurement scales 69, 73, 93–94; and mindfulness 165–166, 169–170; of nurses 140–141; and self-care 115–116, 118; and self-compassion 137–139; of social workers 2, 94–95, 169–170; and training about 81–122; of younger, single, female social workers 22; *see also* depersonalisation; exhaustion; personal accomplishment; workloads

Canadian Association of Social Workers 113, 129
Canadian Nurses Association 43, 56
capitalism 10, 48, 120, 176

196 Subject Index

care leavers 52

caseloads 15, 72–73, 91, 127

Charter for Compassion 35–36

child: abuse 20, 89; and adolescent mental health services 8; care workers 20, 73, 95; poverty 8; of social workers 77; trauma and social workers 19–20, 77–79, 80, 98, 125; *see also* children

child and family social work 20–21, 77, 91, 100; work in 17, 19, 49

child protection social workers 15, 18, 67, 77, 89–90, 95, 146

children: looked-after 52; and mental health problems 53; and poverty 8; and self-harm 8; services 8, 16; and young people and social work 17, 19, 49; of social workers 22–23, 96, 119; and suicide 8; *see also* child

child welfare workers 65–67, 89, 96, 118

class 7, 55, 72, 176, 178

colleagues 3, 15, 71, 103, 112, 124–125, 141, 164, 171; and COVID-19 15–17, 23; discussions with 72, 98, 102, 115, 118, 150; problems with 22; and racism 21; relationships with 92, 100, 104, 120, 165, 174; support of 12, 24, 63, 66, 93, 100, 104, 112, 144, 172; *see also* teams

collective approaches 5, 6, 15, 25, 92; and challenge 54; and compassion 50, 54–55; and compassion satisfaction 92, 102, 104; and discussions 102, 104; and empowerment 163; and mindfulness 172, 176, 178–179; and self-care 120–121; and self-compassion 150, 163; and service users 55

commitment 2, 25, 34, 53, 64, 145; and compassion 38, 50, 53–54; and mindfulness 173–174, 177; to organisations 50, 99, 171; to professional standards 147; to self-care 113–114, 117–118, 122, 124, 126, 128; and self-compassion 140–141, 147–148; to service users 65, 100, 117; and suffering 37, 174

common humanity 36, 43, 52, 136, 141–143, 145–146; scales 131; and suffering 151; *see also* self-compassion

communities 10, 36, 63, 92, 112, 178

Community Care 8–9, 16–18, 23, 27, 31, 57, 66, 81

compassion 2–5, 11, 13, 21, 25, 33–63; active 51–54; and compassion fatigue 64, 68, 76; criticisms of 39–41 debates about 37–39; definitions of 34–37; dilemmas for social work 48–49; education and training for 42–43; foundations of 36–37; and health care 43–44; and mindfulness 161–163, 165; and nursing 43–44; and power 50–51; and professionalism 33, 50–51; and self-compassion 137, 139, 149–150; in social work education and training 46–48; and social workers 45–46; in social work organisations 49–51; a wider focus for 54–55; *see also* organisations; kindness; measurement scales

compassion fatigue 2, 3, 5–6, 14, 19, 22, 41, 45, 63–87; criticisms of 72–76; definitions of 68–69; and empathy 69–72, 98; and mindfulness 166, 168–170; and personal distress 98; scales 69, 73, 76, 81, 93, 97; and self-care 116, 118; and self-compassion 141; and social workers 76–79, 79–81; training for social workers 81–82, 122

compassion satisfaction 3, 5, 12, 14, 21, 23–25, 76, 88–111; and aces 98; and appreciative inquiry 102–104; and compassion fatigue 69, 76; and critical perspectives 100–101; definitions of 93; and empathy 69, 97–98; and ethnicity 96; education and training for 102; and gender 96; limitations of research 97–98; and mindfulness 165–166, 169–170; research and social workers 94–97; scales 69, 76, 97, 102; and self-care 97, 115–116, 121–122; and self-compassion 138, 140–141; and sexuality 96; and wellbeing 115; and a wider focus 99–101

containment 23, 71, 98, 170

continuing professional development 91, 92, 115, 145

control 2, 11, 13, 15, 23, 25; and compassion 49; and compassion fatigue 63–64, 68, 71–73; and compassion satisfaction 93, 100, 104; and mindfulness 164, 172, 176; of practitioners 41, 126; and self-care 113; and self-compassion 143, 149, 151

coping 2, 20, 25; and appraisals 12, 14; and compassion fatigue 66, 74–75, 78, 81; and compassion satisfaction 97, 102; emotion focused 14, 137, 151; and mindfulness 167–169, 172; problem focused 14, 137, 151; and self-care 113–115, 120, 122; and self-compassion 137–138, 143, 151–152; and service users 90; *see also* COVID-19

coronavirus *see* COVID-19

counselling 38, 47, 54; and compassion fatigue 69; external 128; and mindfulness

165–166, 174; and self-care 115–116, 128; and service users 165; and social workers 174

counsellors 3, 68, 74, 115, 140, 165

COVID-19 7, 9, 137; and children 7–9; and ethnic minorities 7; and Muslim people 9; and nurses 138; and poverty 8, 18; and service users 7–11, 15; and social divisions 7; and social workers (*see individual entries below*; young people and women)

COVID-19 and social workers 7–8, 10–11, 15–19, 23, 52; and compassion fatigue 72; and compassion satisfaction 91, 94; and coping with 16; and mindfulness 169–170; and self-care 114, 117; and self-compassion 137–138; *see also* demands; depression

CPAG 8, 26

criminal justice 2, 49, 51–52, 103; *see also* probation workers

crisis intervention work 81

critical reflection 123, 169, 177–178; *see also* reflection

culture 3, 15, 36; of blame 80; and compassion 11–12, 19; and compassion fatigue 73–74, 80; Eastern 148; and mindfulness 161, 171–172, 174, 177; and the NHS 43; and organisations 14–15, 40, 43, 71, 123, 127, 146, 166, 171–172; and self-care 118–120, 127–128; and self-compassion 143, 146, 148, 152; and work 15; Western 148

cynicism 9, 64, 144

demands: administrative 29–52–53, 10; and black workers 74; and compassion fatigue 63, 78, 80; and compassion satisfaction 90, 93, 95, 98, 99, 101; on female social workers 78; from Covid-19 23, 94; and mindfulness 168, 173; organisational 21, 93, 119, 146; and self-care 112, 117–118, 120, 123; and self-compassion 138, 140–141, 146; from service users 79–80; on social work students 122–123; work/life 16, 22–23, 99, 119, 127; *see also* COVID-19; organisations

democratic participation 10

Department for Education 11, 27

Department of Health 43–44, 57

depersonalisation 13–15, 64; and social workers 15, 91; *see also* burnout

depression 10, 12; and compassion fatigue 64, 69–70, 79; and COVID-19 137, 170;

and mindfulness 165–170; and self-compassion 137–139; and service users 9, 79; and social workers 14, 23, 70, 179

(dis)ability 3, 7; and compassion 41; and compassion fatigue 73–74; and COVID-19 9; learning 7; and mindfulness 165, 169, 177–178; and self-care 128; and self-compassion 149, 152; workers 21–3

discourse 55, 75, 104, 111, 121

discrimination 48, 74, 88; and compassion fatigue 63, 72–74, 80–81; and mindfulness 177; and self-care 119, 121; and self-compassion 148–149; and service users 6–7; and social workers 19, 21–22, 55, 63, 72–73, 80, 88, 121

distress 14; and compassion 34–35, 37–38, 42, 45, 54; and compassion fatigue 64, 67–68, 70–71, 79; and compassion satisfaction 98; and self-care 115; and self-compassion 140, 148; of service users 8, 68, 70; of social workers 14, 20, 54, 67, 70–71, 89, 98, 115, 169

diversity 11, 88, 122

domestic violence 9, 45, 78, 91, 98, 100

drug and alcohol use: and service users 8, 79; and social workers 20, 23, 79; and social work students 78

duty teams in social work 91

Dzonsgar Khyentse Rinpoch 161, 180

ecological approaches 3, 47, 73, 100, 104, 113, 176, 179

emotional intelligence 97

emotions 162, 177; positive 7, 90, 97; negative 7, 35, 38, 54, 90, 103, 136, 165–166; and organisations 54; regulation of 144, 148, 170; and social workers 12, 14, 54–55, 71, 95, 103; and social work students 47, 71, 113; *see also* feelings; supervision

empathy: and burnout 15; and compassion 33, 37–40, 42, 44–45, 47, 53–54; and compassion fatigue 33, 37–40, 42, 44–45, 47, 53–54; and compassion satisfaction 97; and emotional exhaustion 15; and mindfulness 162, 164; and self-compassion 137, 139, 150; and service users 25, 53, 64, 69–70; and social workers 38, 45, 66, 69–71, 97; and women 78; *see also* compassion; BAME

empowerment 163, 178; *see also* power

equality 40–41, 101; *see also* inequality

ethics 19, 34–35, 44–45, 68, 113

ethnic: backgrounds 121, 148; differences 177; group 119, 179; minorities 7, 41, 148, 173

198 Subject Index

ethnicity 3, 7, 21, 73, 77, 95, 152; *see also* compassion satisfaction

eustress 12

evidence based practice 64

evidence informed practice 64

exhaustion: and black social workers 119; and burnout 13–14, 64, 69; and mindfulness 164, 168, 171; and nurses 164; and physicians 140; and self-compassion 137–139, 145; and social workers 15, 20, 76, 91, 143, 171; and social work students 168; and work/life conflict 23

families 7–9; and Covid-19 8–9, 17; service users 9, 17, 36, 52, 68; and social workers 17, 52, 77, 100, 104, 174

feelings: anger 54, 70, 119; and compassion 35, 37–39, 42, 47, 50, 54; and compassion fatigue 68–71, 118; and compassion satisfaction 90–91, 95, 98, 101–102, 104; and family care 148; guilt 68, 119, 146; and mindfulness 162–168, 172, 177; and self-compassion 136–139, 141–144, 146, 148, 150–152; of service users 9, 19, 47, 69–70, 95; of shame 138, 146; and social workers 10, 68–72, 80, 95; and suffering 39, 47; *see also* emotions

females: and care for families 119; and compassion fatigue 22; and ethnic minority groups 148; and feminism 119; and job satisfaction 22; and part-time work 96; and self-compassion 148–149; *see also* gender; women

feminist: black self-care 119–120; groupwork 177

gay people 22, 96–97

gender 3, 7, 21; and compassion 41; and compassion satisfaction 96; and mindfulness 169, 177–178; role orientation 149; and self-care 119–120, 125, 128, 169; and self-compassion 148–149, 152; transgender 116; *see also* females; women

The Guardian 8, 9, 15, 24, 26, 31, 91, 110

guilt 7, 68, 144–146; and black feminism 119; and COVID-19 7; and self-compassion 136, 144–145, 152

health 12, 14; and mindfulness 161, 177; and self-care 114, 117–118, 121, 123–124; and self-compassion 137, 142; and service users 7, 19, 75, 79, 121; and social workers 18, 79, 89, 96, 98, 114

Health and Safety Executive 12, 14, 28

health care 2–4, 7, 33, 42–43; and compassion 33, 43, 49; and mindfulness 164–165, 167; organisations 138; professionals 42–44, 165, 167; and self-compassion 138, 140; social workers 117

homelessness people 45

homophobia 176

hope 2, 25, 74, 102, 104; and compassion 40; and compassion satisfaction 93, 99; and mindfulness 163, 172; and self-compassion 137, 140

hospice: professionals 115; social workers 77, 95

hospital social workers 67, 126

"hot-desking" 15

housing 7–8, 19, 52, 79

human rights 88, 178

humour 115

IFSW 7, 28, 68, 84, 113–114, 131, 149, 155

illness 10, 35, 121, 138, 144; and service users 79, 164; and social workers 11, 16–17, 20, 40, 63, 78, 80, 127

imposter phenomena 146

individualism 8, 13, 18, 34; and compassion 36, 41, 45, 55; and compassion satisfaction 92; and mindfulness 175; and self-care 121–122; and self-compassion 143, 149

inequality 8, 40, 48, 55, 79, 119; *see also* equality

injustice 40, 49, 55, 121, 149, 178; *see also* justice; social justice

institutional context 36, 52, 74, 178; of education 113, 123, 152

job satisfaction 24, 90, 92; and child-care workers 20; and compassion fatigue 65, 68; and females 22; and mindfulness 162, 165, 170; and self-care 115–128

Joseph Rowntree Foundation 8, 28

joy 24, 35, 42, 91, 139

justice 34–35, 47, 112, 120, 176; *see also* injustice; social justice

kindness: and compassion 37, 42, 44, 50, 53; and mindfulness 162–3, 174; self 136, 139–140, 142–143, 146, 151; and service users 25; *see also* self-compassion

labeling 7, 25, 68, 169

language 3, 7, 21–22, 24, 104; and compassion 50–55; and compassion fatigue 73–75; and mindfulness 178; and self-care 120, 128; *see also* compassion

Subject Index **199**

LBGTQ 7, 21, 26, 173, 177
leaders: in healthcare 164; in social work 40, 49–50, 145, 147, 164, 171–172
legal duties of social workers 49
Legatum Institute 8, 29
legislation 11
line managers *see* managers
local authority 14, 99, 101, 125, 145, 170, and budget cuts 6, 9, 18; and teams 20, 73
Local Government Association 113, 132
loss 35; and COVID-19 7; education and training in 81; and intersectional racism 119; and service users 8, 10, 79; and social workers 10, 19, 44, 79
low income 18, 19, 66–67

males 22, 48–49, 149, 173
managers 2–3, 13, 23; and compassion 40, 44, 50, 55; and compassion fatigue 64, 81; and compassion satisfaction 102; and COVID-19 15, 17; and disability; and discrimination 21; and self-care 128; and self-compassion 145, 151; and support 18; and workers' home lives 23
MAPPG 161–162, 183
marginalisation 96, 119, 176
measurement scales: compassion 38, 41, 137; compassion fatigue 69, 73, 76, 81, 97; compassion satisfaction 69, 76, 97, 102: mindfulness 163–164; Pro QOL 76; self-care 126; self compassion 136–137, 142, 147, 149, 151
medical models 121
meditation 137–139, 163, 166–167, 176; loving kindness 42, 139; and social workers 118
men *see* males
MENCAP 2, 29
mental health 69; and children 53; and compassion 37, 53; and compassion fatigue 68–69, 78, 80; and compassion satisfaction 95–96; and COVID-19 8, 17; and black professionals 74; and female professionals 78; and mindfulness 161–162; and professional boundaries 37, 51; provision 20, 45, 51, 53, 68; and self-care 114–118, 121, 123–124; and self-compassion 137, 140, 143, 148, 152; services 45; and service users 8, 49, 53, 79; of social workers 17, 22–23, 69, 74, 95–96, 102; and social work 20, 49, 65, 74; and social work students 143, 152, 169
Mental Health Foundation 161, 183
mentors 43

microaggressions 2–5, 14, 25, 36, 74, 78
mindfulness 2–5, 14, 25, 36, 97, 114, 116, 118, 128, 137–139, 142–143, 151, 159–185; and anti-discriminatory and anti-oppressive practice 177; and awareness 36, 118, 170–171; and Buddhism 160–161; and compassion 161–163, 165; and compassion fatigue 166, 168–170; and compassion satisfaction 96, 165–166, 169–70; criticisms of 161–162, 164, 169, 174–178; definitions of 159–160; education and training 142, 160, 162–164; and ethical questions 174–178; and health care 164–166; and measurement scales 162–165, 173; and other professionals 138, 164, 165; and organisations 151, 159–160, 169, 171–172, 178–9; and politics 176; secular 160–161; and self-care 28, 165, 169, 171; and self-compassion 137–9, 142–143, 151, 165, 168, 170, 178; and self-help 161; and self-regulation 164–165, 168–171; and service users 8–11, 17–18, 21, 28; and social work education 166–167; and social workers 167, 169–171; and social work students 143, 167–168; and teams 171–172, 174, 179; and wider perspectives 174–178; and the workplace 161–162; *see also* coping; COVID-19; culture
Mindfulness Association 159, 163, 183
minority groups 44, 79, 119–120, 148
modelling 43, 47, 50, 81, 122, 145; *see also* role
moral 64, 117, 174; compassion 38, 48, 54; dilemmas 17; distress 68; outrage 54; suffering 48
multi-cultural 74; *see also* culture
Muslim people 7–8, 148; *see also* BAME

NASW 113–114, 130, 133
National Audit Office 9, 29
Native Americans 74, 177
neo-liberalism 101; limits to 175; and mindfulness 160–161; and self-compassion 48; and service users 6, 10, 161; and social workers 6, 10; and suffering 48
networks 115
new managerialism 6, 10
NHS 7, 43, 94, 140
NISCC 45, 59
Nursery and Midwifery Council 43, 59
nursing 88; and compassion 4, 34, 41, 43–44, 46, 53; and self-compassion 145; *see also* stress

200 Subject Index

Office of National Statistics 9, 30
OFSTED 97
older people 1, 7, 9, 49
on-line contacts: and COVID-19 16–17, 23, 52; and education and training 122, 126, 138–139, 145, 162, 173; and mindfulness 162, 169, 173; and self-care 124, 126, 145; and self-compassion 138–139, 145; and social work education 145; and social workers 16–17, 52; and social work students 145, 169
oppression 40, 55; and compassion fatigue 63–65, 74, 80–81; internalised 169; and mindfulness 169, 175–178; and self-care 120–121; and self-compassion 143, 149, 172; and social workers 19, 63, 65, 80, 89, 121, 169; and social work students 177
optimism 2, 25, 74, 137; and compassion satisfaction 89, 93, 99, 104
organisations: and appraisals 13; and burnout 64; and climate 40; and compassion 13, 40, 43, 49–51; and compassion fatigue 48; and compassion satisfaction 102; and COVID-19 18; and discrimination 80, 166; and leaders 172; learning in 81, 102, 113, 125, 172; and mindfulness 159–162, 165, 171–172, 178–179; and racism 17; and resources 9, 15, 40, 48, 125; and retention 113; and self-care 5, 112–113, 122–126, 128; and service users 9, 68, 72, 113, 99, 125; and support 99, 125 and teams 99, 102; and turnover 63, 112; and wellbeing 112; and workloads 63, 73, 125; *see also* commitment; culture, demands, self-care; self-compassion; supervision; teams

paediatric social workers 170
palliative care 42, 52–53
pandemic *see* COVID-19
partnership 6, 21, 39, 61, 50–51, 53, 152
patriarchy 176
perfectionism 139, 144, 146
personal accomplishment 14, 24, 64, 92–93, 138
personality: state 98; trait 98
policies: and burnout 64; and compassion 34, 39, 41, 49–50, 54–55; and compassion fatigue 63, 72–73, 80, 92; and compassion satisfaction 101; government 34, 39; national 49–50, 55, 72, 144; nursing 41; and self-care 113, 127 and self-compassion 144–145, 152
politics/political 1, 4, 21; and anti-racism 119; and compassion 40–41, 47, 51,

54–55; and equality 41; and mindfulness 160, 175–176; and self-care 119–121, 123; and suffering 41
post-traumatic: growth 66–67, 88–90, 121; stress disorder 66
poverty 7, 17–18, 48, 52, 55, 79; adult 8; child 8; and compassion satisfaction 88; and mindfulness; 175 and self-compassion 148
power 40, 50–51, 54–55, 72, 102, 121; and black female social workers 119–120; and service users 9, 50–51; and social workers 10–11, 40, 50; and suffering 51; *see also* compassion; empowerment
practice educators/teachers 2; and compassion 47; and compassion fatigue 81; and compassion satisfaction 102; and mindfulness 172; and self-care 128; and self-compassion 145
pressure 2, 4, 12, 81, 145, 171; challenge 11; and COVID-19 7, 9, 79, 91, 94; on ethnic minority groups 119; hindrance 11; and satisfaction 34; and service users 6; and sexuality 97; and social workers 11, 24, 67, 88, 94, 117, 119
pride 2, 7, 24, 50, 91–92
privilege 40, 50, 74, 90, 143, 177
probation workers 23, 103
professional development 81, 92, 10, 112; and compassion 33, 40–41, 50–51; and compassion fatigue 72, 81; and mindfulness 172; self-care 115, 126–128; self-compassion 142–145, 150
professional: associations 55, 112, 143, 152; boundaries 25; capabilities 111, 114; commitment 114; growth 89; identity 45, 92, 114, 144; standards 147, 152; unions 55, 112, 115; *see also* commitment; self-care; values
ProQOL 73, 76, 94
psychologists 3, 94, 126, 138–141, 149

"race" 73, 178; and social workers 7, 21, 74, 118–120, 128
racial bias 96; *see also* discrimination
racism 21, 55, 72, 74, 119, 143, 176
recovery 45, 68, 74–75
reflection/reflective 98, 144; and compassion 42–43, 46–48; and compassion satisfaction 91, 102 critical 123, 127, 169, 177–178; and mindfulness 162, 164, 167–169; and self-care 115–116, 123–124, 127; and self-compassion 150; and the self 150, 168, 177; and social work students 123, 125, 144, 146,

Subject Index **201**

167–168; and supervision 15, 24, 47, 91, 98, 102, 112, 123, 127; and writing 124; *see also* supervision

reframing 13, 16, 103, 139

relationships 90; and compassion 37–38, 41, 43, 49, 52–53; and compassion fatigue 69–70, 72; and compassion satisfaction 89–91, 93, 99–100, 104; and mindfulness 161, 165, 170, 172, 174; and self-care 112, 115, 121; and self-compassion 140, 144

religion 104; and compassion 34, 55; and compassion fatigue 73; and compassion satisfaction 24, 91, 102; and mindfulness 179; and self-care 120; and self-compassion 152; *see also* compassion

reports by social workers 18, 175

residential care 7

resistance 74, 92, 148, 177

resources 13, 73, 162; learning 127; and service users 2, 9, 79, 92, 147; and social workers 15, 34, 72–73, 79, 101, 124, 142; *see also* organisations

retention of social workers 11, 92, 112, 128

rewards: and appraisals 13; and compassion satisfaction 5, 76; and cost cutting 10; financial 163; and service users 6, 104; and social workers 6, 23–24, 45, 90, 94, 104

risk 40; for BAME 7; and burnout 95, 98, 115, 170; and compassion fatigue 77, 79, 80, 98; and COVID-19 16; and empathy 98; and female social workers; and mindfulness 170; and self-care 115; and self-compassion 137; and social workers 11, 49, 77, 79, 78; and trauma 65, 78–80; and work/life conflict 23, 78; and vicarious trauma 66

Rogerian approaches 38, 47, 69

role: ambiguity 11; assessment 17; conflict 11, 18, 169; modelling 43, 47, 50, 81, 122, 145; strain 11, 22

rumination 137, 139–140, 146, 162, 165; and social work students 169; and women 78; *see also* self-compassion

rural 18

safety:10, 65

secondary traumatic stress 64, 66; and ACES 98; and black workers 75; and burnout 76, 94–96, 116; and compassion fatigue 64, 98; and compassion satisfaction 76, 94; measurement of 93; and mindfulness 170; and personal distress 98; and self-care 116; and social workers 64, 66–68,

74, 95, 98, 170; and social work students 94; and vicarious growth 89; and white workers 74

self-care 1–5, 14, 19, 24–25, 36, 43, 67–68, 75, 111–134; and adverse childhood experiences 125; and burnout 115–116, 118; and collectives 120–121; and compassion fatigue 68, 116, 118; and compassion satisfaction 97, 115–116, 121–122; and coping 113, 115, 120, 122; and critical perspectives 24, 120–121, 123, 128; and culture 118–120, 127–128; definitions 114–115; and diversity 122; and ecology 113; and education and training 125–125, 128 and emotions 115, 118, 121, 144; and ethnicity 119; and gender 119–120, 125, 128, 169; and guilt 119; measurement scales 120, 126; and mindfulness 28, 165, 169, 171; and organisations 5, 19, 112–113, 121–128; personal 114–115, 119; physical 114; plans 124, 126; professional 114–115, 121–123, 126, 135; and professional capabilities 114; psychological 114, 116, 121; and "race" 118–119, 128; and retention of social workers 112; and self-compassion 19, 120, 128, 135, 144, 150–152; and sexuality 128; and social work education and training 121–125; and social work students 111, 116–117, 122–123; spiritual 115, 118; and systems 113, 121; trauma informed 118; and turnover 112; and well-being 113–115, 121, 123; *see also* commitment; COVID-19; mindfulness; policies; professional development; reflection

self-compassion 2–3, 135–158; and adverse childhood experiences 146; and collectives 150; and compassion 137, 139, 149–150; and compassion fatigue 141; and compassion satisfaction 138, 140–141; and common humanity 136, 141, 143, 145; and culture 143–144, 146, 148, 152; definitions of 135–136; and discrimination 152; education and training for 137–140, 150; and emotional regulation 136, 141, 144 and gender 148–149, 152; measurement scales 136–137, 147, 149–151; and mindful training 138; and mindfulness 136–137, 139, 142–143, 151, 163, 165, 170, 178; and oppression 143, 149, 172; and organisational settings 24–25, 36, 142, 144–148, 152; and other helping professionals 137–142, 151, 165; and

202 Subject Index

over-identification 136; and professional development 142–145, 150; research 136–138, 168–170; and responsibility 147, 152; and rumination 137; and self-care 19, 120, 128, 135–136, 144, 150; and self-judgement 136; and self-kindness 136, 139–140, 142–143, 146, 151; and sexuality 149; and shame 144; and social work education 144–146, 168–169; and social workers 5, 14, 19, 21, 45, 141–147, 152; and social work students 141–144, 149, 152, 168–169; strengths and limitations; 146–151; and supervision 145, 151; and suffering 136, 149–151; and well-being 137–138; and white workers 148; *see also* coping; kindness
self-kindness *see* kindness; self-compassion
sexism 55, 72, 78, 119, 176; *see also* females; women
sexual assault workers 66, 78, 97
sexuality 3, 41, 55, 73, 149; and social workers 7, 21, 74, 120, 128, 152, 177–178
shame 7, 137–139, 144; and social workers 144–146
Skills for Care 19, 31
social activism 54, 120, 123
social injustice 40, 49, 55, 121, 149, 178
social justice 25, 34, 39, 88, 101, 112; and compassion 54; and self-care 121; and self-compassion 149, 152; and mindfulness 160, 175–177
social transformation 43, 66, 102, 176
social work agency 2, 92, 99–100, 102, 118, 120, 128, 172; climate and culture 71, 171; policy and procedures 64, 145; responsibilities 113, 127, 146; *see also* organisations; workplace
social divisions 3, 6–7, 21, 120, 128, 149
solidarity 34, 121, 176, 178
spirituality: and compassion 34; and compassion fatigue 64, 118; and self-care 115, 118; and social work students 143; and trauma 66, 89
SSSC 45, 60
statutory social work 2, 10, 16, 20, 49, 52
stereotypes 7, 25, 120, 175, 177
stigma 7, 25, 68, 125, 138
strengths 74, 92, 88, 104, 111, 128; and compassion satisfaction 88, 104; and mindfulness 162–163; of service users 4–7, 25, 63, 75, 102, 121; and self-care 11, 128; and self-compassion 136–138, 144, 146, 150; and social workers 92, 102, 144
substance use *see* drug and alcohol use

supervision: and compassion fatigue 72, 77; and compassion satisfaction 24, 91, 94, 98–99, 102; and containment 98; of good quality 77, 91, 94, 112, 115; group 99, 104, 114, 123; limitations of 14, 40, 73, 127; and organisations 40, 72–73, 99; reflective 15, 24, 47, 91, 98, 102, 112, 123, 127; and self-care 112, 115, 124, 126–127; and self-compassion 145, 151; of social workers 14–15, 19, 24; and social work students 47, 123–124, 167; supportive 5, 19, 95; and surveillance 103; *see also* COVID-19; reflection; support
surveillance: by social workers 49, 52; of social workers 10, 41, 44, 103, 126
systems: and compassion 47; and compassion fatigue 80; and compassion satisfaction 100, 104; and internal beliefs/memories; and mindfulness 163, 178–179; and organisations 80, 127

teams 3, 8, 12, 15, 20, 55, 73, 91; and compassion 50, 55; and COVID-19 17–18; criminal justice 103; differences between 20, 73, 99; good practice in 103; and mindfulness 171–172; and self-care 115; and support 12, 24, 63, 66, 71, 99–100, 112; *see also* colleagues
transferrable knowledge and skills 3, 4, 7, 81, 166
transformation/transformative 43, 66, 102, 121, 176, 178
turnover of social workers 11, 63, 65, 68, 112, 115, 128

unions 55, 112, 115

values 3, 92, 101; and compassion 35, 38, 43–44, 47; and conflicts 68; organisational 50, 64; professional 64, 68, 99;" radical" 47; and self-care 126; and self-compassion 144; in social work education 47; "traditional" 38
vicarious: post traumatic growth 67, 88–90, 95, 121–122; resilience 66–67, 88–90, 121–122; trauma 5, 64–67, 73, 81, 88
violence 79: in caseloads 18–19, 66; from students' parents 20; and service users 78–79, 177; and social workers 78; and social work students 72; *see also* domestic violence; sexual assault workers
virtue 34, 43–44
vulnerability: and service users 4, 6, 9, 25, 88; and social workers 4, 98, 121

Subject Index **203**

war situations: and social workers 40
well-being 1, 3–4, 6, 13–14, 24; and
compassion 3–4, 6, 24; and compassion
fatigue 18; and compassion satisfaction
7–8, 24; and mindfulness 4–6, 14–16, 25;
and self-care 5–6, 15, 17–18, 25; *see also*
women social workers
western models 118, 148, 161
white workers 21, 74, 96, 118–119, 148
women social workers: black, feminist 119;
and empathy 78; and job satisfaction 22;
and racism 119; and self-care 115, 119;
and sexual harassment 22; and traditional
caring roles 78; and well-being; *see also*
females; gender
women: black and deaths during COVID-
19 7; Chinese and self-compassion 148;
and domestic abuse/violence 9; and
home schooling 9; and on-line courses
138–139; and gender role orientation
149; Muslim 8; and self-compassion 149;
see also females; gender
work/life balance: boundaries 15–16,
22–23, 69, 99, 127; and compassion

fatigue 69, 71, 73, 78; and compassion
satisfaction 99; and managers 23; and
mindfulness 164; of probation workers
23; and self-care 115, 119; and social
workers 15, 22–23, 99
workloads 11, 15, 17, 19, 63–64; and
burnout 64; and compassion satisfaction
101; management of 64; and mindfulness
170; and self-compassion 141, 146; and
self-care 125
workplace: conditions 15, 22; and compassion
fatigue 73; and compassion satisfaction
99–100; and COVID-19 17; and disability
121; and home boundaries 127; and
mindfulness 159, 161–162, 165–166,
169–170, 172, 174; participation 10;
relationships 15; satisfaction 24; self-care
114, 120–21, 123–126; and social work
students 123–124; support 66; and stress 12;
see also organisations; social work agency

yoga 118, 127, 163
young people 7–8, 17, 52–53
youth justice 91

Printed in the United States
by Baker & Taylor Publisher Services